Capitalism and the national question in Canada

Capitalism and the national question in Canada

EDITED BY GARY TEEPLE

UNIVERSITY OF TORONTO PRESS

© University of Toronto Press 1972
Toronto Buffalo London
Reprinted 1973, 1974, 1975, 1979
ISBN 0-8020-1939-0 (cloth)
ISBN 0-8020-6171-0 (paper)
LC 72-91690
Printed in Canada

Studies in the political economy of Canada (SPEC)

Capitalism and the National Question in Canada is the first collection of essays to be sponsored by SPEC. The group was founded by former members of the University League for Social Reform (ULSR), several of whom had made contributions to its most recent publication *Close the 49th Parallel etc.* They were conscious of the need to foster radical studies of the Canadian political economy and were broadly committed to the establishment of an independent socialist Canada.

Royalties derived from the sale of this book will be used by SPEC to sponsor further research in such aspects of the Canadian political economy as the working class and the labour movement, national culture and ideology, and Canada's integration into the American capitalist system.

IAN LUMSDEN   Atkinson College, York University

Acknowledgments

Several people spent a great deal of their own time on this book. The contribution of the individual authors is obvious, but much of the development and final shape of the book is due to others. It was Ian Lumsden who originally suggested I submit a proposal to the ULSR, and from that point, he was consistently encouraging in this undertaking. In all truth, this book would not exist had it not been for him. Mel Watkins also helped greatly in the first stages and made valuable criticisms of several papers throughout the many months it took to collect and edit them. Danny Drache was encouraging and helpful from the beginning. Jack Warnock, Greg Kealey, and Marvin Ross read several of the papers and provided useful comments. Diana and Larry MacDonald gave of their time in the early stages. Much of the typing and retyping was done by Michaela Faust, who made the University of Toronto an institution helpful to this project. Christine Purden did much of the style editing; her evaluations of the articles were particularly important in making some of the larger decisions. I thank Tom Naylor, whose importance to the book is obvious, for providing some needed wit during the last months of preparation. To Rik Davidson, thanks for the best of advice and assistance and for speeding the book through the press.

Madalen, my wife, contributed much in the criticizing and editing of several papers. Her support and involvement from the beginning were central to the making of this book.

GARY TEEPLE

Contents

Introduction

Canada, it is generally believed, ranks among the independent nations of the world. Before 1867 this country was a colony of France and then England, but Confederation is accepted and understood as marking its entry into nationhood. Since that time, Canada has seldom been described as a colony. Even today, as foreign control over the economy grows more quickly than the growth of industry itself, the belief in national sovereignty remains.

It is often assumed by those who see Canada as an independent capitalist nation that only relatively non-industrialized 'banana republics' qualify for the status of a colony. Canada by virtue of its industry is considered to be an autonomous and not a colonial nation. But when it is recognized that industry *per se* is no criterion of independence, this position is greatly weakened. Most industries in Canada are foreign-owned, and in terms of Canada's total exports, highly manufactured products form but a small part; raw and semi-processed materials and farm and fish produce, on the other hand, constitute the largest portion of export value.

Although little control of industry lies in the hands of Canadian capitalists, it is still held that Canada is a politically independent state. The appearance of autonomy, however, is illusory. The political system of a modern nation-state can scarcely operate independently of its economy. The role of a government in a capitalist country is to regulate social relations in the interests of capital accumulation. If a nation's own capitalists predominate in the ownership of the means of production, the government in pursuing its *raison d'être* will legislate policies to promote their interests – which, in effect, become the 'national' interest. But should capitalists from another country dominate the economy, political subservience shifts to favour the interests of the alien owners of capital. In this case, the nation whose economy is held in sway by foreign capital becomes, as well, a political satellite of the controlling state.

In the Canadian economy, American capital dominates the most important sectors. Without doubt, this is the reason the Canadian government has been so responsive to the political and economic needs of the United States here and abroad and so lax in challenging foreign control when the negative effects are so obvious. The American influence in the economy forces the policies of the Canadian government to fall into line more or less with those of Washington (or Wall Street). Thus, this nation has the political trappings of independence but not the reality because politics under capitalism are ultimately subordinate to the amassing of capital by individuals and corporations, the most powerful of which in this country are American.

This assumption about the political sovereignty of Canada is fed largely by the belief that there is a Canadian ruling class, distinct from American capital. Such enterprises as the CPR, Eaton's, and Weston's, certain names like E.P. Taylor and K.C. Irving, and, of course, the banks are offered as evidence supporting this view. While Canadian ownership of these and other businesses and conglomerates cannot be denied, their nature and position in the economy are often disregarded. In the economy as a whole, American capitalists, and not Canadian, dominate in the most important realm, that of production. American capital prevails in manufacturing, in mining and smelting, and in the 'research and development' of gas and oil. Only the railways, the banks, and certain utilities, such as the supply of power and water, can be considered sectors controlled by Canadian capital. Since these forms of business have as their main role the servicing of the American-controlled sectors, their interests are subordinate to American capital. (Even in its activities in the West Indies and Latin America, Canadian capital has always followed subserviently British and then American capital.) Most of the large concentrations of Canadian capital today perform complementary (or at least non-contradictory) roles in relation to US capital – the form of which is more powerful because it dominates the sphere of production, while Canadian capital prevails largely in circulation, that is, in transportation, communication, retailing, and finance.

This thesis is put forward by Tom Naylor who argues that historically the dominant form of Canadian wealth has been commercial capital which has characteristically expanded in the sphere of circulation. With this form prevailing in Canada until the 1930s when it succumbed to the dominance of American investment, there has been a concomitant restriction of domestic capital invested in the production of goods, that is, in industry. Instead, greater profits in the form of commercial wealth have been made by supplying production centres outside the country with raw materials extracted inside. The effect has been to place Canada in a position subservient to first one and then another industrial metropole.

This dependency on foreign industry prevented the dominant group of Canadian capitalists having a strong consciousness of themselves as the rulers of a nation-state. On the other hand, the ruling classes of industrial nations developed an awareness of themselves – a nationalist ideology – because they owned the means *to create* the wealth of their nations. On the basis of this power, they fashioned the state in their own image for their own ends and were able to maintain themselves at the centre of imperial systems in which other lands were controlled for markets and resource bases. In the face of an industrial power, a nation whose ruling class is founded in commercial wealth, such as Canada, is relegated to a subordinate role – financing extraction and transporting goods to and from the centre of production. These functions are but subsidiary aspects of production. Thus, the kind of consciousness the Canadian ruling class has had of itself developed from its dependent economic role in relations with industrial capitalism in Britain and now in the United States.

Always economically subordinate, the Canadian bourgeoisie could hardly move beyond a colonial mentality. Because the main ideas of a ruling class are those that prevail, the effects of this mentality are reflected in the rest of society. Canadians of other classes, therefore, have been marked by a poorly developed awareness of being members of a nation. Other than the Québécois, Canadians have typically drawn a sense of identity from their European origins. The lack of a strong national consciousness, then, likely derives from the dependent nature of the Canadian bourgeoisie and its influence on the political and social life of the country.

The nationalism of modern industrial nations has arisen generally in the context of their domination of a colonial system. An industrial ruling class will often seek to rationalize its role as a colonial exploiter with a moral declaration of superiority. Thus the activities of the controlling state may be obscured with justifications variously called 'civilization,' 'burden,' 'racial superiority,' 'exceptionalism,' 'democracy,' and even 'God's will.' Yet underlying these notions is the exploitation and subjugation of others. An obvious contemporary example of this bourgeois nationalism is the sense of nationality (blatantly jingoistic as exhibited in the war in Vietnam) that the us ruling class has imparted to Americans of other classes – often regardless of their colour and political persuasion. The domination of the United States over the so-called free world is the present basis of the American belief that its 'way of life' is the best and all other nations are envious of it. In some instances, the envy is there – different classes in nations dependent on the us come to see in the 'American way' worthwhile individual and national goals. But it could hardly be otherwise. With the most pervasive propaganda system ever devised, American values are thrust upon those nations, like Canada, unfortunate enough to be tied to the American empire. A belief in superiority, however, is not inherently attached to all of that which is called nationalism.

The United States has invested more in Canada than in any single country in the world, and since the late 1950s more than it invested in all of Latin America. From these facts it can be surmised that Canada ranks as the most important colony of the us. And out of this colonial position there is emerging a sense of protest which has been dubbed 'the new nationalism' in English Canada. It has arisen largely in areas of society where sections of the middle class prevail, the Canadian haute bourgeoisie having long since been integrated into corporate America via sell-outs and interlocking directorships. But on the issues against which these sections of the middle class have protested American influence, concessions have been forthcoming. As long as the *status quo* is not fundamentally challenged, compromise and accommodation will be used to mitigate the nationalist complaints of professors, teachers, artists, lawyers, engineers, government functionaries, and other technocrats. While some aspects of this new nationalism may ultimately develop revolutionary proportions, for the most part so far, they have been used by sections of the middle class for their own advancement. Much of the middle class is largely servile to the existing capitalist system or indeed capitalist itself and so unlikely to defy the system in a fundamental way.

An examination of the development in Quebec during the first half of the 1960s reveals a situation in which large sections of the petite bourgeoisie were accommodated in government bureaucracies, the arts, universities, and mass media. Similar palliatives are offered by the Parti Québécois. But what has not been so subject to appeasement is the struggle between labour and capital – in the main, American capital. That struggle in the context of the 'national' boundaries of Quebec gave rise to a 'common front' of unions and an articulated class consciousness in the face of American capital and its administrators in Quebec. Any profound challenge to the domination of capital, domestic and foreign, must begin as it has in Quebec in the organized sector of the working class because this sector has the means – at present poorly used – to organize and raise the consciousness of the class which creates wealth but does not benefit from it.

The prospect of such a development in English Canada is greatly hindered by the more complete integration of the unions in the so-called internationals. The contradiction between US control over the unions and the need to fight issues peculiar to Canada, however, will be exacerbated by increasing domestic problems in the US and the growing American domination of the Canadian economy. Branch-plant shut-downs and the consequent displacement of Canadian workers, for example, usually mean more jobs for Americans. It can hardly be expected that American unions would fight shut-downs in Canada when US workers benefit from them and when the AFL-CIO is actively working to influence its *own* government to ensure and increase employment for its *own* workers – albeit to the detriment of those in Canada and Latin America affiliated to the AFL-CIO. Moreover, as the necessity for more decisive labour action on a national scale grows in Canada, the lack of a strong national trade union federation and the cause of its weakness, the international union structure, become increasingly obvious.

It should not be forgotten, despite the rise of a 'new nationalism' among sections of the middle class, that American control over Canadian trade unions has been a major 'national' question since the 1890s. It was the organized sections of the working class which were the first to fight the issue of US hegemony in Canada because American control of the unions came with the groundswell of American investment at the turn of the century. For Canadian unionists the problem was clear. The interests of American capital at home and abroad were those of American labour, as was so frequently argued by

Samuel Gompers, president of the American Federation of Labor. The unity of these interests as pursued by the AFL underlay the contradiction between the need to fight the rising American capital in Canada (as well as domestic and British capital) and American control of the unions by such a centre as the AFL. So it was that Canadian workers began the anti-imperialist struggle long before the middle class even perceived a problem – tied as it was to the interests of the Canadian merchant companies and later American branch-plants.

While this new middle-class nationalism has a certain anti-imperialist tone, its content is largely opportunistic. At present it promises little more than an assurance that some sectors of the middle class will not be denied the dominance they have long held in the social, cultural, and political life of Canada. Assuming that this new found identity continues to develop, it might help to a degree in the struggle the unions must begin to undertake (as they have in Quebec) if we are to change the very system we live in.

As long as the capitalist political order is accepted there will be considerable successful accommodation for those social strata whose interests are not in fundamental opposition to US hegemony. The long-term growth and radicalization of this protest, therefore, is uncertain. Moreover, as long as these middle stratas assume the continuance of the present parliamentary system, their role in finding alternatives to American ascendancy are limited. For example, the Liberal party receives most of its funds from the large US branch-plants which dominate the economy. With clear responsibilities to those who finance the party, it can hardly be expected to limit the expansion of foreign control. As Trudeau's government has stated, the proposed legislation on take-overs (the qualified screening process) is the fullest program it plans to institute to deal with the question. The proposal, moreover, is a sham, promising to 'screen' – not necessarily prevent – only the larger take-overs and ignoring the overwhelming sway already held by the US. As for the Conservative party, it would be unlikely to consider significantly different legislation while its funds come from similar sources.

The New Democratic Party has no stated policy to 'repatriate' the economy. Its acceptance of liberal democracy, furthermore, is basic to its philosophy – and to modern capitalism – thus making it a dubious possibility for leading English Canada to independence. The party's main source of funds come from American international unions which remain ideologically and constitutionally tied to their US headquarters. This connection confronts the NDP with the contradiction – if Canadian independence is to be on its program – of having to win freedom from control by American unions and receiving their funds from the same institutions. For the struggle and debate that is on-going there is a further complication in the widespread idea that the NDP is a socialist party. It is 'left' liberal, but as long as it is perceived as socialist it and its left wings will continue to mislead the struggle for an independent and socialist Canada.

The major liberal democratic parties in Canada, then, represent interests which, in the case of the Liberals and the Conservatives, are mainly American – embodying complicitly most of the large Canadian capital formations in the way of banks, insurance companies, railways, and so on – and, in the case of the NDP, keep the trade union movement divided and weak thereby dampening the possibility of united trade union activities. The Communist Party of Canada remains hopelessly dogmatic; the Social Credit party hopelessly irrelevant to any problem in Canada. Besides being compromised, confused or pointless, none of these parties has fully accepted the right of Quebec to secede, and the only provincial separatist party, the Parti Québécois, is a wolf in lamb's clothing, holding great promise for the middle class of Quebec but little for the working class. What, then, is the alternative for the socialist?

Despite the role played by the 'democratic' parties and institutions in keeping Canada a US colony, the processes of liberal democracy are still largely accepted as legitimate. As long as this remains true, socialists cannot ignore the question of the formation of a new political party. More immediate though, is the question of detaching the trade unions from American control and making them into 'schools of socialism,' centres in which *to begin* the conscious struggle of labour against foreign and domestic capital. In short, the job is to make politics subservient to the interests of working people in Canada, not to those of the owners and managers of capital. Only then will the goal of independence and socialism become a possibility.

It is the intention of this book to further the radical analysis of Canadian society. The perspective and arguments found in the essays are consistent in that they reflect left-wing views. Not all the contributors would agree with what has been argued in this introduction, but certainly they are agreed that the present order is fundamentally unjust and that exploitation of Canadians will end only when socialism is won by and for the working class.

GARY TEEPLE

R.T. Naylor

Graduate of University of Toronto; graduate of London School of Economics;
reject, Nuffield College, Oxford; drop-out, King's College, Cambridge;
teaches in the department of economics at McGill University in Montreal

The rise and fall of the third commercial empire of the St Lawrence

The political economy of Canadian development is often discussed in relation
to two interrelated theories – the 'staple theory,' which focuses on the over-
development of staple industry at the expense of secondary production, and
the 'Laurentian thesis,' a theory of commercial empire based of successive
staple trades. In brief, Canadian history is regarded as a colonial history, characterized by reliance on more advanced economies for capital and markets.
But the logic underlying the two theories has not been adequately explained,
for conventional liberal studies have failed to give explicit consideration to
the pecularities of the Canadian capitalist class and Marxist studies have misinterpreted its character. By comprehending this class as a mercantile one,
accumulating wealth through circulation rather than production, one realizes
that the dominance of a few staple trades leads not to independent capitalist
development, but to the perpetuation of colonialism and underdevelopment.

In the preparation of this paper, special thanks are due to Michaela Faust.

HINTERLAND OF THE NORTH

The roots of the present Dominion of Canada can be found in the year 1503 when the first shipment of gold plundered in the Americas reached Spain.[1] Canadian history since then reveals little more than a struggle between various imperial powers to determine whose dominion it shall be.

While even Canada's remarkably inert and inept ideological elites are being forced increasingly to admit that Canadian history is the history of a French, British, and an American colony successively, the reasons for this relationship of dependence have never been properly assessed. To explain the pattern of dependence, to understand why independence from external constraints has never been pursued by the ruling strata of the Canadian bourgeoisie, explicit note must be taken of the structure of capital and of the capitalist class in both the metropole and the hinterland. Canada would not be a colony were colonial status not of material benefit both to the metropole whose colony it is and to the indigeneous ruling class. Colonial status cannot be explained by technological or geographical determinism[2] or by 'comparative advantage,'[3] but only by reference to the relative stages of capitalist development achieved by both the metropole and the hinterland. The metropole defines the character and extent of economic development in the hinterland area. Moreover, the structural relationships between the colony and the metropole necessarily change as the metropole alters.

In studying a colonial society such as Canada in terms of its social and economic development in relation to the metropole, it seems appropriate to adopt the following methodology. From the structure of the metropole, its dominant class, its stage of development and the structure of capital, and its external economic requirements, we can deduce the character of the imperial linkage. From the form of the imperial linkage follows the political economy of the hinterland and the degree and pattern of development. From the political economy of the hinterland the nature, horizons, and policy of its dominant class can be deduced. The dominant class is directly dependent on the metropole; other classes, in contrast, are defined by their productive relationships with the dominant class and thus are related only indirectly to the metropolitan class structure. That is, while the internal dialectics of class and of capital accumulation may determine the nature of metropolitan expansion, the social structure and the structure of capital in the hinterland cannot be regarded as independent of the metropole. On the contrary, internal changes in the metropole are the immediate cause of socio-economic reorganization in the hinterland.

We are concerned here with transformations in the structure of capital, and hence of the capitalist class, in both metropole and hinterland. Since the Conquest, the key to development in Canada has been in part the availability of capital[4] and, more particularly, its form.[5] We must, therefore, differentiate between various strata of the bourgeoisie according to the particular form of capital represented by each type.

The bourgeoisie as a class fulfil five major and sometimes contradictory economic functions[6]:

1 the omnipresent manager – supervising the utilization of capital and labour in the productive process, the process itself being taken as datum;

2 the rentier, a pure parasite – living off interest and dividends on past investments or rents on past property accumulations without performing any socially necessary role in the capitalistic productive process itself;

3 the 'capitalist' *per se* – embodying investment capital, either owned by the capitalist or borrowed, in a productive opportunity and reaping surplus in the form of net profit;

4 the industrial entrepreneur – creating profitable productive opportunities through various forms of innovative activity, such as discovering a new product, opening new markets either at home or abroad through export of goods or of industrial capital, or reorganizing industrial capacity; and

5 the mercantile-financial entrepreneur – intermediating flows of goods between producers and consumers (merchant), or of capital between savers and investors (financier).

The greatest contradiction among the strata of the bourgeoisie appears between the industrial-capitalist entrepreneur and the mercantile-financial entrepreneur. The first operates in the sphere of production, the second in distribution. Thus, maximization of the mercantile surplus will minimize the industrial surplus. Furthermore, industrial capital is typified by a high ratio of fixed to circulating capital and is concomitantly long-term and often high-risk, while mercantile capital is typified by a low ratio of fixed to circulating capital and is directed towards short-term, relatively safe, investment outlets.[7]

Bearing these distinctions in mind we can analyse the peculiarities of Canadian capitalism, one which continually alters in response to external changes of the metropoles, yet which shows internally a remarkable continuity of historical development. Far from being paradoxical, this continuity in the face of change reveals the fundamental attribute of Canadian capitalism. In its consistency of development lies the key to its need for subordination and its ability to adapt.

Anglo-Canadian capitalism emerged from the confluence of two streams of European capitalist development, French and British mercantilism, and particularly from the dominance of the latter over the former in the peculiar

North American context. The structural basis of mercantilism is the existence of a merchant capitalist class which accumulates wealth through intermediary activities between producers and consumers by filling in regional shortages of goods.

In England prior to industrialism, the merchants' need for national protection and development of transportation facilities and national uniformity of standards coincided with the Crown's requirement for revenue to finance administration and internal development. Whereas previously tolls had been collected by and for the individual urban centres, mercantilism required that tariffs be collected by and for the central treasury.

Initially English overseas expansion took the form of a Crown-sponsored piracy to break into the Spanish bullion monopoly. Elizabeth's share of the spoils brought by Sir Francis Drake on the *Golden Hind* was sufficient not only to discharge her entire foreign debt, but also to establish the Levant Company with a royal monopoly of the Mediterranean trade. In turn the profits of the Levant Company spawned the East India Company.[8]

The Hudson's Bay Company, established in 1670, was virtually the last of its kind in the English-speaking world – on that side of the Atlantic – because jealousy over the Crown's right to grant royal monopolies to favoured individuals led to the passage of the Statute of Monopolies which substantially curbed it. The Statute gave British merchants a unique degree of freedom within the broad confines of the mercantile system, at a time when the King of France still had absolute authority to grant monopolies and subscribed much of the capital himself. In England, after Elizabeth, the Crown ceased to invest directly in foreign trade companies. Instead capital was subscribed from a wide variety of sources on a joint stock basis and was committed for one or a very small specified number of voyages. At the end of the contract period, the capital and profits were paid out to stockholders, and a new subscription, often provided from the same sources as the old, would be sought.[9] This mode of organization, while it kept the ratio of fixed to circulating capital low, had the advantage of both widening the basis from which capital could be subscribed and permitting *de facto* monopolization by the absorption of competing companies into a single venture. The *nouveau riche* merchants began congregating in the City of London where they soon became the chief lenders and funders of government debt.

ANGLO-CANADIAN CAPITALISM, 1760-1846

The British conquest of Canada precipitated the collapse of the French mercantile nexus and an exodus back to France of colonial administrators, representatives of the fur trade monopoly, and some of the seigneurs.[10] A parasitical class of British merchants followed the British army into the defeated colony to feed off the spoils, and quickly assumed control of the fur trade and of vacated seigneuries. Hardly a colonial aristocracy, this group was comprised of 'people on the make,'[11] and their task of 'making it' was considerably facilitated by the legacy of François Bigot, the last Intendant of New France.

During the hostilities, Bigot and his friends cornered the market for colonial grain and other foodstuffs. Since Bigot, as Intendant, determined the buying and selling prices of these goods, in supplying provisions to the various garrisons and royal warehouses he was able to transfer huge sums from the public purse to his own and his friends' pockets. The escalation of expenditure resulting from inflated prices necessitated an enormous issue of paper money. In 1760 the occupying general, James Murray, declared this money worthless, and considerable confusion among the inhabitants ensued. The British merchants took advantage of the chaos and bought up a large amount of the paper money at a tiny fraction of its face value;[12] Britain in turn forced upon France a declaration in the Treaty of Paris that the French government would redeem all the money at one-quarter to one-half of its face value and would provide an additional indemnification of 3,000,000 livres for British subjects holding it.[13] This piece of systematic fraud established the basis of some of the great Canadian fortunes that persist to this day, and represents the foundation of Anglo-Canadian capitalism.

Following the Conquest, further alienation of lands on a seigneurial basis was abolished in favour of free tenure, though the existing seigneuries were left intact. The result was twofold: first, an initial influx of so-called United Empire Loyalists, a group whose primary loyalty was to free land and who by 1812 constituted 80 per cent of the population of Upper Canada; second, a number of large land companies began to develop, hindering further settlement. The fur merchants of the North West Company were foremost among those acquiring huge land grants: as the fur trade declined their activities as land speculators grew apace. By the 1820s the two largest companies, virtual monopolists, were the Canada Company of Upper Canada, founded by John Galt, and the British American Land Company of Lower Canada, controlled by merchants Peter McGill and George Moffat. A *de facto* merger occurred in 1844 when A.T. Galt, son of John Galt, became a commissioner of the Lower Canada company. These land companies bore a special relationship to the colonial governments through the executive councils on which sat most of the commissioners who ran the land companies. The lands were ceded at a very low price, reduced even further because the land monopolies could write off one-half to two-thirds of the price by expenditures on improvements, the costs of which could be passed on to the purchasers. The remainder of the purchase price was paid directly to the executive councils, enabling them to remain financially independent of the assemblies.

Until 1815 there had been no serious shortage of capital in Canada, for the demand for infrastructure was low and some of the (genuine) Loyalists had brought considerable wealth with them or were funded by the London merchant-banking house, Phyn Ellice & Inglis. Moreover, the Napoleonic wars, and subsequently the war of 1812, had resulted in an expanded demand in Britain for Canadian and New Brunswick timber and Canadian grain, and in substantial direct military expenditure in the colonies. But after 1815 capital scarcity became evident as military spending was sharply curtailed. Money coming in on military account had been almost as important as the fur trade and was fundamental to the early prosperity of Upper Canada.[14] In the 1820s and 1830s the timber trade rose to importance, but the fur trade had declined so sharply that timber could not fully offset it. What the timber trade did do was to turn the cargo imbalance in favour of cheap emigration to Canada; and during the first half of the nineteenth century crowds of impoverished, cholera-stricken Irish immigrants arrived to provide cheap labour for timbering, for road, canal, and railway building, and for agriculture. But for several reasons the capital to employ all of this influx of labour was not forthcoming.

The continuation of mercantile colonialism meant the continued domination of merchant capital at the expense of industrial capital, which would compete with Britain. The merchant class and rich Loyalists in Canada aligned themselves with the colonial ruling class, the church, and the land-owning elites.[15] In addition to protectionism, British mercantilism had a long-standing policy of prohibiting the export of manufactured machines and the emigration of skilled artisans.[16]

In the Maritimes also the merchant class dominated. The fisheries had expanded considerably after the fall of New France and the Nova Scotia merchants had had some success in replacing the Americans in the West Indies sugar and rum trade. The War of 1812 also benefitted the Nova Scotia mercantile group: they imported supplies from the United States to sell to the British fleet which was blockading American ports, and the British and West Indian goods which before the war had been shipped directly to the United States were now intermediated by Nova Scotian merchants.[17] In New Brunswick 85 per cent of the population, during the Napoleonic wars, was dependent on the timber trade,[18] and these timber merchants, notably Joseph Cunard, controlled the government.

In all the colonies short-term, low-risk, merchant capital dominated primary staple extraction, whose mode of production was typified by a low ratio of fixed to circulating capital. The system served to maximize the surplus appropriated by the metropole, and consequently minimized the amount of local capital formation.

During the late eighteenth and early nineteenth centuries the mode of production in the agrarian areas was largely petit bourgeois or habitant, neither of which could generate any significant amount of surplus. Petit bourgeois farmers were not self-sufficient, but were fully integrated into an exchange economy conducted largely in kind. This barter system served to build up a dependence on the local merchant who advanced credit.[19]

There was no great market in agricultural labour.[20] Capitalist agriculture did not make any significant inroads until the late 1830s, towards the end of the British mercantile connection. Even then, it was hampered by the big companies who had monopolized most of the prime land. These were mercantile land companies engaging in real estate speculation, not agribusiness. Similarly, the seigneurs of Quebec were developing into straightforward landlords, rather than capitalists, engaging in land speculation, hoarding the best land, and raising rents to exorbitant levels.[21] The existing farmers were forced to parcel out their land to their children, reducing the average size of plots and increasing the general poverty. At the same time, there was a huge influx of Irish immigrants who were unable to afford plots on which to settle. A drain of population to the United States began.

Banking development followed that of the land companies and stemmed from the same class: North West Company fur merchants, Saint John timber merchants, or Halifax shipping magnates. The first bank in Canada was the Bank of Montreal, established in 1817 by fur trading companies and the London merchant bank, Phyn Ellice & Inglis. It was privately owned with special connections with the government of Lower Canada through the Château Clique. Similarly, the Bank of Upper Canada, established in 1818 by grain merchants and canal companies, had direct links with the Family Compact; nine of the fifteen associates of the bank were on the executive and legislative councils in 1818, and this number rose subsequently. The Halifax Banking Company, established in 1825, had a complete monopoly until 1832; five of its eight incorporators dominated the Nova Scotia Legislative Council.[22] These early banks were geared to commerce – fish, furs, grain trading – and did not advance farm or industrial loans; they were merchant banks which extended short-term credit to minimum-risk clients. Building societies emerged in the 1830s, soon to be replaced by loan and mortgage companies to service farmers with mortgage capital,[23] a field from which Canadian commercial banks were barred, first by temperament and later by legislation (which lasted until 1966).

Unlike American merchant capitalists, those in Canada and the Maritimes benefitted from, and identified with, the imperial nexus. In addition to securing a preferred position in the British market, as far back as 1790 the merchant class had succeeded in having a statute passed which permitted American produce brought down the St Lawrence to enter Britain on the same terms as Canadian. The guiding principle of the system was thus free trade in produce with the United States, together with a protected position inside the mercantile system. Similarly, in 1812 the Nova Scotian merchants had a statute passed which provided for a partial relaxation of the Navigation Laws in their favour by permitting their harbours to be opened to American trade which would be transshipped to Britain. By coddling themselves between two metropoles and soliciting favours from the dominant one, the Canadian and Maritime merchant capitalists set a precedent they would follow until the collapse of Canadian merchant capitalism in the early twentieth century.

During the early nineteenth century Britain experienced a rapid transformation. Merchant capitalism was adverse to investment in industry, since industrial investment was necessarily long-term and risky, and showed a lower profit rate than did mercantile pursuits. But a rising industrial class had mounted increasingly successful attacks on the mercantile restrictions, and the merchant and banker clique centred around the City of London. The financing of industrial capitalism was done with the savings of petit bourgeois groups in the outlying regions of England, notably in Manchester, where mercantile restrictions were relatively few.

The first Reform Bill ensured that the industrialists would control the House of Commons. Free-trade sentiment and the disrepute of colonies[24] rose in proportion to the progress of the Industrial Revolution, based first on cotton and later on local supplies of coal, iron, and paupers thrown on the labour market by the successive Poor Law 'reforms.' Then in 1846, prompted primarily by the industrial capitalists' desire to lower money wages by reducing the price of wage goods,[25] the Corn Laws were repealed in Britain, fracturing the Tory party. The Corn Laws were not needed to 'protect' British agriculture; transportation costs provided sufficient protection until near the end of the nineteenth century. Their purpose had been solely to maintain an artificially high price of corn to the benefit of the landlords.

Repeal of the Corn Laws marked the victory of export-oriented industrial capitalism in Britain. Any residual desire to maintain the North American colonies came from the old mercantile concerns, with their interests in the fur or timber trade or colonial securities, and the pro-imperial agitation of the Canadian mercantile bourgeoisie, whose power was on the wane.

As a consequence of the rebellions of 1837-8 against the mercantile classes, the Act of Union was pushed through. Behind the Act of Union and the merging of the debts of the two provinces were the machinations of the merchant oligarchy who needed access to further funds to complete the St Lawrence canal system, and of the Baring Brothers, a merchant banking house in London which saw in Union a means of ensuring the value of Upper Canadian securities by redistributing the burden of the debt over the more populous Lower Canada.

The suppression of the rebellions did not completely end the forces making for the birth of an independent progressive bourgeoisie in Canada. Even the Act of Union did not, for within the confines of the political infrastructure imposed by the victorious mercantile oligarchy the liberal reformers did achieve responsible organization and would shortly form governments. Initially, political gerrymandering permitted the mercantile bourgeoisie to retain control long enough to complete the St Lawrence canals. But the impact of the advance of the Industrial Revolution and the repeal of the Corn Laws broke their power, as surely as it split the Tory party in Britain. To the mercantile oligarchy in British North America, the repeal of the Corn Laws in 1846 was catastrophic.

INTERREGNUM, 1846-66

The merchant class had built up a considerable trade in timber and grain with Britain within the confines of the mercantile regulations, and the now completed canal system permitted them to divert American as well as Ontario grain down the St Lawrence. During the boom period of the timber staple, Quebec with its forest resources and navigation facilities was the hub of economic activity in the Canadas. The reduction in demand for timber caused by the use of steam for transport and coal for industrial fuel during the second wave of British industrialization injured the timber trade, blocked as it was from American markets by tariffs. The curtailing of timber preferences in 1842 continued the process of decline. But grain remained as the backbone of the St Lawrence trade system.

The Canada Corn Act of 1843 consolidated the economic foundations of the St Lawrence system by imposing a nominal duty of one shilling a quarter on imports of Canadian wheat into Britain regardless of British price (the general rule for British protection was to block imports until the British price rose to 80 shillings a quarter). This Act, in conjunction with a tariff against the import of American produce, suited the needs of both mercantile and landed interests in Canada, but – these interests were generally the same people, so interlinked were the merchants, bankers, canal companies, land companies, and legislative and executive councils. Provincial duties were not high enough to block imports of American grain into Canada for milling and shipping to Britain as colonial flour, but just high enough to ensure that Canadian produce got priority. The Canada Corn Act thus simultaneously assured the capitalist farmers a market for their cash crop and made it profitable for

American exporters to Britain to use the St Lawrence route in spite of the tariff and higher costs.[26]

The first blow against the precarious artificial system came in 1845, when the American Congress passed drawback acts which permitted Canadian grain to be exported in bond to New York by way of the Erie Canal, enabling Canadian producers to take advantage of the lower ocean shipping rates from New York.[27] Repeal in 1846 completed the process. It was justified in the British Parliament on the grounds that it would be followed by expanded demand leading to an increase in consumption of Canadian grain.[28] In fact, Canadian grain exports to Britain did rise for the next three years. But the value of these using the St Lawrence route fell.[29] The depression that ensued was commercial, not agricultural. The canals, which had never paid even their own interest costs, suffered a drop in revenue of one-half between 1846 and 1848.[30] And in 1849, speculation and overbuying by Montreal grain factors resulted in a collapse of grain prices, which completed their discomfiture.[31] The Montreal merchant elite began to preach annexationism, while the Reformers, who had gained power in 1847, advocated reciprocity.

The merchants behind the annexationist movement performed a political *volte-face* with respect to the Navigation Laws after the Corn Law débâcle. Previously, they had been content with the restrictions that forced all trade with Britain to be carried in British ships. The Canadian merchants' sole complaint had been regarding a clause that permitted American vessels on the Great Lakes to carry on a direct trade with Canadian ports.[32] In short, they felt the Navigation Laws were not sufficiently restrictive. After the repeal of the Corn Laws, however, annexationists led by Peter McGill and A.T. Galt clamoured for abolition of the Navigation Laws as well, in the hope that this would make the St Lawrence route competitive by opening it to American shipping in the face of American drawbacks.[33] The Navigation Laws were repealed in 1849, but this failed to help the St Lawrence route. At the same time, it did nothing to injure British shipping, whose predominance in international commerce was already so well established that the Laws were unnecessary,[34] however useful they had been to the colonial bourgeoisie.

The Reform movement, which was anti-annexationist, believed reciprocity to be the key to prosperity. In 1849, as a prelude, a free-trade area in national products was created among Canada, Nova Scotia, New Brunswick, and Prince Edward Island. But while annexationism petered out, the mercantile class refused to play dead. In 1852 the Hincks administration contemplated the exclusion of American vessels from Canadian canals unless they went down the St Lawrence[35] – that is, the creation of a Canadian Navigation Law designed to promote American shipping across Canadian waterways with the mercantile elite collecting the crumbs in the form of tolls and commissions. The 'national policy' had begun!

Reciprocity was initiated in 1854. Britain was reconciled to it by the hope that renewed colonial prosperity would permit the colonies to assume a greater part of the burden of their defence. The southern American states supported it as a way of preventing annexation which would tilt the balance of power in favour of the North. The merchant class in Canada, however, continued to invest in the St Lawrence route. A series of railways was initiated culminating in the Grand Trunk charter in 1853, behind which lay the omnipresent Baring Brothers. The final impediment to the railway system was overcome in 1854 with the abolition of the remaining seigneuries in Quebec. But the Grand Trunk scheme to capture the midwest American trade was a total failure. In 1860 the Erie Canal and the New York railways took fifty times as much wheat to New York as the Grand Trunk took to Montreal.[36]

Railway construction in conjunction with reciprocity and capital imports from Britain produced a minor boom for the first three years of the Treaty. Reciprocity meant that, in effect, 'US manufactures would be enabled to enter the Canadian market, and US importers would take over Canadian natural resources ... on a greatly increased scale.'[37] Reciprocity was explicitly predicated on the idea that Canada would provide raw materials and the United States finished products. The indigenous capitalist class which centred around the much-lauded Montreal merchants lacked both the imagination and the financial wherewithal to develop and dominate an industrial economy, and would subsequently rely on American entrepreneurs for the former and British financiers for the latter.

The end of capital imports following completion of the excessively expensive, graft-ridden railway system precipitated a severe deflation. In 1857 Galt, the minister of revenue and a member of the Grand Trunk syndicate, faced with a drop in tariff revenue, raised the tariff to acquire the funds to meet the railway debts. The Grand Trunk system was teetering in bankruptcy with operating costs totalling 85 per cent of its gross revenue. The Galt tariff irritated the American government and helped to precipitate anti-reciprocity sentiment in the United States. The Civil War and the part played in it by Canadian merchants completed the process.

With their by now remarkable propensity for backing the wrong side, the merchant class in Canada, which the railway boom had restored to power, were avidly pro-South during the war. Secession would mean the breaking up of the marketing patterns of the American Northwest farmers and a loss of their access to the Mississippi route for cheap shipment of surplus produce to the east or to foreign markets.[38] Concomitantly with reciprocity this meant an enhancement of the value of the St Lawrence route. The Grand Trunk began at last to pay off.[39] The Bank of Upper Canada, which was intimately connected with the Grand Trunk, together with other Canadian banks, also extended its operations during the Civil War and by and large managed to replace the eastern American banks in moving the crops of the Northwest farmers.[40] Abrogation of reciprocity was an act of retaliation for British and Canadian merchant support of the South. If abrogation were followed by a rescinding of bonding privileges, the province of Canada would be isolated from Europe several months a year, curtailing the power of the Montreal merchants. But this class had one more card up their sleeve – Confederation and the national policy.

Canadian Confederation resulted not from a drive for independence led by a dynamic capitalist class[41] but from the inability of the Canadian bourgeoisie to find a new dependency. The national policy was one of mercantilism, of consolidation and expansion within a strong state structure. Like American mercantilism, it had to fail, though for very different reasons. Canadian mercantilism was a belated reaction to structural changes in the metropoles in 1846 and 1866: the triumph of export-oriented British industrial capitalism over the landed and mercantile class coalition, and of protectionist American industrial capital over the staple-producing, low-tariff South. During the course of consolidation of Canadian mercantilism, the metropoles again underwent major structural change, with the dawning of the age of corporation capitalism in America and the rise of formal imperialism in Britain.

Industrial capitalism stagnated in Britain after 1870, but commerce and finance rose to new importance. Historically, these two sectors were closely related; they had been built up during the mercantile period and had not declined during the rise of industrial capitalism. It was the resurgence of the old mercantile bourgeoisie in a new guise that determined the course of British economic policy for the next few decades, and this resurrection provides the answer to the riddle of the rise of finance-capital.

Because of British supremacy in trade and shipping, world trade was increasingly conducted in sterling, the 'key currency' during the heyday of the gold standard. Other countries began keeping their international reserves in short-term, interest-bearing deposits in British banks which could then channel off the funds into lucrative long-term portfolio investments abroad, the British banking system earning an interest rate differential.

While the banking system grew fat on the returns from overseas export of finance capital, it also drained off funds that were direly needed to rejuvenate Britain's ailing industrial base. This shifting of capital flows from industry to finance together with a continued free trade policy ensured that the much-needed cartelization of British industry did not occur. Thus, finance and trade both came to rely on the underdeveloped world as the major recipient of finance capital and as the only market which Britain's inefficient industrial system could capture.

During the last third of the nineteenth and first third of the twentieth centuries, portfolio flows from Britain to the old colonies and semi-colonies occurred on an enormous scale. Investors who put their money into foreign countries sought to use the resources of government to minimize the risk. For unlike trade, where all that was needed was the securing of a single payment for goods exchange, with the rise of finance capital the risks to the metropole increased. It was now a matter of ensuring an uninterrupted flow of interest payments back from the hinterland to the metropole.[42]

Finance capital emerges not from industrial capital, as is usually supposed, but from merchant capital, through the pooling of merchants' resources and their development of a banking structure, and through the earnings of the entrepôt trade. Like merchant capital, finance capital is a low-risk type of venture; but, unlike merchant capital, it is long-term. British portfolio investors looked for the most stable form of bulk investments, such as government bonds and railways. By 1893, British capital invested abroad was 15 per cent of the total wealth of the United Kingdom, nearly half in the form of loans to foreign and colonial governments. Of the rest, the largest proportion was invested in railways, banks, telegraphs, and other public services owned, controlled, or vitally affected by governments; the bulk of the remainder was placed in land or industries directly dependent on land values. A strong state structure in the hinterland to defend the loans was essential, as Canadian experience during this period showed.

CANADIAN MERCANTILISM: THE THIRD
COMMERCIAL EMPIRE OF THE ST LAWRENCE, 1867-1918

The system known as mercantilism in Europe consisted of a series of policies aimed at internal economic consolidation and/or expansion. It was the economic counterpart of the political process by which states were integrated and strengthened. While there were as many particular manifestations of 'mercantilism' as there were states engaging in such policies, the basic common factor was the existence of merchant capital as the principal mode of accumulation. In Britain, mercantilism might be said to have displayed three salient characteristics. (1) The edification of state power was theoretically the ultimate goal, with national wealth supposedly regarded as simply a means to attain it. Economy was held to be subservient to society and society to the state structure. (2) A strong paternalistic state directed the process through regulation of industry and trade, consolidation of the public finances, expansion of the tax base, rationalization of public administration, and the provision of social overhead capital; and all in coalition with a merchant, rather than an industrial, bourgeoisie. (3) Policies were adopted to stimulate industrial development by tariffs and subsidies, and by encouraging an inflow, or blocking an outflow, of skilled labour and capital – capital then largely in the form of bullion. The balance of trade doctrine, however, is not a necessary part of all mercantilism; only when international capital movements take the form of specie flows is a surplus on the balance of trade necessary to attract it. Under certain conditions, to be examined shortly, a balance of trade deficit is necessary.

Canadian Confederation and the subsequent national policy are an unambiguous example of mercantilism in action.

As to the edification of state power as primary, no less an authority than Sir John A. Macdonald concurred: 'There are national considerations ... that rise far higher than the mere accumulation of wealth, than the mere question of trade advantage; there is prestige, national status, national dominion ... and no great nation has ever arisen whose policy was Free Trade.'[43] Subsequently, of course, Macdonald and his henchmen made fortunes out of railway swindles, establishing that under ideal circumstances national and personal interests would coincide. Macdonald's conversion in practice from being a disciple of Sir James Stuart to one of Adam Smith, and the ensuing CPR scandals, heralded the birth of Canadian liberalism.

The second characteristic was very much in evidence – a strong state structure, with considerable interference with and direction of the course of expansion, even to the extent of establishing state-chartered monopolies.

The British North America Act was derived from a political theory of branch plant imperialism: lower levels of government were formerly weak and dependent on Britain; now they were to be weak and dependent on Ottawa, which was in turn answerable ultimately to Westminster.[44] The Act was essentially a document in public finance, reserving for the federal government every power critical to controlling the pattern of economic development.[45] All taxes other than direct (which then implied land taxes), regulation of trade and commerce, banking, credit, currency, bankruptcy, canals, telegraphs, navigation, and all residual powers went to the federal government. Provincial revenue requirements were expected to be met by a paltry subsidy.[46]

Power over money matters was to rest exclusively with the federal government, direct taxation would be politically unpopular, and the meagre subsidy was expected to remain permanent. Liberal democracy in Canada was thus set back three decades. Strangling the provincial assemblies' powers over the purse meant that the mercantile oligarchy would have no further difficulties in raising capital for their particular purposes, as long as they controlled the federal government, and popular protest was relegated to the provinces. As an additional safeguard the old legislative council was restored, federally appointed, to its former grandeur in the guise of the Senate. As if this were not enough, the federal government also assumed the imperial government's power of disallowance over colonial (provincial) legislation.

The Reformer Dorion who opposed the scheme objected to the assumption of imperial disallowance powers and denounced the Tory party as one which 'always sides with the Crown'; the Tory constitution would result in Canada having 'the most illiberal constitution ever heard of in any country where constitutional government prevails.'[47]

By contrast, the cretinous George Brown was quite explicit in his reasons for supporting Confederation. Canadian 5 per cent bonds had fallen seriously in London to the level of 71. But Brown pointed out that on the day the Confederation resolutions reached London they rose to 75. When the full texts arrived there they rose to 92,[48] lending considerable credence to the view that the Baring Brothers were the true Fathers of Confederation.[49]

The anti-Confederate Joseph Howe expressed the similar view that imperial pro-Confederation sentiment was vested in two groups: those who wanted to rid Britain of the colonies and those who were worried about their investments in Canada and wanted colonial union so that the revenue of the Maritimes would be attached to those of Canada, enabling them to secure payment of the debts.[50] In New Brunswick the electorate rejected the plan. The local manufacturing group, already under attack from American exports, feared a further assault by Canadian ones. The Saint John bankers were frightened by the possible competition of the (federally controlled) Canadian banks and the loss of their local monopoly. And most merchants had closer ties with the United States than with Canada. But imperial pressure, Canadian campaign funds, the impending end of reciprocity, better guarantees for the Intercolonial, and the drying up of British capital sources turned the tide and coerced the Maritimes into Confederation.[51]

The centralization of economic and political power is a sharp contrast to American patterns, and one of Canada's greatest national myths holds that this centralization was due to the disingenuous and beneficent wisdom of the Fathers of Confederation who wanted to save their country from a débâcle like the American Civil War. (The real explanation will be evident shortly.) A further noteworthy contrast is the relegation to the provinces of such mundane matters as civil rights. Moreover, while the American states were left responsible for their own public debts with, in some cases, catastrophic effects on their ability to pay them or raise new loans in international capital markets, the federal government in Canada assumed the burden of provincial indebtedness with immediate advantages in terms of international credit rating. The taxation powers also proved of signal advantage in raising capital for development purposes, permitting the federal government to channel off savings which were then handed over in seldom repaid loans and grants to the railway interests who controlled the federal government.[52]

In addition to securing high credit ratings internationally, federal control over banking and currency also prevented the pursuit of cheap money policies (which favour the debtor by reducing the real burden of his debt by inflation at the expense of the creditor). The debtors were farmers; the creditors, financiers and railway magnates. The conservatism of the banking structure and its government-protected concentration helped after, as well as before Confederation, to perpetuate a staple-extracting economy.[53]

The dominant position of the state structure also was manifested in the western expansion. American expansion was led by the pioneer settler, fleeing the rise of agribusiness with the state structure following in his wake, but in Canada the state structure – that is to say, the CPR and its military arm, the Canadian Pacific Mounted Police – went first, expropriating the Indians and Métis and allocating new lands to the settlers who followed. The horizons, and to a remarkable extent the personnel, of the federal government and the CPR were often inseparable.

Far from being the response of a rising industrial capitalism striving to break down intercolonial tariff walls, Confederation and the national policy were the work of the descendants of the mercantile class which had aligned itself with the Colonial Office in 1837 to crush the indigenous petite bourgeoisie and nascent industrialists. As we indicated earlier, the direct line of descent runs from merchant capital, not to industrial capital but to banking and finance, railways, utilities, land speculation, and so on – activities dependent upon and closely connected with the state structure. Banks function as intermediaries between savers and investors and grew out of merchant capitalists pooling their resources. Transportation – and in this period that means railways – intermediate flows of goods between producers and consumers. A few examples will make the linkages clear.

Donald Smith, later Lord Strathcona, commenced his career as the Labrador commissioner of the Hudson's Bay Company. As early as 1857, he had become a shareholder in the Bank of Montreal along with other officers of that company and of the North West Company which it had absorbed. The HBC itself was a classic mercantile corporation concerned with entrepôt activities. It ruled a subject population of 147,000 Indians and 11,000 whites and Métis in an empire larger than continental Europe. The mark-up on merchandise sold to settlers and Indians was between 100 and 400 per cent; private trading was outlawed and a capital offence. The Indians were thus forced to rely exclusively on the Company for gunpowder; and the few settlers that had managed to squeeze into the territory, part of Selkirk's legacy, depended on it as their sole market for agricultural produce. Over half the profits were remitted to England.

In 1863, the Grand Trunk syndicate purchased majority control of the Company with a view to extending their line to the Pacific coast. And in 1869 they duly surrendered vast tracts of land to the Dominion government in the expectation that it would be ceded back to them as a land grant for railway development, with a net gain of the Dominion purchase price of the land. There were exceptions to the surrender of HBC lands – one-twentieth of the total and the area around the trading posts were reserved for the Company. These tracts around the posts were subsequently to become urban centres and increase astronomically in value, and, of course, the Company held the title. But who held the title to the HBC itself?

In 1870 the wintering partners of the Company sent Donald Smith to England to present their claims to a share of the proceeds of the sale of the company lands to the Dominion. The sale of land had greatly weakened the Company's position and its stocks were trading at a very low price; Smith was quick to take advantage, and he bought up the majority holding. In 1874 he duly appointed himself land commissioner of the Company, thereby acquiring control over the remaining company lands.[54]

The Indians and Métis, whose existence had been crucial to the profit position of the Bay, now represented an impediment to settlement. Burning the prairies to drive away the buffalo helped as a solution to the Indian problem, as did another land transfer. After the HBC's surrender of lands to the Dominion government, huge areas were duly transferred to the CPR and other railway enterprises linked to it. The CPR proved itself a good corporate citizen of the new Dominion by bringing troops into the territory to clear the Métis off the lands it had been granted. Eminent among these railway magnates who received the lands taken from the Hudson's Bay Company was, not surprisingly, the malignant Donald Smith.

The list of eminent financiers and railwaymen of the period is a veritable 'who's who' of Canadian politics for two generations. And without exception, the linkage runs from merchant capitalism to finance, transportation, and land speculation. The Maritime timber merchant Cunard founded a trans-Atlantic steamship company that still bears his name. The Molson family branched out from breweries into banking and a St Lawrence steamship company. Sir Hugh Allen commenced as a grain merchant and subsequently moved into steamships, railways, and insurance. John A. Macdonald was one of the incorporators of the Kingston Fire and Marine Insurance Company in 1850 and of the Trust and Loan Company of Upper Canada; he subsequently became president of the Manufacturers' Life Assurance Company.

The Montreal and Kingston Railway Company of 1851 included among its incorporators A.T. Galt and George Moffat of the land monopolies, John Young, A.N. Morin, L.T. Holton, and George Etienne Cartier. P.J. Chauveau, first premier of Quebec after Confederation, headed the promoters and incorporators of the Quebec and Saguenay Railway Company. Sir George Simpson of the Hudson's Bay Company was an early president of the North Shore Railway. The Quebec clerical elite were especially zealous stockholders in these concerns: by tithes, by rents on their lands or by borrowing from their communicants at virtually no interest, the church raised capital to invest widely in steamships and railways.[55] The Grand Trunk promoters included Peter McGill of the Bank of Montreal and the Annexation Manifesto, Galt, and Cartier. As McNab might have put it – politics are my railways.

The example of Cartier is particularly revealing of the historical lineage. His grandfather had been a merchant dealing in early staples – salt, fish, and wheat. His father was a founder of the Bank of Montreal and of the railway company St Laurent–Lac Champlain.[56] Cartier himself rose to prominence through the Grand Trunk and as Macdonald's right-hand man.

The conservatism of the political philosophy espoused by the Fathers of Confederation, and their much vaunted distaste for the mass liberal experiment to the south, reflects little more than their material position as big merchants, bankers, and transportation magnates, rather than industrial entrepreneurs. A search for a genuine, deep-rooted Canadian liberalism would have ended here. Canada was born a conservative political economy because this is the ideological counterpart of merchant capitalism.[57] Liberalism is the ideology of the industrial entrepreneur; industrialism breeds a philosophy of laissez-faire. But merchant capitalism works through the state structure to enforce its monopoly position. The willingness of Canadian political and business elites to use the state structure to control and develop the economy and enrich themselves is not the consequence of conservatism, but its cause.

Like the Hudson's Bay Company it replaced, the Canadian Pacific Railway was a mercantile, state-chartered monopoly. Initially two companies attempted to secure the contract. The dominant triumvirate that emerged after Macdonald's return to office in 1878 consisted of Donald Smith, who represented the landed interest, George Stephen of the Bank of Montreal, the financial interest, and the American entrepreneur William Van Horne, who was responsible for construction, that is, for all activities requiring productive talent rather than just political influence. Lands taken from the Bay were ceded back to the CPR together with enormous gifts of cash, land guarantees, already completed lines, and tariff and tax exemptions. The fact that transcontinental expansion led by the CPR followed the route of the fur trade is thus a scant surprise. And, as the CPR route made them potential urban centres, the lands around the fur-trading posts left in the hands of the HBC, alias Donald Smith, increased enormously in value.

Third among the attributes of a mercantile system (after a powerful state and much state regulation) were the policies adopted to stimulate territorial and population expansion and industrial development.

From 1868 to 1874, Canadian exports to the United States had grown 30 per cent in spite of the abrogation of reciprocity. But the great depression beginning in 1873 led to a collapse of primary product prices which ruined timber merchants and destroyed Quebec's cereal-based agriculture, forcing a partial switch to dairy products.[58] In Ontario, the collapse of grain prices ruined a large number of farms and produced a rush to the cities, where the farmers attempted to break into retail trade. The resulting oversupply of small merchants meant a rate of business failure in Canada of three times that of the United States. While charges of US dumping were bandied about, the real cause of the crisis was agricultural, and the main result was the fall from office of McKenzie's low-tariff administration. The National Policy of high tariffs followed Macdonald's return to office.

The tariff was not needed to protect existing industry, which was small and highly competitive with imports.[59] Even as late as 1876, evidence before a Commons select committee showed most witnesses to be overwhelmingly in favour of reciprocity. The purpose of the tariff was not to 'protect' existing industry but to expand the scale of the economy by attracting capitalists and blocking the outflow of population. Macdonald in 1878 could not have been more specific: 'We have no manufacturers here. We have no work-people; our work-people have gone off to the United States ... These Canadian artisans are adding to the strength, to the power, and to the wealth of a foreign nation instead of adding to ours. Our work-people in this country, on the other hand are suffering from want of employment ...

'If these men cannot find an opportunity in their own country to develop the skill and genius with which God has gifted them; they will go to a country where their abilities can be employed, as they have gone from Canada to the United States.

'If Canada had had a *judicious system of taxation*, they would be toiling and doing well in their own country.'[60]

The National Policy of the Tory merchant-capitalists was also supported by the Quebec clergy as a means of keeping their flock at home, settled on lands on which the hierarchy collected tithes and rents, and riding the railroads in which they were major stockholders.

The economic 'nationalism' pursued by the Tories did not contain any internal paradox. Attracting foreign capitalists and branch plants was explicit policy, a mercantile device for capital accumulation, and its short-run results were fully anticipated. The Tory politicians used mercantilist fiscal devices conceived in, and appropriate to, a world where international capital transfers took the form of bullion flows. It worked for Canadian mercantilists in the nineteenth century; in the twentieth century, it was their undoing.

Given that the National Policy was explicitly intended to attract foreign capitalists it cannot be analysed with the conventional liberal economists' tools, for these are designed to consider the effects of a tariff on an existing industrial structure rather than in augmenting the supply of factors of production available to the economy.[61] While industrialists do generally seek protection in the form of tariff walls from their governments, they do not seek government policies which aim to increase competition, especially from the very same foreign industrialist that the tariff is supposed to exclude. Preventing competition is what industrial protection is all about, and this is not what Macdonald's tariff was intended to do. Not only was there little industry to protect, but the consequence of the tariff was the antithesis of protection.

Clearly, it was not industrialists who initiated this policy but the merchant-capitalist class. The merchant, the banker, the railway and shipping tycoon, and the landholder all benefit from the absolute expansion of economic activity, while in the long run the local industrial entrepreneur loses. The dominance of merchant capital means the draining off of funds into mercantile pursuits and away from industry. Together with the tariff, the result is the stultification of industrial capital. In previously open sectors where no domestic industry existed, the future potential of the local industrialist is reduced by the establishment of foreign branch plants. In cases where domestic industry does coexist with imports, the tariff-induced branch plants increase competition and reduce the prices at which the merchant class can purchase output for their intermediary activity. In other cases, the tariff leads to rapid cartelization.[62]

Canadian manufacturers were certainly eager for 'protection,' but not of the sort the National Policy gave them. The complaints were many and vehement from established capitalists as each province, city, and even town pursued its own mini-National Policy by offering every manner of bribe – tax concessions, land, low utility rates, loans, and even cash grants to branch-plant industry.[63] The real winner was the mercantile sector of the Canadian bourgeoisie working through the Tory party.

The essential policy of the Montreal merchants from 1763 had been strict mercantilism within the British Empire together with free trade with the United States. American production of American goods was intermediated by Canadian merchants via the St Lawrence route. Confederation and the National Policy were simply an adaptation of the old pattern, in the light of free trade in Britain and the abrogation of reciprocity by the United States; but now the intermediation was to be internal. The branch plants represented a shift in the locus of production to inside the border, production which could be shunted off to other parts of the internal mercantile system by the same merchant class in a slightly new guise.

The contradiction between the requirements of Canadian merchant capital and those of Canadian industrial capital was thus decided in favour of the merchants. Industrial capital needs cheap raw materials, easy credit conditions, and low transport costs; merchant capital relies on regional scarcities of raw materials and goods to obtain high prices extracted through credit costs, transportation rates, and merchandise mark-up. Merchant capital, typified by a low ratio of fixed to circulatory capital, also needs rapid turnover, and cannot undertake long-term risky investment. It is, therefore, oriented towards abetting the quick extraction of staple output, rather than industrial processing.

Another adjunct of the National Policy was the encouragement of immigration. Canada was largely agrarian during the 1870s, and it was difficult to coax the inhabitants off the land in the East either to settle the West or to be proletarianized. Immigration policy was the response. At first, the policy of western settlement was a failure; this is usually attributed to the greater lure of the American West. It is often maintained that Canada's West was not settled until the American West was filled. Perhaps so, but filled with what? The enormous migration to Canada in the last decade of the nineteenth and first of the twentieth centuries contained a large proportion of Americans who clearly could not be fleeing from the settlers of the American West, but rather from the rise of agribusiness, the bankruptcy of the family farm, and the imposition on them of tenant farmer status.[64]

Another reason for the early failure of Canadian immigration policy was land monopolization. Upon receiving its land grant, the CPR immediately sold 5 million acres for cash to the North West Land Company, a consortium of British capitalists including Donald Smith who was rapidly replacing the Baring Brothers as the simulacrum behind Dominion development policy. Together with Smith's Hudson's Bay Company, the North West Land Company controlled five-ninths of the arable land. Early attempts to squeeze high prices out of the land blocked an inflow of European settlers.

Even where settlement did occur, western farmers were exploited by both the CPR's transportation monopoly, and the tightly cartelized banking system. The eastern banks (operating through western branches) would offer only short-term credit, whereas the farmers required long-term loans. The role of the banks thus reinforced the farmers' dependency on a single cash crop since the earnings in good years would have to be used to pay off the debts contracted in the bad years.

Agribusiness was alien to the Canadian West. The mode of production remained largely petit bourgeois, with increasing mechanization displacing farm labour. The upper middle classes in the urban areas were, by and large, branch managers of eastern banks or eastern mercantile chain stores, Eaton's, Simpson's, and the Bay.[65] The land companies were mercantile, concerned with speculative land sales rather than agricultural production. The grain elevator companies were eastern-based and tightly cartelized; by 1900, three-quarters of the elevators in western Canada were owned by five companies.

An important source of capital at this time was British portfolio investment, which was encouraged to a large extent by the centralization of monetary control in Canada with the resulting high credit ratings in international finance capital markets. Private Canadian firms had been unable to draw on the London capital markets because of their small size and concomitant risks. Only quasi-public bodies could do so. And the merchant banks prior to 1900 were providers of short-term credit only. British finance capital filled the void.

Prior to the First World War, British capital invested in Canada greatly exceeded American, and there were fundamental differences in form. About 90 per cent of British investments in Canada up to 1913 consisted of purchases of Canadian securities, of which the greatest proportion was government and financial institution bonds and debenture stock without voting rights. Enormous borrowings by governments were not restricted to the federal and provincial levels: even small municipalities overloaded themselves with public debt to pursue their little national policies of bribing firms to locate within their domain. The provinces, robbed of revenue sources by the terms of Confederation, had no other means of raising capital. Most of the remaining ten per cent of British investments went into the speculative purchase of town and agricultural lands, or was invested in British insurance companies, in mortgages, loans, and securities. This pattern fits in perfectly with the general character of British portfolio investment throughout the world during the pinnacle of empire. The sole objective was to obtain interest in stable investments. In most of the very few cases where a majority of the common stock was held by British investors, the control of the enterprise 'by tacit consent of the British shareholders remained with the Canadian minority shareholders.'[66]

That Canada was, prior to the First World War, the most favoured colony of the British empire in terms of the amount of portfolio investment can be credited to the readiness of the Tory merchant-capitalists (and the Whig railway group after 1900) to use the state structure to guarantee loans to other private or public undertakings. By 1912, government bond guarantees for private railways totalled a quarter of a billion dollars. British portfolio investments built up other transportation projects as well, and the public utilities, the banking, and the financial sector.

The pattern of American investment prompted by the tariff on manufactures was quite different. Less than 40 per cent of American investments in Canada prior to 1913 were security purchases, and most of these came at the end of the period. The great majority were direct investments in branch plants. Often the capital utilized was far greater than the amount of American capital actually invested, the remainder being obtained by borrowings from the growing Canadian banking systems and thus, at one level removed, from British portfolio investment, or by floating loans directly in Britain. The Americans retained control through their ownership of the common stock 'often representing nothing but ... the productive technique and the promotional ability of the American interest in the project.'[67] This pattern of British finance capital, American industrial entrepreneurship, and Canadian natural resources – the proverbial North Atlantic triangle – was an elaborate magnification of that set by the CPR triumvirate: George Stephen representing finance, William Van Horne the industrial ability, and Donald Smith the Hudson's Bay Company lands.

By 1911, when Laurier's government was overthrown, the Liberal party, through the influence of the new railway syndicates with their dependence on British loans, was evolving into a big-business Whig party and coming close to outdoing the Conservative party in pro-British sycophancy. But the bulk of Liberal support was from those with agrarian and Maritime low-tariff interests. Reciprocity divided the party, causing some defections, and the Tories used anti-American slogans to maintain the National Policy with the full realization that the tariff was the key to the influx of branch plants. Reciprocity might have meant a withdrawal of industrial capacity across the border,[68] which Sifton, a dissident Liberal, predicted would put an end to 'the industrial development of Canada by American branch plants,'[69] an event which would have benefitted some Canadian industrialists while injuring the mercantile class.

'No trunk nor trade with the Yankees' meant home production of American goods rather than imports. In 1911 the branch plant system and the mercantile bourgeoisie won once more.

By the late nineteenth and early twentieth centuries, the international division of labour that has continued to prevail until the present was well established. The branch plant secondary sector prompted by the tariff with free entry of many parts was strongly biased towards assembly operations. The close control exercised by the American parent over its Canadian subsidiary assured the perpetuation of this division of function. In the primary sector, not covered by the tariff, the typical pattern was the extraction of resources and the export of raw materials for processing in the United States.[70] In the few instances where significant processing of resources did occur within Canada, this reflected not 'comparative advantage,' but conscious policy decisions.

Given the abundance of British portfolio capital available, part of it supporting American direct investment, and given the good credit rating of the
federal government, it is clear that the influx of direct investment to take advantage of the tariff and to loot natural resources cannot be explained by a
shortage of capital. Any deficiency of local savings, if such existed, could be
easily offset by the credit Britain could offer in exchange for cannon fodder
for the imperial wars. The answer most in vogue at present is a 'shortage of
indigenous entrepreneurship.'[71] This explanation is false in the sense that 'entrepreneurship' can be either industrial or mercantile, and Canada, much to
its misfortune, has had no lack of the latter throughout its history. With respect to industrial entrepreneurship, if we interpret deficiency thereof as im-
plying that American capitalism possessed some special attributes permitting
it to take advantage of productive opportunities which Canadian capitalism in
the particular period under consideration did not, then the explanation is tau-
tological, and thus trivial in so far as it fails to make specific reference to the
objective social conditions of the period, especially the pattern of dependence.
The real problem was the stultification of indigenous industrial capital by the
continued dominance of merchant capital in alliance with British finance capital, together with the historically rooted characteristics of American capitalism.

In contrast to the conservatism of British finance capital and Canadian merchant capital, both of which tended to avoid risk and to rely on the security
of the state structure, American investments in Canada were made in speculative and risky enterprises requiring modern industrial techniques and venture-
some management, investments which offered a chance of unusually high profits as well as losses.[72] These attributes of American investment were not
accidental, but were the result of the particular process of historical development followed by American capitalism.

With the stimulus to industrialization provided by the Civil War and the
post-war high tariffs, the entrepreneur's local single factory grew into the vertically integrated national corporation.[73] During the critical post-war phase of
American expansion, a financial elite began to emerge alongside the industrial
system; but it never achieved a position of dominance. This pattern was the
result of two events. First, the dismantling of the Bank of the United States
and the outlawing of branch banking crippled the growth of finance capital.
Second, and related to the first, was the absence of state interference with
business after the 1830s with the collapse of state credit and the series of
bank failures that followed the repudiation of debts by Mississippi and Florida. Clauses were introduced into many state constitutions prohibiting the
states from engaging directly in business ventures and from providing aid to
private corporations through bond guarantees.[74] After 1848, similar clauses
were introduced into the constitutions of all new states, setting the course of

American development more definitely in the direction of private independent enterprise.[75] Independent of the state structure and independent of the financial system, the corporations were forced to turn inside themselves for a capital resource, and internal financing wherever possible became a cardinal rule of corporate behaviour. Corporation capital in its American form thus merged industrial capital and finance capital into a single organic whole, and finance capital never became a potent force on its own. After reaching the limits of possible expansion in the form of the vertically integrated national concerns, the corporation's horizons expanded as well to take a global view in the form of expanding export markets. The export advantage was admirably suited to permit America to feed off the taproot of other imperialisms. British finance capital was made available to Canada through the flotation of loans which were then used to buy New York bills of exchange. In turn, this exchange was used to pay for imports from the United States. The adjustment of the British balance of payments to the capital invested in Canada was effected through British exports to the United States. In spite of its heavy borrowings during this period, Canada maintained a favourable balance of visible trade with Britain. But its imbalance with the US was much greater than its borrowings there. Hence 'the capital borrowed by Canada in Great Britain largely entered Canada in the form of American commodities.'[76]

The American corporations, forever the innovators, advanced to their highest stage, that euphemistically called 'multinationality' through direct investments abroad on an enormous scale. Export of direct investment is accompanied by export of industrial organization, consumer taste patterns, social philosophy, and inevitably metropolitan law through the subsidiary. Unlike earlier experiences, in the American empire the flag follows trade.

THE SECOND INTERREGNUM, 1919-39

As we have seen, the Macdonald tariff produced industry in Canada but no Canadian industry,[77] because it was not intended to produce Canadian firms. It was a mercantile rather than an industrial protective tariff, designed explicitly to augment the quantity of productive factors available to the economy by attracting foreign capital. To the merchant capitalist ruling class, the nationality of the industrial sector was irrelevant: what counted was its size and its location in central Canada. The federal government did not play the role of entrepreneur, as is often suggested, but that of financial intermediary and provider of social overhead capital. And the so-called Laurentian thesis that the country's development followed the route blazed by the fur traders reveals more about the direction of intercorporate linkage than it does of principles of development economics.

It is not surprising then, that the tertiary sector, the sector servicing industrial capital – banking and finance, transportation, communications, and utilities – has to this day the least percentage of foreign control. Built up by British finance capital, directed by Canadian merchant capital and the federal
government, it has remained dominated by the descendants of the merchant
capital class. Constructed during the era of transcontinental expansion, this
sector was really a branch plant of British imperialism that owed its subsequent independence not to the promotional abilities of the Tory merchant
class, but to the fact that British imperialism utilized portfolio rather than
direct investment to link hinterland and metropole. Government policy to
protect this sector from foreign take-over cannot explain the absence of foreign control; for without a strong, indigenous vested interest, there would
have been no government policy.

In spite of the influx of American direct investment prompted by the tariff,
Canada remained firmly a British appendage until the end of the First World
War. British finance capital invested in Canada was three times the level of
American industrial capital. At this stage, American natural resources, with
the important exceptions of forests and some minerals, were still abundant.
American capital had moved into lumber in the 1830s and into silver and cop-
per in 1846. By 1880 over half of the mining in Ontario and Quebec was
American-owned.[78] The overwhelming share of mining finance was done by
equity and very little by funded debt. Mining shares were held by banks, but
only as collateral against call loans; and these shares were confined to companies whose property contained ore bodies of an established asset and value.
British investments in Canadian mining were minimal.[79] But the total value of
mining as a percentage of GNP was fairly small. An index of the strength of
the British connection during this period was the fact that, despite its free
trade rhetoric, the Laurier administration was pressured into introducing a
double schedule into the tariff giving preference to British export goods, although Britain still refused to budge from its free trade position. The preference simply served to force more American branch plants to establish themselves to avoid losing the Canadian market to British exporters. Canadian
industrial capital was still not strong enough to challenge the hegemony of
Tory merchant capital and British finance capital.

The years between the wars were the era of the wheat staple. Like fish, fur,
and timber before it, the ratio of fixed to circulating capital was low, predominantly because it was in the interests of the banks and transportation monopoly to keep it low. The farmers needed long-term capital to improve the
farms and develop the crop base, but bank lending was restricted to short-
term credit, reinforcing their dependence on the unstable single cash crop.

Prairie depressions led to massive abandonment of farms and to dust bowls. The prairie surplus appropriated through the transportation monopoly and its grain elevator connections, the agricultural implements cartel fostered by the tariff, and the absence of anti-trust laws, and the banking cartel's ability to demand higher interest rates in the west than those prevailing in the east, all supplied revenue that could be used to pay off the imperial loans. The markets too were European, providing the east-west linear nexus to the flow of economic activity that validated the national policy. The tariff, by fostering branch plant manufacturers in central Canada, complemented the system by permitting railway overheads to be spread over the coming and going.[80] The result was to create a relatively homogeneous class structure in the West. The petit bourgeois base and the upper middle class which was largely representative of eastern mercantile concerns, together with the colonial character of the western economy, would in the end prove a thorn in the side of the mercantile elite by breeding strong, unified folk movements in opposition to the mercantile central authority.[81]

The system could sustain one transcontinental railway system, but not three. Yet transcontinental expansion was necessary if the new railways were successfully to tap the grain and merchandise flows. The new railways, unlike the CPR, had been built with a high proportion of funded debt which left them immediately with enormous fixed interest charges to bear. The sole way of covering the charges was immediate development of traffic in raw materials. The result was the fostering of rapid exploitation of mines and pulpwood. The costs of rapid depletion and the damage done to the future economic potential of outlying areas were ignored for the benefit of metropolitan centre finance and railway interests. The railways, like the banks, must bear their share of the responsibility for perpetrating an extractive economy.[82] But even this did not suffice to prevent bankruptcy. The Tory government sought a solution through nationalization of the Canadian Northern, the Grand Trunk, and the Grand Trunk Pacific. The CPR and Bank of Montreal had hoped to merge the bankrupt line with their own and objected to nationalization. When Arthur Meighen subsequently nationalized the Grand Trunk and Grand Trunk Pacific, the CPR and Bank of Montreal groups switched allegiance to the Liberal party.[83] For the Tories it was the beginning of the end.[84]

East of the Ottawa River, few cheers for the national policy could be heard. Most of the branch plants were in Ontario. The flood of western wheat had completed the destruction of Quebec cereal agriculture. The logging industry was in decline with the most accessible stands suitable for lumber depleted by merchant capital's need for rapid turnover. The Quebec shipbuilding industry did not survive the triumph of steam power. The Vieilles Forges near Trois Rivières, seat of Quebec's iron industry for two centuries, had collapsed in the face of American branch plant competition and were abandoned in 1883. Nearly 300,000 people emigrated from Quebec between 1881 and 1911. Also, Quebec had no coal deposits, and its iron and asbestos were still inaccessible in the Shield.[85]

In the Maritimes, Confederation and the railways destroyed the national geographic protection of their fledgeling industry. The western prairies satellite favoured central Canadian manufacturers through geographic advantages. The coal mines had been expected to form the basis of industrialization: instead the coal was shipped to Ontario to feed branch plant manufactories there. The fisheries were on the decline. The Maritimers lived more than just rhetorically on the wrong side of the tracks.[86]

After the First World War, the British imperial system was in decline, but not yet dead, for the legacy of its period of hegemony, the enormous portfolio indebtedness incurred, was to prove its heaviest burden on Canada. But the political influence of Britain declined, and the political and economic influence of the United States grew *pari passu.* American imperialism had extended into Canada to take advantage of British imperialism, of the Canadian-European linkage based on the St Lawrence and its legislative extension along the 49th parallel by the tariff. On 28 April 1925 the British empire died, when the chancellor of the exchequer, Winston Churchill, announced Britain's return to the gold standard[87] which meant that her already weak balance of trade position would continue to deteriorate and her debts to the United States pile up. The passing of the Statute of Westminster marked the formal transfer of Canada from Britain to the United States, giving the Canadian bourgeoisie the constitutional authority to beg favours from Washington as they previously had from London.[88] Canadian independence from the United States had always been conditional on its continued dependence on Britain, on the fact that it was in the material interests of British capitalism to prevent Canadian capitalism from engaging in a wholesale sell-out to American capitalism. With the Statute of Westminster, the precarious balance was upset.

The British system of international *haute finance* could operate only in the context of stable, freely convertible currencies. The post-war bouts of monetary instability had damaged it seriously. With the collapse of the gold standard during the great depression, the system disintegrated completely. But the depression also meant a collapse of world wheat prices and a concomitant severe rise in the real burden of fixed interest charges on railway and utility debts payable to Britain from Canada, charges that amounted during some years to 25 per cent of the total foreign exchange earnings of the economy. The great pillars of the Tory national policy crumbled along with its mentor.

The policy response was predictably myopic: an attempt to lessen the burden of the problem by increasing its extent, through soliciting more foreign investment, increasingly in the form of branch plants. Much as American exports had earlier fed off loans of finance capital from Britain to Canada, now American direct investment firms cashed in on the collapse of finance capital and the weakness of the Canadian economy in the face of the enormous burden of fixed interest charges. American exports had earlier requited the transfer of British finance capital into Canada: now American industrial capital requited the return flow of interest payments to Britain.

The Ottawa Agreements were a last ditch stand of British imperialism, largely dismantled at American request after the war; however, in effect they strengthened, not the British hold, but the American one. Imperial preference was now a two-way stream, and American direct investment firms were quick to take advantage. The Dominion government defended its tariff policy on the explicit admission that in 1931 alone tariff changes had caused ninety new branch plants to blast their way into Canadian markets.[89] In 1846 the British metropolis had failed the Canadian merchants and ruined their grain trade by adopting free trade – and the response was annexation, an invitation to American .take-over; in the 1930s the British metropole failed them again ruining their grain staple, and the response was further invitation to American take-over. The third commercial empire of the St Lawrence had definitively ended.

In all the provinces, the need for additional revenues to cope with the depression in the wake of federal apathy meant the cultivation of economic ties with the United States. Several forces were at work to increase the degree of continental integration at the expense of the European link. New staples were emerging. Pulp and paper, minerals, oil and gas, and hydroelectric power, unlike the old staples, required a high ratio of fixed to circulating capital which Canadian merchant capital and British finance capital were not equipped either materially or emotionally to provide. The investments would be necessarily risky in the initial stages. The 'natural' markets for the new staples were American. These resource industries fell within the provincial sphere of authority. And unlike the old staples which were intermediated by the Canadian mercantile bourgeoisie on their way to European markets, the American corporations could exploit the new staples directly; and the corporation, rather than the market, would determine the division of labour. The extensive links south established by Canadian railways and banks facilitated the process of destroying the linear nexus on which the national policy was predicated. American corporation capital responded with predictable alacrity.

After the Second World War a flood of American direct investment into Canada occurred as industrial branch plant capitalism and the Liberal party succeeded in wresting the country from the British nexus and transferring it in total to the American. In 1949, Canada's balance of international indebtedness as a proportion of GNP was at the lowest point of the century, and virtually all the external debt was American direct investment. The British 'connection' was completely paid off.

As with the Tories three-quarters of a century earlier, the theoretical basis of Liberal policy was out of date. The Tory party had worked with precepts from the British mercantile period, appropriate in the short run to their material position as merchant capitalists and colonial financiers, but inappropriate in the long run to the world of direct investment flows that would overthrow them. The Liberals derived their faith from an earlier period of market-oriented industrialization; it was a faith woefully inadequate in the new world of international corporation capitalism.

CANADA IN THE AMERICAN CORPORATE EMPIRE

The high tariff structure alone cannot explain the post-war rush of American corporate capital into Canada. While the Macdonald tariff can be given the bulk of the credit, or blame, for intrusions into the secondary sector until the depression (though not of course the unprotected primary sector), the post-war influx cannot be so easily attributed to Macdonald's failure to read Ricardo.[90] The post-war period has been one of successive rounds of multilateral tariff reductions; at the same time, it has been one of unprecedented international flows of direct investment. Hence, liberal economists who claim that the branch plant structure of present-day Canadian industry is attributable to the tariff are in the curious position of maintaining that high tariffs *and* tariff reduction *both* stimulate direct investment. While a tariff may be a partial explanation of why foreign investors set up new capacity in a protected economy, or why independent industry is established under inefficient conditions, it can never explain actual take-overs of already existing independent firms – and these account for a major share of post-war American expansion.

In a world where capital flowed internationally at the same speed as the Royal Navy, an interest rate differential was the signal of a capital shortage to which a portfolio flow would respond. But direct investment is the external counterpart of the internally retained earnings of a corporation: it does not pass through the banking structure, and it responds not to interest rates, but to the future level of profits it is expected to generate. Hence it does not necessarily move to an area where capital is scarce. The converse is more likely the case. It is aimed at the most dynamic outlet, an economy that has already proven itself capable of generating the surplus to sustain real capital formation and the income to clear its product markets. This dictum is indisputable in the case of direct investment in manufacturing for sale in the hinterland.

But it also holds for direct investment in resource industries; for here the investment is directed, not at the hinterland, but at the metropolitan market.

But if capital is available in the hinterland, why does not the indigenous capitalist class undertake the process of industrial development? In Canada, the process of penetration by direct investment has been aided considerably by the legacy of merchant capital, an overdeveloped transportation and financial infrastructure which drains funds away from industry. The tightly cartelized banking system cannot provide long-term risk capital, but is concerned primarily with liquidity. Life insurance companies prefer fixed interest securities and government bonds and mortgages, and invest only in very gilt-edged securities, which naturally are those of big established American concerns. In fact, the Canadian Insurance Company Act operative prior to the Second World War required that common stock investments be limited to shares presenting a continuous dividend record for seven years preceding the date of purchase. These factors, together with the reluctance of American firms to issue minority shares in their subsidiaries, twist the Canadian capital market so that Canadian capital continues to flow into utilities, agriculture, housing, merchandising, and government bonds,[91] thus robbing industry of funds. The National Policy also submerged local industry, by encouraging branch plants which could draw on parental income when short of funds. Any part of Canadian industry that has survived the National Policy and the resurgence of merchant capital has been tightly cartelized and closely held for generations, often within the same family.

Empires built on direct investment are the highest stage of imperialism. Mercantile empires are premised on exclusivist sources of primary staples with markets regulated by the imperial government; laissez-faire empires are predicated on the free exchange of staples and finished products. In both cases, the colonial surplus is appropriated through the act of exchange itself by the imposition of adverse terms of trade. Portfolio investment empires are based on self-liquifying loans, and the surplus is extracted through a return flow of interest payments. But direct investment empires are founded on the take-over of the actual production process, and they grow on their own volition by reinvestment of alienated hinterland surplus.

During the regime of British finance capital, the imperial nexus required a strong state structure to mediate flows along an east-west nexus. The National Policy produced a linear monocentric political economy ruled from Ottawa by Toronto and Montreal merchant capitalists who, in turn, were answerable to Westminster. Staples flowed from west to east; manufactures from east to west; finance capital from London to Montreal and Toronto, and interest payments back to London. But the linkages under the rule of corporation capital are very different.

The new staple industries and the rise of branch plant industrialism provided the provincial governments with the means to regain the financial powers they had been robbed of by Confederation. The rise of provincial powers has been contingent upon their hastening the development of resource extraction from which they can collect royalties. The royalties and other tax sources in turn can be used to try to bribe secondary industry to locate within their spheres of authority. In cases of direct investment in secondary industry, firms tend to cluster together to protect their market share and encroach on those of their competitors. This tendency to urbanization is not a new one. In 1913 over 70 per cent of the American branch plants were located in the seven largest urban centres. In 1934, when the number of branch and plants had almost trebled, again 70 per cent were to be found in these centres.[92] The rise of branch plant industrialism has led to the secular stagnation of rural areas, a tendency greatly enhanced by rapid resource depletion policies fostered by tax give-aways and by the rise of American corporate farming leading to bankruptcy of the family farm. Concentrations of direct investment tend to fragment national markets and balkanize the state structure. Pressure groups and lobbies increasingly cluster about the provincial levels of government, and federal-provincial relations degenerate into an interminable squabble over the distribution of the spoils as each province requires an increasing share of total government revenue to bribe branch plant industry or resource-extracting firms into locating in its sphere of authority. Trends in the federal-provincial division of effective power during this century reflect little more than the ratio of American direct to British portfolio investment, the first co-operating with Canadian industrial capital and the Liberal party, the second with Canadian merchant capital and the Tory party. The advance of industrialism is normally an integrating social force producing nationalism; it is clear that second-hand industrialism is a disintegrating social force producing Pearsonian 'internationalism.'

Indigenous industrial capitalism in Canada was historically a weak force, stultified by the domination of merchant capital and the branch plant industry the Tory group fostered to complement its mercantile scheme. Despite the impetus given Canadian industrialism by the Second World War, the generation gap between it and American corporation capital was enough to guarantee its submergence and assimilation into continental American capitalism. At the same time, the old mercantile bourgeoisie was evolving into a corporate capitalist class.

When one considers the realities of the concentration of power inherent in the direct investment process, the contention that it is a two-way stream,[93] that it involves 'interdependence rather than dependence' as Jean-Luc Pepin claims to have devined, becomes an absurdity. While a strong case can be made for the view that European and American firms are engaged in a process of interpenetration that is best regarded as a form of international oligopoly, not completely subservient to any one state structure[94] - that is, that the corporate division of the world economy is taking precedence over the national division - the Canadian situation is exceptional.

First, *with certain very important exceptions*, Canadian ownership of US stock is widely spread out, and hence belongs in the realm of portfolio investment since it does not involve control. Second, within the United States, most of the stockholders are rentiers; directors of the corporation rule with only partial legal ownership of the common stock, while asymmetrically, in the hinterland, the parent corporation both owns and rules. Third, the outflow of Canadian investment capital that does occur is prompted, not by 'interdependence,' but by the highest stage of dependence, by the fact that parent corporations prefer 100 per cent ownership of their offspring and this effectively blocks equity participation in the hinterland. An infant industry may fail to mature because of congenital defects; it may also fail to grow up and assume responsibility because of an excessively domineering parent.[95]

The Canadian industrial bourgeoisie has thus been relegated to the position of managing branch plants for foreign masters; of serving, McLaughlin-style, as junior partners in continental American capitalism. But it is quite different with the old mercantile bourgeoisie. The railway, banking, and financial interests began very early to establish links with the United States. By 1929 over 77 per cent of Canadian direct investment in the United States was accounted for by railways and transportation interests, the banks, and the insurance companies.[96] A large share of the remainder was accounted for by the breweries and distilleries, very old Canadian businesses with close links to the mercantile bourgeoisie. Of Canadian direct investments in the United States today that actually involve control over an enterprise, the same groups - banking and finance, transportation, breweries and distilleries - account for the overwhelmingly large share. And with the exception of the CPR's mining complex, the mercantile bourgeoisie typically diversified into mining and manufacturing by buying up already established concerns, rather than setting up their own.[97]

But the independent sector of the Canadian bourgeoisie, largely the descendants of merchant capital, is small in relation to the total. Control of the Canadian economy lies overwhelmingly with the branch plant group. The National Policy and Canadian federalism were uniquely mercantile creations. The industrial bourgeoisie, through the Liberal party, has usurped the power structure only to find that a necessary condition of their rise to dominance is the disintegration of the mercantile structure they long sought to control. The spread of branch plant industrialism and extractive industries breeds increasingly greater contradictions, while the concomitant rise of provincial government powers makes them more and more difficult for the federal state structure to resolve.

The concentration of manufacturing in a few increasingly uninhabitable urban centres leaves pockets of poverty and structural unemployment scattered across the country. The dependence on capital-intensive staple exports is simultaneously the export of future employment: GNP rises rapidly, while technological unemployment rises even faster. The growth of 'multinational' firms means reinforcement of the imitative and dependent character of Canadian industry, which means as well an increase in the amount of bribes the corporation can demand as a precondition of operation; it means that the pattern and pricing of international trade is an administrative decision taken in American boardrooms; that the choice of growth points and the extent of development is subservient to the global profit position of American corporations. Coyne, Gordon, Kierans – the rate of defection and dissent in establishment circles grows. Yet the response of the Canadian bourgeoisie is the expressed desire to build a foreign corporate empire of its own.

Canadian branch plant quasi-imperialism actually has a long and dishonourable history as junior partner to British or American concerns. During the reign of British merchant capital, a salt, fish, and rum trade was established between Halifax and Jamaica, which was followed in 1837 by the establishment by the Halifax Banking Company of a partnership with the London-based Colonial Bank to service the British Caribbean. During the regime of British finance capital, and until the opening of the Panama Canal by competing American shipping interests, the CPR established itself in the imperial mail service to Hong Kong and the Far East by building up a Pacific steamship fleet to complement the railways. It was the CPR's expansion in the service of British imperialism that helped prompt the American seizure of Hawaii.[98] During the same period, Canadian banks began a process of penetration into Central America and the Caribbean that has continued to escalate. The Bank of Nova Scotia followed the rum trade into Jamaica in 1889. By 1910 Canadian banks had a network in Bermuda, Cuba, Mexico, the Bahamas, Puerto Rico, and Trinidad. Apart from Jamaica, where the Bank of Nova Scotia is dominant with 45 branches, the Royal Bank of Canada together with Barclay's DCO controls most of the banking business in the eastern Caribbean. And at present, Canadian insurance companies control 70 per cent of the Caribbean insurance business.[99]

Railways and transportation concerns and utility companies too have significant Caribbean and Central American holdings. These were pioneered by William Van Horne, who, after completion of the CPR, established railway ventures in Guatemala and Cuba. Van Horne began his Cuban activities in the wake of the Spanish-American War, when no Cuban authority would challenge him. By 1900, his syndicate had moved into utilities, acquiring electric railway and lighting franchises in Port of Spain, Kingston, and Demerara. The utility operation, Brazilian Traction, Light, and Power (the modern Brascan), established in 1912 in tramways, railways, and hydroelectric power, also had links to the Van Horne group.[100]

A series of other major Canadian utilities operations grew up – Mexican Light and Power, Jamaica Public Services, and Canadian International Power Company Ltd. These, like the banks, are currently on the wane. For with the eclipse of the British empire, a rising nationalism was directed against them, skilfully used by Latin American leaders to divert attention from the real problem, American and British industrial, mining, and agribusiness companies.

First went merchant capital, then banking and finance, railways and utilities, and more recently hotels and playgrounds for millionaires – all service industries either imitative of British companies or lackeys of American ones. The only significant 'Canadian' imperialist operation in the area of industrial capital has been the American-controlled Alcan. Thus, Canada's parasitical pseudo-imperialist ventures conform precisely to the pattern of development of Canadian capitalism itself, both in timing and in form.

CONCLUSION

Despite the selfless courage of a Walter Gordon or the vulgar opportunism of a J.J. Greene, the policy of the bourgeoisie throughout Canadian history has been remarkably consistent. It has been a policy of subordination to a metropole. If one metropole fails, another has always been forthcoming.

In the first empire using the St Lawrence, French merchant capital exploited *coureur de bois* and Indian labour to return the rich rewards of the fur trade to the French crown and aristocracy, stultifying local capital formation and thus preventing the emergence of a Canadian bourgeoisie which would challenge their authority and that of the metropole. After the Conquest, English merchants did likewise, until the mercantile revolution in the American colonies and the subsequent border settlement destroyed the first commercial empire of the St Lawrence.

Then Anglo-Canadian merchants, factors and representatives of British joint-stock mercantile companies, in collaboration with a Franco-Canadian landed class, intermediated flows of primary staples from the US to Britain along the St Lawrence route. When the British industrial revolution, the triumph of the British industrial bourgeoisie over the London-based mercantile class, abrogated their special concessions and destroyed the second commercial empire of the St Lawrence, the Canadian mercantile class opted for annexation.

But the Reform Movement, at the zenith of its political power, triumphed with reciprocity. Growing out of merchant capital, Canadian banking, railway, and financial interests created the Canadian Confederation to extend their intermediary activities across the continent, and relying on British finance capital and pro-British imperial xenophobia to offset the impact of the branch plant American industry that was a necessary adjunct of the mercantile system they created. Confederation represented the restoration of the old mercantile ruling class in a new guise, and their triumph over the Reform party in the wake of the abrogation of reciprocity. But they misjudged the long-run consequences of the policy. With the collapse of the British empire, Tory mercantilism, which earlier had held a substantial share of the lion's power in Canada, was a spent force in spite of its subsequent attempts to wave the tatters of the Union Jack and invoke the spirit of the CPR's man in Ottawa. The Diefenbaker years were a populist resurgence led by a backwoods squirearchy without the power previously given the party by the mercantile bourgeoisie, by this time an integral part of continental capitalism.

Industrial capitalism in Canada, a suppressed force, from the days of reciprocity until the present, through the Liberal party or its predecessors, had pursued a policy of consistent continentalism. But like the Tory party before it, the Liberal party became a victim of the contradiction implicit in a policy of imperial subordination. American industrial capitalism had transformed itself into multinational corporation capitalism, rendering the ruling class of the hinterland as a class *per se* virtually irrelevant to the management of the northern periphery of the continental system.

The contradiction of continuity in change resolves itself in disintegration. A Canadian capitalist state cannot survive because it has neither the material base nor the will to survive, the former contributing substantially to the latter. It remains to be seen if it can survive in some other form.

Yet in a very real sense Canada has fulfilled the dreams and aspirations of its founders. A few years before Confederation, when territorial expansion westward was being considered, George Brown peered into his crystal globe and declared perceptively, 'If Canada acquires this territory it will rise in a few years from a position of a small and weak province to be the greatest colony any country has ever possessed.'[101] History has been kind to George Brown and his northern vision.

NOTES

1 It was gold that prompted the first European land grabs in America and financed the formation of companies in Britain which were the vanguard of British colonization efforts during the mercantile period.

2 As in the Innis-Creighton school of political economy. See H.A. Innis, *The Cod Fisheries* (Toronto 1954), and *The Fur Trade in Canada* (Toronto 1956); D. Creighton, *Empire of the St. Lawrence* (Toronto 1970); W. Easterbrook and A. Aitken, *Canadian Economic History* (Toronto 1965); and F. Ouellet, *Histoire économique et social du Quebec* (Montreal 1971).

3 As in the orthodox Chicago neo-liberal school. See H.G. Johnson, *The Canadian Quandary* (Toronto 1963), and J. Dales, *The Protective Tariff in Canada's Development* (Toronto 1966).

4 See H.C. Pentland, 'The Role of Capital in Canadian Economic Development before 1875,' *Canadian Journal of Economics and Political Science* XVI, 4 (Nov. 1950), 458.

5 It will be a central theme of this paper that the type of capital must be stressed at least as much as, if not more than, its quantity. In Canadian history at least, capital has shown itself to be more mobile intra-sectorally and internationally than inter-sectorally and intra-nationally.

6 See J. Schumpeter, *The Theory of Economic Development* (New York 1961), 129-33, and J.A. Hobson, *The Industrial System* (London 1927), 158. Note that the activities of the industrial capitalist and entrepreneur are quite complementary. In fact, the industrial entrepreneur cannot exist without the presence of the capitalist; for the former in isolation, as Schumpeter portrays him, boils down to the archetypal petit bourgeois.

7 With respect to other socio-economic classes, industrial and merchant capital imply the existence of different contradictions. A proletariat *per se* is an adjunct solely of industrial capital. Mercantile wage workers do not create surplus value; they simply help the merchant to divert part of the surplus generated in the sphere of production into his own pockets. See K. Marx, *Capital,* III (Moscow), 288. Merchant capital in fact impedes the process of proletarianization. Where merchant capital dominates at the expense of industrial, the tendency is greater for production to assume the character of the petit bourgeois mode, the family farm, or the free artisan. Hence, class antagonism can often take the form of petit bourgeois versus merchant capital, rather than proletarian versus industrial capital. (See K. Marx, *Pre-Capitalist Economic Formations* (London 1964), 107-10.)

8 J.M. Keynes, *Treatise on Money,* II (London 1920), 156. Ironically it was East India Company servants, led by Thomas Munn, who led the propaganda attack on the royal bullionism which had created their company in the first place.

9 E. Heckscher, *Mercantilism,* I, rev. ed. (London 1962), 399.

10 The bulk of the ruling class, the clerical elite, and the great majority of the seigneurs remained in the colony. By the end of the French regime, these groups were, however, composed largely of Canadian commoners who had little incentive to return to France. Small merchants, too, tended to remain. Among those groups that went back to France, the decision was often not voluntary and a Bastille sentence awaited them. See G. Fregault, *François Bigot: Administrateur français,* II (Ottawa 1948), for an account of the incredibly blatant frauds perpetrated by, and the subsequent fate of, the colonial ruling elite at the end of the French regime. Bigot, Cadet, Pean, and others were placed in the Bastille for activities which in a British colony would have earned them a place in the House of Lords – proof positive that the Conquest was a progressive event for the colony.

11 S.D. Clark, *Movements of Political Protest in Canada, 1640-1840* (Toronto 1959), 87.

12 R. McIvor, *Canadian Monetary, Banking, and Fiscal Development* (Toronto 1958), 8-10.

13 A. Shortt, ed., *Documents Relating to Canadian Currency, Exchange, and Finance during the French Period* II (Ottawa 1925), 765 *et passim,* contain the original documents describing the machinations involved.

14 Pentland, 'The Role of Capital,' 458.

15 S.B. Ryerson, *Unequal Union* (Toronto 1968), 97.

16 As late as 1833, the prohibition on the export of specified machines was renewed and the Board of Trade denied licences for the export of spinning frames, textile equipment, and certain machine tools. This helped to prevent the rise of competitive cotton industries elsewhere. See R.G. Weiss, 'Economic nationalism in Britain in the nineteenth century,'

in H.G. Johnson, ed., *Economic Nationalism in Old and New States* (London 1967).

17 W. Copp, 'Nova Scotian Trade during the War of 1812,' in G.A. Rawlyk, ed., *Historical Essays on the Atlantic Provinces* (Toronto 1967), 83.

18 W.S. Macnutt, 'The Politics of the Timber Trade in Colonial New Brunswick, 1825-40,' in Rawlyk, *Historical Essays*, 120.

19 V.C. Fowke, 'The Myth of the Self-Sufficient Canadian Pioneer,' *Transactions of the Royal Society of Canada* LVI, III (June 1962), 25-6.

20 H.C. Pentland, 'The Development of a Capitalistic Labour Market in Canada,' *Canadian Journal of Economics and Political Science* XXV, 4 (Nov. 1959), 450.

21 N. Vallerand, 'Histoire des faits économiques de la Vallée du St Laurent, 1760-1866,' *Economie québécois* (Montréal 1969), 56.

22 McIvor, *Canadian Monetary, Banking, and Fiscal Development*, 60.

23 W.M. Drummond, 'The Financing of Canadian Agriculture,' in J.F. Parkinson, ed., *Canadian Investment and Foreign Exchange Problems* (Toronto 1940), 265.

24 With the notable exception of India. Fears of a resurgence of the Indian textile industry were sufficient that even the most ardent free traders did not consider decolonization here.

25 See D. Ricardo, 'On Protection of Agriculture,' and 'The Influence of a Low Price of Corn on the Profits of Stock,' in E.K. Gonner, ed., *Economic Essays of David Ricardo* (London 1956).

26 While the Canadian canal system was superior to the American, New York's advantages over Montreal as an ice-free ocean port were sufficient to tilt the cost advantage to the American route in the absence of fiscal intervention. See G.N. Tucker, *The Canadian Commercial Revolution, 1845-1851* (Toronto 1964), 39-40.

27 Easterbrook and Aitken, *Canadian Economic History*, 290.

28 E. Porritt, *Sixty Years of Protection in Canada, 1846-1907* (London 1908), 49.

29 D.L. Burns, 'Canada and the Repeal of the Corn Laws,' *Cambridge Historical Journal*, II (1928), 261.

30 Tucker, *The Canadian Commercial Revolution*, 50.

31 Burns, 'Canada and the Repeal of the Corn Laws,' 264.

32 Tucker, *The Canadian Commercial Revolution*, 84-5.

33 Vallerand, 'Histoire des faits économiques de la Vallée du St Laurent,' 75.

34 J.S. Mill, *Principles of Political Economy*, Ashley ed. (London 1921), 902. Adam Smith had given the Navigation Laws his blessing, but by Mill's time they were simply 'an invidious exception to the general view of free trade.'

35 D.C. Masters, *The Reciprocity Treaty of 1854* (Toronto 1963), 11.

36 Vallerand, 'Histoire des faits économiques de la Vallée du St Laurent,' 82.

37 Ryerson, *Unequal Union*, 236.

38 W.A. Williams, *The Roots of the Modern American Empire* (New York 1969), 11.

39 Masters, *Reciprocity*, 125.

40 A. Shortt, 'Origins of the Canadian Banking System,' in E.P. Neufeld, ed., *Money and Banking in Canada* (Toronto 1964), 143-4.

41 Ryerson, *Unequal Union*, 242, for example, argues that Confederation was the result of a drive by growing industrial capital to harmonize tariffs among the various British North American colonies. He maintains as well (270) that there was a direct lineage between the old mercantile and the new industrial ruling classes. Somehow, within thirty years of suppressing the rebellions, merchant capital with its long historical roots is supposed to have transformed itself into industrial capital. Creighton, too, seems to assume that his beloved Montreal merchants suddenly vanished, as if the Corn Law repeal repealed their malignant existence as well. Our interpretation will be very different. The merchants, unfortunately for all but them, remained very much in control for some time to come.

42 E. Mandel, *Marxist Economic Theory*, II (London 1968), 452.

43 Statement in 1878 *Parliamentary Debates* cited in G.D.W. Goodwin, *Canadian Economic Thought: The Political Economy of a Developing Nation, 1814-1914* (London 1961), 58.

44 D. Creighton, *Dominion of the North* (Toronto 1969), 306-7.

45 A. Dubuc, 'The Decline of Confederation and the New Nationalism,' in P. Russell, ed., *Nationalism in Canada* (Toronto 1965), 114.
46 A.T. Galt, in P.B. Waite, ed., *The Confederation Debates* (Toronto 1963), 53-5.
47 A.A. Dorion, in *ibid.*, 92-3.
48 George Brown in *ibid.*, 67.
49 Dorion in *ibid.*, 89-90, 147, pointed out the role of the Grand Trunk in the proceedings.
50 Joseph Howe, 'Confederation Considered in Relation to the Interests of the Empire' (Sept. 1966), in J.M. Beck, ed., *Joseph Howe: Voice of Nova Scotia* (Toronto 1969), 180-1.
51 See esp. A.G. Bailey, 'Opposition to Confederation in New Brunswick,' in R. Cook, ed., *Confederation* (Toronto 1967).
52 G. Myers, *History of Canadian Wealth* (Chicago 1914, Toronto 1972), provides a hair-raising account of the theft involved.
53 McIvor, *Canadian Monetary, Banking, and Fiscal Development*, 67. The major challenge to the tight money policies pursued by the banks came from the Alberta Social Credit in the 1930s. This was countered by the federal power of disallowance.
54 H.A. Innis, *A History of the Canadian Pacific Railway* (Toronto 1923, 1970), 197.
55 Myers, *Canadian Wealth*, 17.
56 L. Bergeron, *The History of Quebec: A Patriot's Handbook* (Toronto 1971), 129.
57 Not because of any mysterious geist of conservatism as George Grant would have it, or because of any transfusion of British Toryism before the political culture became congealed as Horowitz interprets it. Cf. G. Grant, *Lament for a Nation* (Toronto 1965), and G. Horowitz, 'Conservatism, liberalism, and socialism in Canada, an interpretation,' *Canadian Journal of Economics and Political Science* XXXII (May 1966), 143-71.
58 A.G. Gosselin, 'L'Evolution économique du Québec: 1867-1896,' *Economie québécois*, 109-14.
59 W.A. Mackintosh, *The Economic Background of Dominion-Provincial Relations* (Toronto 1964), 27-8.
60 *House of Commons Debate* (7 March 1878), 857-9. Cited in M. Bliss, 'Canadianizing American Business: The Roots of the Branch Plant,' in I. Lumsden, ed., *Close the 49th Parallel etc.* (Toronto 1970), 35.
61 Dales, *Protective Tariff*, admits to the fact that the tariff did increase the scale of the Canadian economy but claims its long-run effect was to reduce per capita income below the level which it would have achieved without it. But he arrives at such a conclusion by utilizing the oldest static resource allocation concepts and in so doing contradicts his own initial premise. For to conclude that the existing allocation of resources as a result of the tariff is less efficient than the configuration of industry that would exist without it must assume the same resources are available both before and after the tariff, a premise explicitly contradicted from the outset. Curious logic – even for an economist.
62 While the tariff did stimulate the textile industry, it led to mergers and overproduction: the textile industry was well underway before the tariff and was based, especially in Quebec, more on pools of cheap, docile labour rather than on the mild pre-1878 tariff. Between 1880 and 1890 production increased two-and-one-half times, but cartelization of this formerly small-firm industry proceeded at such a pace that by 1892 70 per cent of total Canadian production came from two companies. The stimulus to iron and steel came from the railway boom, not from the tariff. And the farm machinery industry was well established before the tariff. Gosselin, 'L'Evolution économique du Québec,' 130-3.
63 Bliss, 'Canadianizing American business,' 33.
64 R. Luxembourg, *The Accumulation of Capital* (London 1963), 408.
65 S. Lipset, *Agrarian Socialism* (New York 1968), 49-50.
66 J. Viner, *Canada's Balance of International Indebtedness, 1900-1913* (Cambridge 1924), 285.
67 *Ibid.*, 285.
68 Bliss, 'Canadianizing American Business,' 37.

69   M. Wade, *The French Canadians* (Toronto 1968), 592.
70   As early as 1846, the Annapolis Iron Mining Company started a full range of operations
     including manufacturing at Moose River, Nova Scotia. This was quickly abandoned, and
     the firm insisted that in the future only mining was to be done in Nova Scotia; processing
     was to occur in the US for resale to Canada and the Maritimes. See Ryerson, *Unequal
     Union,* 221.
71   See K. Levitt, *Silent Surrender: The Multinational Corporation in Canada* (Toronto
     1970); S. Hymer, 'Foreign Direct Investment and the National Economic Interest,' in
     Russell, ed., *Nationalism in Canada*; and M. Watkins, 'A New National Policy,' in T. Lloyd
     and J.T. McLeod, eds., *Agenda 1970* (Toronto 1968).
72   Viner, *Canada's Balance of International Indebtedness,* 12, or C.K. Hobson, *The Export
     of Capital* (London 1963), 29.
73   See esp. A.D. Chandler, *Strategy and Structure: Chapters in the History of the Industrial
     Enterprise* (Cambridge, Mass. 1962) for a historical analysis of the successive stages of
     corporate growth and evolution.
74   H.E. Dougall, 'Some Comparisons in Canadian and American Railway Finance,' in H.A.
     Innis, ed., *Essays in Transportation* (Toronto 1941), 19-20.
75   Hobson, *The Export of Capital,* 111-12.
76   Viner, *Canada's Balance of International Indebtedness,* 282.
77   Watkins, 'A New National Policy,' 161.
78   H. Marshall, F. Southard, and K. Taylor, *Canadian-American Industry* (New Haven 1936),
     6
79   J.M. Watson, 'Mining Finance in Canada,' in Parkinson ed., *Canadian Investment,* 234-7.
80   H.A. Innis, *The Fur Trade in Canada* (New Haven 1930), 404-5. See also his 'Unused
     Capacity ...,' in *Essays.*
81   See C.B. Macpherson, *Democracy in Alberta* (Toronto 1970), 21.
82   H.A. Innis, 'Government Ownership in Canada' (pamphlet), 265.
83   D. Creighton, *Canada's First Century* (Toronto 1970), 149-50.
84   The decline and fall of the Tory party reflected that of the British empire. Big business
     Whiggery had been ascendant since the first world war, and the depression saw that it
     was firmly seated in power. Like the British Tory party after the repeal of the Corn Laws,
     the Canadian Tory party became a vehicle of petit bourgeois protest led by a backwoods
     Tory squirearchy who articulated, in the language of liberal democracy, their frustrations
     at being squeezed out of the political and economic centres of power. In Britain this
     group was known in the mid-nineteenth century as 'Tory radicals'; in Canada in the twen-
     tieth it was dubbed 'red Tory' by academic circles. The depression too spawned petit bour-
     geois folk movements in the West to challenge eastern mercantile hegemony.
85   W.F. Ryan, *The Clergy and Economic Growth in Quebec (1896-1914)* (Quebec 1966), 31.
86   B. Archibald, 'Atlantic Regional Underdevelopment,' in J.T. McLeond, L. Lapierre, C. Tay-
     lor, and W. Young, eds., *Essays on the Left* (Toronto 1971), 110.
87   See esp. D.E. Moggeridge, *The Return to Gold, 1925* (Cambridge 1969), and J.M. Keynes,
     'The Economic Consequences of Mr Churchill,' in *Essays in Persuasion* (London 1944).
     This, incidentally, is the same imbecilic Winston Churchill who on assuming the role of
     prime minister some years later announced in the Commons that 'I did not become His
     Majesty's first minister to preside over the dissolution of the British empire.'
88   Innis, *Essays,* 405-6.
89   *Financial Post* (8 August 1931), cited in Marshall, Southard, and Taylor, *Canadian-
     American Industry,* 247.
90   As Dales, *Protective Tariff,* would have us believe. The survey taken in 1931 by Marshall,
     Southard, and Taylor, *Canadian-American Industry*, 199, showed that the tariff was re-
     sponsible for 76 per cent of the branch plants, while the recent survey of A.E. Safarian,
     Foreign Ownership of Canadian Industry (Toronto 1966), 209, showed that the tariff was
     unimportant in explaining the post-war rush.
91   H. Aitken, *American Capital and Canadian Resources* (Cambridge, Mass. 1961), 120.

92 Marshall, Southard, and Taylor, *Canadian-American Industry,* 221.
93 C.P. Kindleberger, *American Business Abroad* (New Haven 1969), 140.
94 See S. Hymer and R. Rowthorn, 'Multinational Corporations and International Oligopoly: The Non-American Challenge,' in C.P. Kindleberger, ed., *The International Corporation* (Cambridge, Mass. 1970), and R. Rowthorn, *International Big Business, 1957-1967* (Cambridge 1971), for a refutation of the thesis outlined in J.J. Servan-Schreiber, *The American Challenge* (Middlesex 1968).
95 One consequence of this pattern of dependence has attracted considerable attention. In 1956 it was noted that 'the Toronto Stock Exchange ranks second only to the New York Exchange in volume of shares traded. For short periods it even exceeded the New York Exchange in volume.' Professor Inman's words, expressed in *Economics in a Canadian Setting,* once a standard introductory text book published by one of Canada's leading houses, Copp Clark Publishing Co. Ltd., contrast sharply with the current situation wherein the total annual demand for additional equities in Canada has been estimated to be double the supply of new issues. While fifteen American exchanges increased their trading volume by 170 per cent between 1962 and 1967, the six Canadian ones increased trading by only 38 per cent. Significantly, since Professor Inman's words were written, his textbook has been supplanted with a branch plant edition of Paul Samuelson's rave best-seller and the Copp Clark Company itself succumbed to a foreign corporation in 1963.
96 Marshall, Southard, and Taylor, *Canadian-American Industry,* 249.
97 The CPR exception can be accounted for by the fact that, unlike other railroads, it was built up largely with cash and land grants rather than bonds, and hence commenced without heavy fixed interest obligations and with a resource goldmine in its land grants, which its tendency to equity financing permitted it to exploit itself.
98 R.W. Van Alstyne, *The Rising American Empire* (Chicago 1965), 178-80.
99 K. Levitt and A. McIntyre, *Canada-West Indies Economic Relations* (Montreal 1967), 24-7.
100 L.C. and F.W. Park, *Anatomy of Big Business* (Toronto 1962), 138-9.
101 Cited tenderly in Creighton, *Dominion of the North* (Toronto, new ed. 1962), 291.

Gary Teeple

teaches part-time at the University of Toronto

Land, labour, and capital in pre-Confederation Canada

IT IS axiomatic that the development of industrial capitalism depended on the creation of a landless, property-less working class and a capitalist class investing in manufacturing industries. In England, the peasants and yeomanry who were forced from the land during the two centuries preceding the Industrial Revolution formed the basis of the body of landless workers which became the industrial proletariat.[1] In the eighteenth century in the midst of the same capital accumulation that produced the 'free' wage-labourer,[2] the industrial capitalist rose to dominance.

Once the working class and the industrial capitalists were fully established, industrialism flourished in England. It similarly prospered in the United States at a later date. The American Revolution placed an indigenous merchant bourgeoisie in a position of dominance, and then, through trade, land speculation, and the Civil War,[3] this bourgeoisie accumulated the capital necessary to build large-scale industry. By the mid-nineteenth century the complement to this accumulation, a working class, was emerging comprised largely of recent immigrants from Ireland, Germany, Scandanavia[4] – and Canada.

The proletariat in England was created from the indigenous English, Irish, and Scottish agricultural classes. The 'enclosures' and other land restrictions and practices prevented these classes from returning to the land and the only alternative was 'free' wage-labour – the basis of the industrial capitalist accumulation of wealth and mode of production. The colonies which were settled by immigrants, however, raised a problem. There were no enclosures, land was in abundant supply, and – in theory, at least – every man could be his own master on his own land. In this situation, it was argued, the new immigrant would settle on the land and thereby effectively prevent 'the existence of a class of labourers for hire'[5] and, consequently, the development of industrial capitalism.

This argument was put forward in 1833 by E.G. Wakefield, who studied the attempts at colonization in Australia and British North America. Without some barriers or restrictions to land settlement, workers would not remain dependent on wage-labour, and without this pool of labourers industrial capitalism could not develop in the colonies.[6] If the abundance and availability of land prevented the formation of a working class, as Wakefield reasoned, the solution lay in making it so expensive that the immigrant would have to work for a time before he could afford to purchase property of his own. It was Wakefield's theory that by the setting of a 'sufficient price' on available land – that is, a price prohibitive to the ordinary immigrant – a pool of landless labourers would be artificially created. Once the immigrant had saved enough, through wage-labour, to purchase property, he would likely withdraw from the labour market. Thus, in order to maintain the labour supply, the fees collected from land purchases would be used to bring a 'substitute' immigrant into the colony. The immigrant labourer, in fact, would pay 'the capitalist for leave to retire from the wage-labour market to the land.'[7] According to this theory of systematic colonization, a created labour market of this type would spur the development of industrial capitalism in the colonies.[8]

The intent of Wakefield's theory was to create in the colony a working class that would encourage colonial capitalists and those in the mother country to develop industry in the colony. His logic contained an assumption, however, regarding the nature of the ruling class in the colony. What Wakefield saw in England was a rising industrial bourgeoisie in the midst of the industrial revolution, a class willing to invest in manufacturing and dependent on a large pool of landless labourers. Such was not the case in British North America, but it was nevertheless assumed to be. In the colony there was an aristocracy in firm control whose power and wealth accrued from government office, ownership of the land, and trade in furs and later in grain and timber. It was a merchant capitalist class, not a class of industrialists.

Thus, although some of Wakefield's theories can be seen in the Imperial Land Acts after 1827 in British North America, in fact the land policies and practices of the ruling class from the Conquest to Confederation had produced similar results to his theory of systematic colonization. Because of the abuses of land granting, land was so monopolized as to make it almost impossible for the greater number of immigrants to own any property.[9] Even before some of Wakefield's policies were enacted, land was not readily available to the immigrant without financial means, and the outcome was the creation of a class of landless labourers in the colony. The lack of industrial growth due to the presence of a mercantile ruling class and the monopolization of land had by 1800 created widespread unemployment among the immigrants and by 1820 had produced a 'glut of labourers.'[10] For these reasons, British North America had a surplus of labourers from the early 1820s on and immigrant workers were unable to find the abundance of work or land which had been their dream in emigrating.

LAND GRANTING PRACTICES AND POLICIES, 1760-1825

At the centre of the problem was the nature of the colonial administration. After the Conquest, both Nova Scotia and Quebec had colonial governors appointed from England; similarly, though later, the governors of New Brunswick and Upper and Lower Canada administered the policies set out by the imperial government. The power of these colonial administrations rested on their monopoly of office, and the rights and privileges attached to their appointed positions.

Chief among these rights was control of the land, which was the sole pre-rogative of the governor and lieutenant governors in the colonies. It was they who granted the land and interpreted the imperial policies on this most abundant resource. This right, founded on the control of office, led to the formation of what might be called a landed aristocracy. In each colony a coterie of appointed officials existed who received and granted free to select others – friends and business concerns – vast areas of much of the best land.

Prior to the Constitutional Act of 1791 the process of monopolization of the land largely for speculative purposes had begun, without a hint of modesty. The whole of Prince Edward Island was granted in one day to a few dozen 'absentee proprietors'[11] in 1767, and attempts to settle the island had only limited success.[12] Similarly, in Nova Scotia between 1760 and 1773, 'when the population of the Colony was only about 13,000,' the magnitude of the grants amounted to '5,416,849 acres of the most valuable land in the Colony, in the most convenient situations bordering on the coast, principal rivers and harbours.'[13] Most of these grants went to individuals or land companies in Britain or the United States. Alienation of the land in Nova Scotia was so extensive by the time the Loyalists arrived in the late 1770s and 1780s that legal processes of 'escheat'[14] had to be carried out against 'the proprietors of the unimproved land'[15] in order to obtain property to settle those Loyalists who wanted to farm.

Speculation in land was greatly encouraged by the free grants to the Loyalists, as well as those grants received under the Proclamation of 1763 by the militia, soldiers, and sailors. In both cases, the land usually fell into the hands of private speculators, businessmen, or politicians. As early as 1789, the problems related to land speculation in New Brunswick[16] became the basis of a short-lived movement of political protest. Its spokesman, James Glenie, recognized the main reason that land was not widely settled and business was stagnant in the provinces of Nova Scotia and New Brunswick: the land practices of Colonel Carleton 'drove by degrees the labouring class of settlers out of the Province ...'[17] Glenie claimed that the government escheated the lands granted to the soldiers, gave these lands to their 'friends and adherents,' and aided in the monopolization of the land near Fredericton.[18]

The conditions underlying and motivating this protest are revealed in the following description of the ruling class of the province: 'the concentration of power rested upon a simple but highly effective system of exploitation of the colony's two main resources of the time, land and offices, by a small, socially privileged group of people situated largely in the capital of the province ... The acquisition of much of the best land of the colony by a few favoured loyalists ... the appointment of the local land-owning aristocracy to positions of political office ... reflected the dominance in the political life of the province of a class whose main preoccupation became that of maintaining its privileged position.'[19]

As Glenie indicated, monopoly of political office and land drove many of the settlers and immigrant labourers out of the province well before 1800. Indeed, it has been argued that 'on balance, the Maritime Provinces probably lost more people by emigration than they gained by immigration in the first two decades after the Peace of 1783.'[20] Conditions were such, however, that while many found it impossible to purchase land or effectively settle it once they had, there was little employment because of the lack of an internal market. The land monopoly barred extensive settlement and thereby curtailed growth of both the population and local business. The result was a class of people in the province who could not settle and, because of lack of employment, could not accumulate the means to emigrate as others had done. With no alternative, these labourers became beggars, thieves, vagabonds or squatters.

A decade before 1800, New Brunswick passed a law designed for 'poor relief' entitled: 'An Act for preventing Idleness and Disorders and for punishing Rogues, Vagabonds and other Idle and Disorderly Persons.'[21] It was directed at 'all persons who not having any visible means of supporting themselves, live idle and refuse to work for the usual wages, and all persons going about to beg alms.'[22] Clearly this Act was directed at the unemployed in the 1780s; to be unemployed was to be 'idle and disorderly.' The point is, however, that the land practices of New Brunswick had prevented large-scale settlement on the land, deterred the development of business, and the consequence was a body of landless, unemployed labourers.

By 1790, land had been so lavishly granted to the Loyalists and notables of Nova Scotia and New Brunswick that an order was given by the imperial government forbidding 'further grants of land.'[23] These provinces were clearly loyal, but the imperial government was concerned about American encroachment in the old Province of Quebec. In an attempt to consolidate the colonial territory of Quebec and to further isolate the French (who remained a conquered people under an alien military regime),[24] the Constitutional Act was decreed in 1791. Through the Act, the structure of government was set out for Upper and Lower Canada, all land that was vacant was to be granted 'only according to English laws and custom,'[25] and two-sevenths of all the land granted was to be set aside for support of the Protestant clergy and for revenue for the government. Without doubt, the Constitutional Act was the vehicle by which England sought to secure its hold in North America. In essence, the Act was to tie a government, a church, and a people to the land as a conservative bulwark against the liberal ideas of the American Revolution. In practice, it formed the basis of autocratic rule in the form of the Château Clique in Lower Canada and the Family Compact in Upper Canada, for the Act gave to the appointed lieutenant-governors the right to make appointments in the province and to interpret and carry out the imperial land policies.

The alienation of land was to become one of the chief means of accumulating wealth for these ruling cliques in Upper and Lower Canada, as well as the main impediment to both the development of industry and the employment of immigrant labourers. The essence of Wakefield's theory – the creation of a landless class of wage-labourers – was by and large realized by 1820. Three decades earlier, pauper peasants and farmers whose harvests had failed or whose lands had been expropriated under the acts of enclosure had sought a solution in emigration from England. But the concentration of land ownership in the British North American colonies produced a situation that closely resembled the one they were escaping: land was largely inaccessible to those without means.

The free land grants to the Loyalists greatly contributed to this concentration of ownership. Indeed, it has been shown that, in keeping with the purpose of the Act of 1791, 'the Government attempted to create a landed aristocracy by giving an additional grant of 200 acres of land free of expense to all (of the Loyalists) who had entered Canada before ... 1798.'[26] There were as well free grants to 'the children of the Loyalists when they came of age,'[27] often as much as 1000 acres.[28] The result of these excesses was simply that the Loyalists received extensive tracts of land, far more than they ever intended to settle or develop. In fact, of the free grants prior to 1838 in Upper Canada alone, the Loyalists had been given 3,200,000 acres of land of the total 5,786,946 acres distributed in 'non-fee' grants.[29] 'Loyalist rights,' that is the land grants they or their children received, became a standard article of trade, and speculators could buy them for a small fee or even 'a gallon of rum.'[30] That most of these lands eventually ended up in the hands of private speculators is indisputable.[31] 'Local businessmen or prominent politicians in York'[32] were the main recipients, and these speculators or 'companies of associates'[33] had little intention of carrying out the settlement regulations attached to these grants.

The grants which had been given to the soldiers and sailors under the Proclamation of 1763, as with those granted to the militia and soldiers of the War of 1812, by and large found their way into the hands of their officers or other speculators.[34] Perhaps former military men made poor settlers; or more likely the pattern of land granting made settling a very difficult undertaking. In any event, few of these men ever remained on the land,[35] but chose rather to sell them to their officers or abandon them.[36]

Many officials in the governments were involved in amassing these grants to soldiers for themselves, but they also acted directly to distribute land for their personal ends, particularly through the system of township granting. This was an early institution in British North America, beginning in 1763, having its heyday in the decade before 1800 in Lower Canada, and ending after great abuse in 1818.[37]

In theory, the purpose of this system was to grant land to groups of 'associates' who were to settle immigrants on *part* of the grant in return for the remainder, which was always much more than that given to the settlers. Since one had only to apply in order to obtain such a grant, the petitions for townships were numerous. In Lower Canada, 'by ... 1796, "almost all the good lands ... (had) been petitioned for"; and by ... 1798, applications for twenty million acres had been received.'[38] As there were only 17 million acres of surveyed land in Upper Canada by the time of the Rebellions, these figures give some indication of the extent of the land grab even before the turn of the century.

These petitions were seldom from *bona fide* leaders of associations, but rather from speculators who did very little, and often nothing, to carry out the requirements of the grant.[39] The worst offenders, and some of the largest recipients, were members of the government. In Lower Canada, Governor Prescott's attempts to revise the system were thoroughly discarded by his successor, R.S. Milne. He himself accepted a grant of about 48,000 acres and thought nothing of the 12,000 acres 'given to each of the members of the Executive Council constituting the Land Commission.'[40] Before he left his post, he had given about 1½ million acres to sixty people, through the system of township leaders and associates.[41]

Political favourites, merchants, and a coterie of colonial officials from the governor to the land surveyor were among the land speculators of the time.[42] Very little of the land was developed or opened for settlement, as the speculators were interested only in the profit they could make from the rising prices of land as immigration increased. The monopolization of such vast lands by so few was clearly a deterrent to settlement and a force in conjunction with immigration in creating a large body of landless labourers early in the nineteenth century.

The withholding of land for speculative purposes stemmed not only from these brazen abuses of land granting, but also from the Constitutional Act. Vast acreages were set aside in 1791 for the support of the Protestant clergy and as a source of revenue for the government of each province. These reserves amounted to almost one-third of the total land in Upper and Lower Canada[43] and were clearly designed for speculative purposes, the object being to raise their value through the labour of the settlers surrounding them.[44]

The checkerboard pattern in which the reserves were laid out in each township was to meet with harsh and constant criticism. In 1828, a committee in the British House of Commons reported that they retarded 'more than any other circumstance the improvement of the Colony.'[45] In fact, they were not only 'lands withdrawn from settlement,' but also a formidable barrier to communication between settlers and markets. Both clergy and Crown reserves were obvious hindrances to immigrants desirous of settling on the land.

Since it was never clear how these reserves were to be used or administered,[46] for the most part they remained wild. Although some leasing did occur, it was always very limited. By 1822, less than 10 per cent of all the Crown reserves were being leased and by 1821 only a very small sum 'had been received in rents from the clergy reserves.'[47] What must be understood about these leases is that few were settled. The common practice, no doubt encouraged by those in power with interests in the timber trade, was to strip the land of timber and move on, often not even paying the rent.[48] If some of these reserves were settled, frequently the occupiers were squatters, for few people had the money to rent property.[49]

The demand for the reserves rose by the mid-1820s, because by this date 'desirable' lands in both Upper and Lower Canada were 'no longer available.'[50] In 1825, many of the reserved tracts were 'sold' to the newly formed land companies[51] at cheap rates, and a year later others were sold by auction.

Such were the land granting practices and policies of the colonial autocrats governing in the British American colonies prior to 1825. It was a systematic distribution of land only in one sense; fewer and fewer favourites, relative to the growing population, monopolized more and more of the land. Farmers who had managed some success and local businessmen who wanted to grow were forced to protest against these land practices because of their prohibitive nature. As early as the 1780s in New Brunswick, these classes argued against the land abuses stemming from a monopoly of political power. In 1794 and 1796, there were riots in Lower Canada partly in protest of the 'exorbitant rents'[52] demanded by French seigneurs, English merchants, and others who had bought the seigneuries. Moreover, much of the best land in the Eastern Townships had been alienated to these companies of associates, who were inevitably English or American; as a result, the Canadiens' sense of isolation increased and, indeed, the expansion of their farming was seriously curtailed. In Upper Canada, the corruption of the administration and the land monopoly brought protest in the first decade of the nineteenth century. Certain magistrates were censured for their practice of exploiting the settler and driving him from the land. These magistrates, who were often also merchants, were accused of charging exorbitant rates for articles to the settlers and receiving 'payment by mortgages upon their grants,' thereby frustrating the efforts of the settlers, who were forced into dependency on the merchants. By foreclosing on these mortgages, some magistrates acquired 'immense Tracts of Territory.'[53] Thorpe voiced the grievances of the inhabitants who were agitating against this 'shopkeeper aristocracy,' describing the government and the effect of its policies as follows: '[The administration is] surrounded by the vilest miscreants on earth, who have gorged themselves on the plunder of every Department [in the government], and squeezed every Dollar out of the wretched Inhabitants, who have long stunted the growth of the province and have now driven it to the verge of ruin.'[54]

THE IMPOVERISHMENT OF IMMIGRANTS BEFORE 1825

While enclosures and other land-holding changes had driven thousands from the land in Britain, their arrival in British North America provided little relief for their destitution and few hopes for a return to the land. The ruling colonial administrations had indeed 'gorged themselves' with the land, and there was little to be had without substantial savings. That the majority of the immigrants arrived destitute is unquestionable.[55] Clearly, then, many were effectively barred from the land, unless they were aided by a colonizer, or unless they were 'Loyalists' or formerly in the military. Almost always, payment of some sort had to be made before a plot of land could be occupied.[56] Elsewhere, quit-rents would be demanded, a practice which did little to encourage settlement, but much for speculation.[57]

Immigration to the Americas increased after 1815. The end of the war with Napoleon brought widespread unemployment in the British Isles; the harvests failed in 1816 and 1817; in 1818, emigration was over 18,000, and some 15,000 (mainly Irish and Scotch) arrived in Canada.[58] The potato crop failed in Ireland in 1821, and emigration from Ireland increased from this date on.[59] These people, who owned neither land nor property, arrived in Halifax, Quebec City, and Montreal in search of the land or employment the colonies supposedly could offer.

Because land monopoly prevented extensive settling of these people and also inhibited the development of industry, the immigrants were faced with two alternatives: moving on to the United States[60] or poverty in British North America. That thousands were forced into the latter is evidenced by the rapid development of 'welfare' schemes after 1815. The increased numbers of immigrants after this date exaggerated the existing poverty. The provincial capital of New Brunswick, Fredericton, saw its poor rate triple between 1814 and 1817, according to one writer.[61] By 1814, there had been enough poor in the town to warrant the establishment of an almshouse. A House of Industry was built in 1822 in order to encourage work habits for the 'idle.' Saint John had an almshouse, as did several other parishes in New Brunswick by 1819.

These almshouses and work houses should be distinguished from the 'aid' or 'emigrant societies' which gave help to destitute and indigent emigrants upon their arrival in New Brunswick. Undoubtedly, many of these destitute ended up in the colony's workhouses, but the problems must be separated. *Arriving* without the means or knowledge to attain work or land but desiring it was one problem and the other was the general lack of employment possibilities in the country.

Poor relief developed later in Nova Scotia than in New Brunswick, but by 1817 there existed 'An Association for the Relief of the Labouring Poor.'[62] This institution provided 'soup, wood, and some employment' to hundreds of men who by that date had 'tramped in from the rest of the province (and Newfoundland) looking for work.' In the year of its formation (1820), the Halifax Poor Man's Friend Society helped 4213 men, women, and children who were unemployed and in great need. The records of its business do not go beyond 1825, but during its brief years of existence, it claimed to have helped at least 1000 persons per year and about 1500 in 1825. Clearly, there was much unemployment among the inhabitants of the colony; it was not only the immigrants who were destitute.[63]

Upper Canada had so many poor and unemployed by 1792 that its jails were crowded, for there were no alms or poor houses.[64] In the statutes of this province in 1799, the 'use of apprenticeship as a device of poor relief ... had been made explicit.'[65] Generally, however, the care of the poor was the concern of private groups exercising their paternalistic morality. By the 1820s, there were several organizations 'whose sole purpose was to meet the needs of the poor.'[66] As for Lower Canada, unemployment was extreme enough for the legislature in 1818 to incorporate 'a House of Industry in Montreal.'[67]

These examples are testimony to the vast unemployment and impoverishment of the landless class of labourers in British North America before 1825. There are no statistics for pauperism in Canada at this time, and the argument that there were great numbers of people able to work, yet without jobs, can only be supported by alluding to this available evidence.

SETTLEMENT COMPANIES

The land policies up to 1826 had been fickle and intemperate. They had been misinterpreted, frequently corrupted, and deliberately tampered with. The consequences were well in evidence by the early 1820s as begging and destitution increased. The immigration rate was rising rapidly and workable land had to be found to settle the thousands of new arrivals. The government did not so much search for a solution as seek to further the speculation in land by using the increased demand for it as a means of profiteering. Most of the land companies formed were associations of speculators not unlike the 'associations' that existed under the township system of granting land. More land, then, was thrown into the hands of speculators, and extensive settlement became more difficult.

The Canada Company in Upper Canada was the largest of these settlement companies. In 1826, it received about 3½ million acres of Crown land in the province[68] – an amount so large that thereafter the government was left only a single 'block of excellent land' near Georgian Bay.[69]

Although this company did more to settle immigrants than most, it speculated with its grants, as had previous companies of associates. In the Report on Grievances, chaired by W.L. Mackenzie in 1835, testimony is given concerning the absolute rule of the Canada Company over its lands and its practices in land-jobbing.[70] Aside from the deleterious effects of speculation, the majority of the Company's profits went to England, and little of its accumulated wealth remained in the Canadas. During the prosperous years from 1854-1857, the Company ceased selling or leasing its land, in full knowledge that demand was drastically raising prices.[71]

The Company's relations with the government were very close indeed, Canada West was described as a company province. One writer said, it was the 'universal sentiment ... [of the people of Canada West] that the Canada Company controlled the Government and had its "tools" in the Legislature.'[72] They were not far wrong: in 1855, A.T. Galt, an associate of the company, became the Chairman of the Select Committee on the management of the public lands; this position meant that, as a government official, Galt was to keep watch over his private enterprise.

Similarly espousing a willingness to promote large-scale emigration and settlement, in 1834 the British-American Land Company was formed and given at a low price over a million acres of land in Lower Canada.[73] Its connections with the government, too, were very close: two of the commissioners of the Company were the Honourable Peter McGill and the Honourable George Moffat; and from 1844 to 1854, A.T. Galt also was a commissioner. Although in four years the company sold several thousand acres, this accomplishment was somewhat tempered by the fact that the land was some of the richest in the Eastern Townships – it could be sold even at inflated prices. Financial difficulties beset the Company by 1838, and its aid to settlement ended soon after. Its speculative practices had given the Company large resources, however, and Galt later invested these in the International Railway Company and in several manufacturing concerns.[74]

The failure of the British-American Land Company to encourage large-scale settlement over a long period was repeated by the New Brunswick and Nova Scotia Land Company. Formed in 1831, it purchased half a million acres in 1833, on which it was to encourage settlement. It did settle some of its lands, but these went to 'practical farmers with a capital of from £200 to £600.'[75] The majority of the immigrants were poor, and all they received from the company were promises. None of the promises for the poor materialized. The Company demanded excessive prices for its lands, as did the British-American Land Company, and this aggravated the already scarce land situation. Most of the company's efforts were focused on settling partially cleared lands with farmers who could afford them, and on 'denuding the land of its best timber.'[76] Settlement, in general, was badly neglected.

The 1820s and 1830s saw the best of the Crown lands sold to land companies, which speculated with these lands and kept them largely unsettled. By the 1850s, the pressure of immigration of the previous decade increased the value of land in the northern districts of Canada West. Ostensibly, then, to promote settlement, the land company idea was repeated. This time about one-quarter of a million acres was given to the Canadian Land and Emigration Company.[77] Lumbering was its main concern, and its lands in the Parry Sound and Haliburton areas remain sparsely settled to this day.[78]

The land companies did little more than to continue the earlier hoarding practices. Speculation was their preoccupation and lumbering their fastest way to profits. These companies, however, were part of a larger attempt by the imperial government to reverse the 'improvidence' of the earlier grants to political favourites, the militia, and Loyalists and the speculation involved in these exorbitant, near monopolistic, grants. Yet had the companies been successful in settling the land, they would have been antagonistic to Wakefield's policies. In name, they were settlement companies; in practice, they were land-jobbers.

New Brunswick, for example, had granted or sold well over 2 million acres by 1825, and Nova Scotia 4,750,000 acres. In Lower Canada, by the same date, the seigneuries amounted to about 8½ million acres, and the government (especially under R.S. Milne) had alienated another 3,356,000 acres. The remainder, approximately 5½ million acres, was granted partly to the British-American Land Company and partly, as before, to politicians and notables.[79] Ninety-five per cent of all the surveyed and alienated land in Lower Canada had been undeveloped in 1825. The development of land in Upper Canada was not much better, but according to Durham, about one-tenth was developed by 1838. Of about 17½ million surveyed acres, over 13½ million had been granted and only 1,147,019 acres remained to the Crown.[80] In 1834, however, only 1,003,520 acres had been recorded as under cultivation.[81]

IMPERIAL LAND POLICIES

By the middle of the 1820s, the British government had recognized that the unemployed immigrants arriving in the North American colonies were not settling there but were in fact moving on to the United States. To correct the situation, that government began a series of land policies which were altered frequently until Confederation. One of the earliest new 'instructions' was to grant free land to retired military personnel; this was instituted in 1826 to help ensure loyal citizenship. Since few ever settled their grants, more land was added to the holdings of speculators.

The New South Wales System was begun in 1827, only to be abandoned in 1831. This system, ill-defined as it was, had good intentions of making land available to poor immigrants. The principle was to sell Crown land by auction at an 'upset' price.[82] In practice, however, additional fees were superimposed for surveying, locating, and patenting the auctioned land, thus substantially increasing the initial price. Confusion over administration of the system remained until 1831, and the ones to benefit were the land-jobbers who almost invariably outbid the immigrant.[83] This policy of sale only increased the monopolization of the land already well advanced in the late 1700s and its effect was to drive many more immigrants to the United States in search of jobs and land.[84]

By 1831, Wakefield's ideas had triumphed. The principles of the Land Act of 1831 reaffirmed the policy of sale of 1827 for the alienation of all Crown lands not in the hands of land companies.[85] Wakefield's advocates set about applying his theories, apparently oblivious to the growing mass of unemployed that were already numerous in the towns and cities. The net effect of this Land Act was to continue to discourage *bona fide* settlers from staying in Canada and to increase the accumulation of Crown lands in the hands of speculators. Continuation of these Wakefieldian policies took place under the Land Act of 1841 which, in fact, was framed to encourage settlers to remain in Canada instead of going to the United States.

The very text of the Act of 1841 was contradictory. On the one hand, it stated that no free grants would be made to anyone;[86] and on the other hand, it declared that the governor-in-council could make free grants of land (50 acres) to any British male subject on the colonization roads. Not surprisingly, since the colonial governments were very closely involved in the timber trade and in land speculation, the intent of the Act was lost. The low prices designed to encourage poor immigrants onto the land created the effect of a gold rush for land-jobbers. Speculators bought the land for timber, and few immigrants found the means to settle. The Land Act further impeded them by requiring of the 'prospective settler ... proof of being able to maintain himself until the raising of the first crop.'[87] For a small family, this 'proof' would amount to £47, and most immigrants simply did not have the money.[88]

It is possible that the policy of placing settlers on the colonization roads was an attempt to produce a cotter class,[89] a group of labourers who would have sufficient land to sustain themselves for part of the year and who would be hired seasonally (during the winter) to work for the timber merchants. Since it appears that the purpose of the colonization roads was to exploit the timber of the province,[90] rather than to encourage settlement, and since there had been an earlier attempt to settle indigent immigrants on small parcels of land, forcing them to seek seasonal employment,[91] the idea is not without some foundation. In all, about sixteen of these roads were built between 1845 and 1878. Adjacent farms were begun and abandoned with regularity, and by the early 1860s a few of the settlers who had started remained.[92]

It was in this Land Act of 1841 that the principles of creating a 'labour supply' in the colonies were most fully expressed. It is therefore somewhat ironic that, by the time Wakefield's policy of systematic colonization was instituted, the problem of labour for industry was largely solved. By 1841, there was no shortage of workers who were landless and in search of jobs. The question had become one of how to keep the immigrants and settlers in the Canadas, to prevent their emigration to the United States.

One last attempt to attract and keep settlers in Canada came in 1859. The policy changes were such as to give a discount to those who bought land with cash, to allow a poor man credit and no settlement duties, and to allow the selling of land en bloc, in townships. It was not a compromise of great help to the poor or even the prospective settler with capital, for the best lands in Upper and Lower Canada had been 'filled' by the 1840s.[93] The compromise of 1859 did help speculators, however; the Canadian Land and Emigration Company profited well under this new township granting system.

It would be incorrect to suggest that none of these immigrants settled on the land in Canada. Clearly, many thousands came with sufficient savings to enable them to buy some land, generally at the speculator's price; but in turn, they raised the price of surrounding land through improvements to their own. Many indigent immigrants also were settled on the land, especially through 'assisted' settlement programs such as those of Selkirk, Robinson, and Talbot. But in comparison to the thousands who were unable to settle, the efforts of these colonizers amounted to very little. In fact, their settlements were frequently ill-fated.[94]

If poor immigrants were not 'assisted,' their chances of acquiring land were almost impossible. One writer states that 'Settlement in the Canadian backwoods, *even on free grants*, was virtually impossible without capital.'[95] It is variously estimated that from £47 to £300[96] was required to settle. Even when the necessary tools were supplied, as well as food stocks for at least a year, as in the Robinson settlement, the trials of cutting a farm out of the wilderness were formidable. Moreover, once a settler was established on the land, he encountered problems of a different nature. If the company land agent did not harass or even drive a settler from his farm,[97] the magistrate merchants were always at hand, ready to take advantage of a pioneer's need for manufactured goods and, in the absence of much money in circulation, willing to extend credit. The result was often disastrous for the settler.

EMIGRATION FROM THE CANADAS

It has been argued so far that, from a very early date, land in Canada was accumulated and controlled by a small number of people. In addition, wages were not at a sufficient level to allow widespread purchases of land by the indigent immigrants who had secured employment. That thousands could find neither work nor land is evidenced by the large emigrations to the United States and by the misery and suffering of great numbers of unemployed who remained in the British North American provinces.

Some of the earliest emigration has been summarized as follows: 'Durham claims that sixty per cent of the total immigration into the British North American Colonies found their way across the international boundary. Of the 39,163 who arrived at Quebec between 1817 and 1820, not 100 families settled on the lands of Lower Canada. Another report claims that about an average of two-thirds of all the immigrants arriving at Quebec between 1818 and 1826, passed over into the United States, and John Richards maintains that scarcely any remained of the 29,000 immigrants of 1827-28, ... Merivale says that of the ½ million British emigrants to the North American Continent between 1830 and 1840, fully three-quarters settled in the United States.'[98]

Durham's Report confirms this early exodus. It states: 'immigration has been checked [by the excessive quantities of land ... owned by persons who never intend to cultivate them] , and out of the immigrants who have reached the colonies, more than half have sought a refuge in the United States.' This same Report says of the Wakefieldian Land Act of 1831: 'The young men of the colony, unable to purchase the wild lands on the terms now imposed, and who would constitute our most valuable and hardy settlers, are leaving us by hundreds.'[99]

The decline in immigration to Canada and the rise of numbers going to the United States was evident by 1834. It was the rebellions, however, which produced a more massive movement of settled farmers from Upper Canada. The struggle for reform had been lost, taxes remained high, and farmers and immigrants alike in 1838 'appeared "like swallows in autumn" preparing for their flight to the south.'[100] The movement was so extensive that 'small towns such as Port Hope and Pickering were almost abandoned, and in one district which had formerly contained over five thousand people, an observer did not see a single man at work in the fields, although the season was far advanced.'[101] It was this exodus which finally forced the government to move, and the result

was the Land Act of 1841 – an act which blindly instituted Wakefield's policies even though there were already many unemployed immigrants and emigrating farmers. As we have seen, the Act was not successful and the exodus
continued.

The chances of employment increased in the early forties,[102] but immigration to British North America also increased, varying annually between 30,000
and 40,000.[103] The cities of Canada were filled with these crowds, and thousands left to find work in the United States. One writer made these estimates
of the emigrants from Canada: 'In 1849, 73 per cent of all British emigrants
to North America ended up in the United States, in 1850 the percentage rose
to 79.' 'In 1851 "nearly all" of the 3,470 new arrivals in New Brunswick
passed on to the south.'[104]

Shipbuilding and lumbering, two sources of much employment, were at a
standstill in the mid-forties.[105] With ever-increasing numbers arriving in Canada, emigration to the south increased. Many French-Canadians had joined
this exodus. The reasons were the same: land was too expensive and jobs were
too scarce.[106]

By the middle decade of the century, 'A.C. Buchanan, chief emigrant agent,
estimated that of the total number arriving at Quebec and Montreal in 1856,
41% went on to the United States. He pointed out that practically all of the
Norwegians, one-half of the Germans and Irish and one-sixth of the English
and Scottish settled in the latter country. In 1857, out of 72,251 immigrants
entering Canada, 37,034 went on to the United States.'[107] More serious in the
view of the government was the 'alarming movement of French Canadians to
the eastern manufacturing states and to the western agricultural states.'[108]

In 1857, a Special Committee of the Legislature of the Province of Canada
concluded that the main reason for this exodus lay in the 'unwise land policy
in Canada.' The Committee pointed out, as one writer put it, that 'under this
policy [or the lack of such] ownership of land had become concentrated in
the hands of a few individuals and companies which did little to cultivate the
lands or to settle people upon them. As land owned by absentees was practically exempt from taxes, the farms of struggling pioneers in the same community had to bear a heavier burden of tax.'[109]

During the 1860s the United States had need of an unprecedented number
of workers, thereby encouraging even further emigration. Also in 1862, under
the Homestead Act, inexpensive land became readily available in the United
States. Canada, in contrast, did not liberalize its land policies until after Confederation. But by this time, Canadian-born residents in the United States
numbered about half a million, not including the thousands of immigrants
who simply passed through Canada.[110] The fate of those who emigrated from
Canada is part of the history of the American working class. For those who

stayed in Canada, there are as yet few chronicles of their suffering in the pre-Confederation period.

Unemployment, however, did affect many of those who stayed, in particular the Irish who had been brought to Canada in order to build the canals. The winter months offered no wage-labour for them and being reduced to desperation they often formed 'gangs of labourers [which] sometimes took provisions forcibly from houses or taverns.' In the late 1820s and early 1830s, the Irish in the cities 'were regularly dependent on charitable agencies for survival.'[111] In 1834, Toronto had such a large and poor shanty town on its outskirts that W.L. MacKenzie wrote of it and the poor districts of Toronto: they 'throng with persons unlicensed selling beer, whiskey and other strong liquors, and affording ... room for Gambling and Vice in its blackest shapes ... I never saw anything in Europe to exceed the loathsome sights to be met in Toronto.'[112]

Lower Canada was not much better. 'The hovels' of Quebec and Montreal in the 1820s were described as containing '"crowds of British emigrants, who were struggling with those complicated horrors of poverty and disease", too poor and too ignorant to go on to Upper Canada.'[113] By 1831, 'one in every 399 persons in Lower Canada was living upon alms; in 1844, one in every 151 of the population was a recognized pauper subsisting upon alms.'[114]

During the 1840s and 1850s in both Canada West and Canada East (Upper and Lower Canada), the government found it necessary to build 'houses of correction,' and a number of hospitals and 'lunatic asylums' as well as jails and penitentiaries and orphanages – all in response to the begging and misery that was so common. In 1837, Toronto set aside money for the establishment of a House of Industry, but built it a few years after the rebellions.[115] In the same year, the City granted £250 'for the relief of the poor and distressed' in the City. A further grant of £350 was given a year later because of what was termed 'the prevailing distress of the City of Toronto arising from the number of paupers.'[116] Hamilton, Kingston, Montreal, and Toronto, all were similarly forced to build poorhouses to accommodate their unemployed workers in the decades preceding Confederation.

CONCLUSIONS

By the 1860s, large-scale capitalist production had not developed in Canada, and the creation of a large capitalist proletariat was thereby prevented. As long as industrial capital was subordinate to the interests and the laws of the ruling class, there could be no industrial working class. There did arise a class of landless labourers who potentially could have supplied this essential prerequisite to the development of industrial capital. This class came into being because the alternative to wage-labour, farming, was effectively prohibited for

large numbers of immigrants from the 1820s to Confederation. Land was not
widely available because the ownership of public lands had been heavily concentrated from the time of the Conquest. It was through the oligarchic ownership of the land, expressing itself in speculation, official policies, the reserves,
and the land companies, that the widespread distribution of land among the
majority of needy immigrants was prevented. The direct result of this land
monopoly, combined with the predominance of mercantile capital, was the
creation of thousands of landless labourers who were either forced to subject
themselves, at best to a syndrome of seasonal labour and 'relief,' at worst to
pauperism, crime, and the houses of industry or forced to emigrate to the
United States in search of land or jobs. This human misery in the towns and
cities of pre-Confederation Canada was the terrible irony of Wakefield's
schemes for systematic colonization; his policy was obsolete before it was applied, for the ruling class in the Canadas had created a capitalist 'labour market' but little industry to make use of that 'market.'

The central fact of the Canadian ruling class before and after Confederation
was, and is, its foundation in mercantile capital.[117] This form of capital is accumulated in the process of circulation of goods; that is, money is made by
buying and selling articles (raw materials *or* manufactured goods), not by producing the article, this latter process being the basis of industrial capital. It is
this central characteristic of the Canadian ruling class which explains why,
even to the present time, Canada has not become the industrial nation with a
large population that it might have been.[118] The point is, as Marx argued, that
'wherever merchant's capital still predominates we find backward conditions.'[119] These conditions include low growth in population, conservative social and political traditions, and indeed, many of those characteristics of a
past era which industrialism throws to the winds. Marx explained the reason
for this inhibition of industrialism: 'The independent and predominant development of capital as merchant's capital is tantamount to the non-subjection
of production to capital, and hence to capital developing on the basis of an
alien social mode of production which is also independent of it. The independent development of merchant's capital, therefore, stands in inverse proportion to the general economic development of society.'[120] In other words,
as long as merchant's capital is dominant and enters into the capitalist mode
of production only in a limited way, industrial development stagnates. A merchant class can be 'an obstacle to a real capitalist mode of production[121] – and
indeed, it was an obstacle to the development of industry in Canada. It was
because of this merchant class that the purpose of Wakefield's theory (to create a labour force) was accomplished by the 1820s, while the desired effect
of this labour pool (the stimulation of industrial development) did not take
place in the pre-Confederation period.

The genesis of the mercantile capitalist in Canada is found in the British merchants at the time of the Conquest. Like so many vultures, they 'were first at Quebec at its fall'[122] and then followed the troops to Montreal, where they established their colonial headquarters for the fur trade. The position of this merchant class was central in the new colony as a result of its 'alignment' with the military government. A unity of interests was to be expected, for one motive of the military conquest was to seize the profitable fur trade. This oligarchy of colonial officialdom and merchants soon appropriated the land by way of gifts and grants. Thus, the wealth and power of the ruling class in the British North American colonies came to be founded in office, trade, and land.

The main source of wealth, however, derived from the fur trade and, later, from the timber and grain trade. Essentially, the merchant class gained profits in the transfer of goods to and from the colony. From this point of view, large-scale settlement of the colony had no immediate value to the merchants as long as the population was sufficient to extract and transport the staples. The immense accumulation of land frustrated the growth of the population, and therefore of industry; yet it presented no contradiction to the owners, because their investment in the land was minimal while their control was almost absolute.

Control over the British North American colonies was oligarchical. The majority of colonial officials, merchants, and land-jobbers were of a single mind, with ultimate control resting primarily in England. Because this oligarchy controlled and sapped the country and greatly inhibited settlement, there was little opportunity for the development of large indigenous merchant and farmer classes. The strength of the colonial ruling class was demonstrated in the rebellions of 1837. The uprising failed because the classes who were demanding democracy were small, and because the lack of adequate roads conspired against what unity of effort could be mounted. The colonial ruling class controlled too much and their interests precluded the development of large indigenous classes of farmers, labourers, and professionals which could have launched a successful struggle.[123]

Because settlement was inhibited by land grabbing, so too was the development of local markets, the poverty of which in turn hindered the growth of a local manufacturing class. The market in manufactured goods was controlled by the 'shopkeeper aristocracy' who preferred to trade these articles rather than produce them.

Manufacturing in Canada grew in relation to the development of external trade – that is, in tune with the interests of the merchant ruling class. In an effort to increase the volume of the timber and grain trade, the canals and later the railways were constructed. It was in the context of the requirements of railroad building that local industry developed in the 1850s and 1860s. Yet because the ruling class interests remained the same (that is, mercantilist rather than industrial), manufacturing developed in a limited way - sufficient for the needs of railway construction and a small population. The population was kept small, in comparison to that of the United States[124] which was rapidly industrializing in this period, because the interests and practices of the ruling class in Canada were tied to staple extraction - wheat, timber, and minerals - and did not require the vast army of labourers needed by American industry.[125] The capitalist class that ruled Canada increased its wealth primarily through the development of trade and communications systems, rather than through the production of finished goods.

'The less developed the production [that is, industrial manufacturing],' Marx wrote, 'the more wealth in money is concentrated in the hands of merchants or appears in the specific form of merchant's wealth.'[126] As industry develops and industrial capital predominates, merchant capital is relegated to a secondary position in the development of the nation's wealth. Because in Canada a mercantile bourgeoisie has reigned, the growth of industrial capital has suffered. In pre-Confederation Canada, the effects of this ruling class on the labouring class were two-fold: thousands of immigrants and established settlers in Canada were driven south several decades preceding 1867 and thousands more were faced with seasonal labour or the almshouse, vagabondage, and crime as the alternatives to the work and land that was so scarce.

NOTES

1 K. Marx, *Capital,* I (New York 1967), chap. 27, 752.
2 *Ibid.,* 757. Wealth had been accumulated over the preceding centuries through trade, the plantation system, national debts, and commercial wars.
3 G. Myers, *History of Great American Fortunes* (New York 1910), 400. He writes: '... it was during the Civil War that Northern capitalists of every kind coined fortunes from the natural disasters and from the blood of the very armies fighting for their interests.'
4 C.F. Wittke, *We Who Built America* (New York 1939).
5 Marx, *Capital,* 767. See also: E.G. Wakefield, *A View of the Art of Colonization,* London, 1849, and *England and America,* New York 1834.
6 It was this realization that caused Marx to say of Wakefield that he had 'discovered in the colonies the truth as to the conditions of capitalist production in the mother-country.' That is, capitalist production requires a body of labourers with no alternative for their livelihood but wage-labour.
7 Marx, *Capital,* 773.
8 Wakefield's importance to the colonization schemes affecting Canada was not trivial. His influence was manifest in at least two decades of land policies when immigration was high. His ideas were perhaps best employed in the Land Act of 1841, which to a large extent emerged from Durham's Report - Wakefield reputedly being the author of Appendix B of the report.
9 Yet their presence increased the demand for land and thereby pushed up the prices and increased the profits of those who monopolized it.

10 H.C. Pentland, 'Labour and the Development of Industrial Capitalism in Canada,' unpublished PHD thesis, University of Toronto, 1960, pp. 19 and 109.

11 C.P. Lucas, ed., *Lord Durham's Report on the Affairs of British North America* (Oxford 1912), vol. 3, 65.

12 *Ibid.*, 65. In 1838 Durham wrote: 'the greater number [of the grants] ... remain chiefly in a wild state.'

13 N. MacDonald, *Canada, 1763-1841: Immigration and Settlement* (London 1939), 319.

14 Formally, this process refers to land reverting to the Crown on death of the owner when there is no will. In practice, it was confiscation by the colonial government for their own purposes.

15 Lucas, *Lord Durham's Report,* 76.

16 It was created by the division of Nova Scotia in 1784.

17 S.D. Clark, *Movements of Political Protest in Canada, 1640-1840* (Toronto 1959), 160.

18 *Ibid.,* 161.

19 *Ibid.,* 165.

20 D. Creighton, *Dominion of the North* (Toronto 1962), 187.

21 B. Greenhous, 'Paupers and Poorhouses: the Development of Poor Relief in Early New Brunswick,' *Social History,* 1, no. 1 (1968), 104.

22 *Ibid.,* 104

23 MacDonald, *Canada, 1763-1841,* 73.

24 Clark, *Movements of Political Protest,* 173.

25 MacDonald, *Canada, 1763-1841,* 74.

26 *Ibid.,* 52.

27 R.L. Jones, *History of Agriculture in Ontario, 1613-1880* (Toronto 1946), 33.

28 J.H. Richards, 'Lands and Policies: Attitudes and Controls in the Alienation of Lands in Ontario During the First Century of Settlement,' *Ontario History,* 50-51 (Autumn 1958), 195.

29 *Ibid.,* 195.

30 Jones, *Agriculture in Ontario,* 33.

31 MacDonald, *Canada, 1763-1841,* 53.

32 W.A. Jackson, 'The Regressive Effects of Late Eighteenth Century British Colonial Policy on Land Development Along the Upper St. Lawrence River,' *Annals of the Association of American Geographers,* XLV (1955), 264.

33 H.M. Morrison, 'The Crown Land Policies of the Canadian Government, 1838-72,' unpublished PHD thesis, Clark University (1933), 4.

34 R. Gourlay, *Statistical Account of Upper Canada,* 1 (1822; New York 1966), 574.

35 Lower makes it clear that most of the 'soldier-settlers' failed to maintain themselves as farmers. Several of the 'disbanded soldiers were even given implements, log-cabins, and food to help in farming the land in anticipation of a crop after the first year.' The people at Drummondville (such a settlement) were inexperienced settlers and after a year 'were plunged in abject misery.' A.R.M. Lower, 'Immigration and Settlement in Canada, 1812-1820,' *Canadian Historical Review,* 3 (1922), 41.

36 Lucas, *Lord Durham's Report,* 11. The total grants allotted to these military men amounted to 1,276,526 acres in Upper Canada. Less than one-tenth was ever settled or cleared, according to Durham. In Lower Canada, militia claims amounted to about one-half million acres 'by far the largest part of which is still perfectly waste and unsettled,' wrote Durham in 1839.

37 *Ibid.,* 73.

38 MacDonald, *Canada, 1763-1841,* 78. Also see G.F. McGuigan, 'Administration of Land Policy and the Growth of Corporate Economic Organization in Lower Canada, 1791-1809,' in W.T. Easterbrook and M.H. Watkins, eds., *Approaches to Canadian Economic History* (Toronto 1969), 107.

39 L. Gates, *Land Policies of Upper Canada* (Toronto 1968), 31.

40 G. Myers, *History of Canadian Wealth* (Chicago 1914; Toronto 1972), 67.

41 *Ibid.*, 65, and MacDonald, *Canada, 1763-1841,* 83.
42 MacDonald, *Canada, 1763-1841,* 335, 357, 365.
43 In Nova Scotia and New Brunswick, 500 acres 'were set aside in each parish for the support of the clergy.' See R.G. Riddell, 'A Study in the Land Policies of the Colonial Office, 1763-1855,' *Canadian Historical Review,* XVIII (1937), 395.
44 *Ibid.*, 396; and A. Wilson, *The Clergy Reserves of Upper Canada* (Toronto 1968), 13.
45 Jackson, 'Regressive Effects,' 265.
46 R.G. Riddell, 'The Policy of Creating Land Reserves in Canada,' in R. Flenley, ed., *Essays in Canadian History* (Toronto 1939), 300.
47 Wilson, *Clergy Reserves,* 44.
48 *Ibid.*, 53.
49 MacDonald, *Canada, 1763-1841,* 229.
50 *Ibid.*
51 Riddell, 'Land Policies of the Colonial Office,' 396.
52 Clark, *Movements of Political Protest,* 204.
53 *Ibid.*, 225.
54 *Ibid.*, 226. 'In Upper Canada, since 1825, the government has had scarcely any lands left to part with, that is, lands which were attractive to settlers.' Merivale goes on to say that after this date it would appear that those who settled on the land would have had to do so on land 'purchased from private owners.' Without doubt these were settlers of some means. H. Merivale, *Lectures on Colonization and Colonies,* 2 (London 1841), 97.
55 H.I. Cowan, *British Emigration to British North America, The First Hundred Years* (Toronto 1961), chap. 2.
56 J.E. Howe, 'Quit-Rents in New Brunswick,' *Canadian Historical Review* (1927), 56.
57 *Ibid.*, 56. Quit-rents were a sum paid in lieu of feudal duties.
58 Cowan, *British Emigration,* 39.
59 H.T. Pammett, 'Assisted Emigration from Ireland to Upper Canada under Peter Robinson in 1825,' *Ontario Historical Society, Papers and Records,* XXXI-33 (1936), 56. Throughout the remainder of the decade, the thirties and the forties, the immigrants were for the most part the same – poor and destitute – and numbered many thousand each year.
60 As settlers in British North America were evicted from the land, and as immigrants arrived who lacked the means to settle, a flow of migration began to the United States. In 1806 alone, an estimated 70,000 persons emigrated from the Canada's to the United States. R.B. Splane, *Social Welfare in Ontario, 1791-1893* (Toronto 1965), 5.
61 Greenhous, 'Paupers and Poorhouses,' 111.
62 G.E. Hart, 'The Halifax Poor Man's Friend Society, 1820-27: An Early Social Experiment,' *Canadian Historical Review* (1953), 112.
63 *Ibid.*, 110-12, 120.
64 Splane, *Social Welfare,* 68. In Upper Canada, in 1810, 'a statute was passed to declare the common goals in the several districts of the province to be houses of correction to which might be committed "all and every idle and disorderly person, and rogues and vagabonds, and incorrigible rogues, or any other person or persons who may by law be subject to be committed to a house of correction."' M.K. Strong, *Public Welfare Administration in Canada* (Chicago 1930), 24.
65 Strong, *Public Welfare,* 43.
66 Splane, *Social Welfare,* 76.
67 Strong, *Public Welfare,* 36.
68 Myers, *History of Canadian Wealth,* 85.
69 Morrison, 'Crown Land Policies,' 51.
70 *Reports on Grievances,* House of Assembly, Upper Canada, 1835, 25, 26.
71 Morrison, 'Crown Land Policies,' 107.
72 *Ibid.*, 51.
73 MacDonald, *Canada, 1763-1841,* 295.
74 Myers, *History of Canadian Wealth,* 87.

75 MacDonald, *Canada, 1763-1841*, 307.

76 *Ibid.,* 308, 309.

77 Morrison, 'Crown Land Policies,' 111-12.

78 'In 1871,' writes J.H. Richards, in 'Laws and Policies,' 207, 'after seven years of settlement, the total population on the Company Lands was only 655. Indeed, some of the townships have shown no recorded settlement down to the present and one, Longford, after being sold for its pine, passed through various hands, and was, in 1948, in the possession of the Longford Reserve Limited, of Cleveland, Ohio.'

79 MacDonald, *Canada, 1763-1841*, 313.

80 Lucas, *Lord Durham's Report*, 52.

81 *Reports on Grievances*, 54.

82 Riddell, 'Land Policies of the Colonial Office,' 390.

83 *Ibid.,* 368.

84 MacDonald, *Canada, 1763-1841, 324.* W.L. Mackenzie confirmed this exodus and the monopoly when he wrote in the *Colonial Advocate* in 1828 about the hardship of getting land and how so many 'valuable settlers' were leaving the country.

85 Riddell, 'Land Policies of the Colonial Office,' 399.

86 H.M. Morrison, 'The Principle of Free Grants in the Land Act of 1841,' *Canadian Historical Review*, XLX (1933), 392.

87 *Ibid.,* 405.

88 H.Y. Hind, T.C. Keefer, *et al., Eighty Years' Progress of British North America* (Toronto 1863), 305.

89 Pentland, 'Labour and the Development of Industrial Capitalism,' 229.

90 Morrison, 'Crown Land Policies,' 91.

91 As early as 1819, the granting of 50-acre lots 'to impecunious settlers' was authorized. It was not clear whether or not they were to serve as part-time labourers. In 1833, 1834, and 1835 the government of Upper Canada located sixty families on 5-acre lots. In this case, it was more clearly a question of producing a group of seasonal labourers. See Lucas, *Lord Durham's Report*, 65.

92 Morrison, 'Crown Land Policies,' 97.

93 Richards, 'Land and Policies,' 200.

94 See Cowan, *British Emigration*, 288.

95 V.C. Fowke, 'The Myth of the Self-Sufficient Canadian Pioneer,' *Transactions of the Royal Society of Canada*, LVI (1962), 29. (emphasis added)

96 See Cowan, *British Emigration*, 57, and Jones, *History of Agriculture*, 67.

97 *Report on Grievances*, 25.

98 MacDonald, *Canada, 1763-1841*, 522-3.

99 Lucas, *Lord Durham's Report*, 80, 14.

100 R.S. Longley, 'Emigration and the Crisis of 1837 in Upper Canada,' *Canadian Historical Review*, XVII (1936), 30.

101 *Ibid.,* 34.

102 Pentland, 'Labour and the Development of Industrial Capitalism,' 239.

103 Morrison, 'Crown Land Policies,' 54.

104 Cowan, *British Emigration*, 195.

105 MacDonald, *Canada, 1763-1841*, 55.

106 Myers, *History of Canadian Wealth*, 103.

107 P.W. Gates, 'Official Encouragement to Immigrants by the Province of Canada,' *Canadian Historical Review*, XV (1934), 27.

108 *Ibid.,* 28.

109 *Ibid.*

110 G.E. Jackson, 'Emigration of Canadians to the United States,' in W.P.W. Kennedy, ed., *Social and Economic Conditions in the Dominion of Canada* (1923), 27.

111 Pentland, 'Labour and Industrial Capitalism,' 222.

112 *Ibid.,* 227.

113   *Ibid.*, 237.
114   Myers, *History of Canadian Wealth,* 104.
115   Splane, *Social Welfare,* 70.
116   Strong, *Public Welfare,* 28. In 1851, the Census of the Canada's reported in Upper
      Canada: 86,224 farmers and 78,584 labourers, and in Lower Canada: 78,264 farmers
      and 63,365 labourers. These labourers are distinct from any and all crafts or skilled
      trades and probably do not include the vagabonds and slum dwellers at that time.
117   See R.T. Naylor's paper in this volume for an historical analysis of mercantile capital in
      Canada.
118   In 1959 over 90 per cent of all Canadian exports were 'farm and fish products' and 'raw
      and processed industrial materials.' Highly manufactured goods other than auto parts
      accounted for less than 10 per cent. In 1969, farm and fish products and raw and pro-
      cessed materials declined to about 2/3 of total exports, owing mainly to the rise in per-
      centage of auto parts made in Canada. Economic Council of Canada, *Patterns of Growth,*
      Seventh Annual Review (Sept. 1970), 78.
119   *Capital,* III, 327.
120   *Ibid.,* 328.
121   M. Dobb, *Studies in the Development of Capitalism* (New York 1968), 123.
122   W.H. Atherton, *Montreal, 1535-1914,* II (Montreal 1914), 45.
123   As Stanley Ryerson put it: 'the forces for a successful bourgeois-democratic revolution
      had not matured sufficiently.' *Unequal Union* (Toronto 1968), 113. The American Revo-
      lution of 1776, on the other hand, was successful because historically there was the oppor-
      tunity for the development of strong indigenous merchant, farmer, and professional
      classes in the face of colonial rule. In Canada, the colonial rulers, merchants, and land-
      owners had profound common interests.
124   After 1847, more and more immigrants from the United Kingdom were going to the
      United States as opposed to the Canadas. In 1847, 142,154 immigrants landed in the US
      and 190,680 in British North America. A year later, 188,233 went to the US and only
      31,065 to the Canadas. For the next ten years, up to 1857, the average annual emigra-
      tion from Britain to the US was 175,000 and to the Canadas 35,000. Morrison, 'Crown
      Land Policies,' 88-9.
125   To this day, the population of Canada is small because of the historical *rule* of merchant
      capital. Industry has been encouraged to the degree that it fulfils certain needs of the
      population; but it is a truncated, branch plant system, having its headquarters outside
      the country (predominantly in the US), because large-scale indigenous industry is anti-
      thetical to large-scale merchant capital.
126   *Capital,* III, 326.

Roger Howard and Jack Scott

Roger Howard is a graduate student at the University of British Columbia;
Jack Scott is editor of *Progressive Worker* and of *Class Struggles in Canada,
1789-1899*

International unions and the ideology of class collaboration

A CRUCIAL factor in United States domination of Canada has been the role of American international unions in the organization of Canadian workers. In broad terms, international control over Canadian unions has meant the development and maintenance of a class-collaborationist labour movement; as a result, the growth of working-class consciousness in Canada has been inhibited and the union struggle limited to economic concerns. How such a situation aids the exploitation of the working class in Canada and profits the American and Canadian ruling classes, and how it happens that Canadian unionists accept the situation, are the questions which will guide our historical discussion.

Beyond these issues, it is our intention to deal with the roots of class collaboration in the unions. We believe that, in addition to the creation of an independent movement, the overcoming of a class-collaborationist ideology is essential to the development of a revolutionary movement in Canada.

THE ARRIVAL OF INTERNATIONAL UNIONS

The penetration of Canada by American unions began in the 1860s under the auspices of individual unions, 26 years before the founding of the American Federation of Labor. At this time, Canada consisted of a group of disunited provinces, politically and economically differing in their interests, and practically isolated from one another by the geography of the country. This geography facilitated north-south communication: thus, during the latter half of the nineteenth century, there was nothing to prevent a free flow of labour across the Canada–United States border. The first union problem encountered in connection with this labour mobility was the exchange of cards between separate national unions in the same craft. Indeed, the creation of common, cross-boundary organizations was initially proposed as a solution to card exchange problems, and also as a means by which labour might be strengthened, financially and organizationally.[1] There is little doubt that there appeared to be strong practical reasons for such a close association, without either side having it clearly in mind to dominate the other. In practice, however, the superior strength of the United States unions led to dominance and, soon, to conflict.

These factors perhaps explain why the internationals were able to gain a foothold in Canada with apparent ease. But they do not explain why the AFL and later the AFL-CIO strived, and strive today, to maintain control over the affairs of Canadian unionists. This question is extremely important when it is realized that 70.8 per cent of organized workers in Canada belong to international unions, while only 24.5 per cent belong to national unions.[2]

Explaining why American unions cling to Canadian subordinates, John Crispo writes: 'International unions by tradition have no thought or desire of giving up their status unless compelled to do so. This reflects a mixture of pride and idealism and a feeling that they have an obligation to their long standing Canadian members ... Their reluctance [to leave] is due in part to the idealism that motivated many of these unions when they originally came into Canada.'[3] Altruism, idealism, or solidarity are explanations that might acquire a ring of sincerity if the AFL-CIO were to recognize the right of Canadian workers to secede. But American unions fight furiously for control of Canadian locals and, in recent years, have spent millions to defeat efforts to establish an independent Canadian movement.[4] Idealism is hardly a satisfactory explanation for such an overwhelming desire to retain control. For a solution to this problem, we must examine the motivations of American unions in their foreign relations and their connection with American foreign policy and the State Department's goals in the world.

THE ROLE OF AMERICAN UNIONS
AND THE AMERICAN EMPIRE

The motives and effects of the penetration of American international unions into Canada become clearer when examined in the context of the developing role of US unions in the origins and expansion of the American economic empire. Very early in its history, the AFL adopted policies and practices that meant class collaboration at home combined with the promotion of the interests of American business abroad. This co-operation, in exchange for access to decision-making for labour leaders, was enthusiastically offered as soon as the general lines for the expansion of American economic power became clear.

As early as 1901, in a speech to the National Civic Federation (an organization of industrial and labour leaders), Samuel Gompers proclaimed a 'community of interests' between capital and labour: 'There is in our time, if not a harmony of interest ... yet certainly a community of interests, to the end that industrial peace shall be maintained ... I want to see the organization of the wage-earners and the organization of employers, through their respective representatives, meet round the table ... there to discuss the questions of wages and hours of labor and conditions of employment and all things consistent with the industrial and commercial success of our country ... We want better relations with the employing class. We are contributing our quota toward that desirable end.'[5] What this quota included soon became apparent, when Gompers used his influence in the AFL to break strikes against the Buffalo Union Furnace Company and the Manhattan Elevated Company, both owned by prominent members of the National Civic Federation.[6]

The origin of this attitude, aside from the personal ambitions of labour leaders to become part of the industrial élite, lies in part in the nature of the AFL itself. The AFL was made up overwhelmingly of craft unions of skilled workers. With the development of industry, an increasing proportion of the working class consisted of unskilled workers, largely immigrants, blacks, and women. It is almost impossible to organize the unskilled into craft unions. But organization by industry instead would mean, by and large, the elimination of the already existing craft structures. This alternative, of course, was rejected by the leaders of the AFL; in fact, they co-operated with the government and employers in destroying industrial organizations, such as the Knights of Labor, Industrial Workers of the World, and One Big Union. This situation was to continue until grassroots pressure led to the organization of the Congress of Industrial Organizations. (Even here the CIO worked completely within the limits of the capitalist system as laid out by the New Deal.) Thus, class collaboration in the United States developed out of an organization that represented a relatively small and relatively privileged section of the working class.

When the victories of the Spanish-American War (1898) made clear the growing international economic and military power of the United States, the leaders of the AFL expanded their vision to a classic conception of what is now known as neo-colonialism: 'The nation which dominates the markets of the world will surely control its destinies. To make of the United States a vast workshop is our manifest destiny, and our duty, and thus side by side with other nations, in industrial and economic rivalry, all basing the conditions of the workers upon the highest intelligence and the most exalted standard of life, no obstacle can be placed to the attainment of the highest pinnacle of national glory and human progress. But to attain this end is the acquirement of the Philippine Islands with their semi-savage population necessary? Surely not. Neither its gates nor those of any other country of the globe can long be closed against our constantly growing industrial supremacy.'[7]

Although opposed to outright colonialism, because of the threat of immigration of 'semi-savage' cheap labour, the directors of the US labour movement have supported American domination of the world's markets from its beginnings to the present day. They view the labour movement as an integral part of the US economic empire and stand ready to do their 'duty.'

In spite of several early ventures,[8] it was not until the First World War that the union leadership became really integrated into the new institutional structures of capitalism and imperialism. Representatives of the AFL were invited to sit on the Council of National Defense, an advisory body that worked out the mobilization of the American economy for war, and the War Labor Board, which arbitrated labour disputes for the duration. But there was a price for admission to the charmed circle of power. Although union standards were maintained in those areas where they had already existed through organization, the *status quo* was frozen in all other regards. The open shop was maintained in government-run ventures, and there were informal agreements to maintain a no-strike policy and to discourage new organizing.[9]

The integration of labour bureaucrats into the integral structures of the American system was continued and strengthened after the war, particularly in the New Deal period and during the Second World War. But our major interest lies in the role of US unions in the empire. This role is most clear in Latin America, which, aside from Canada, is the most important area of US domination.

American unions have carried out two major functions in Latin America. On the one hand, they have attempted to mollify class conflict by organizing 'responsible' American-style unions. On the other, they have worked to support general US economic and political policy by binding Latin American unions into regional organizations dominated by American labour.

For example, in 1918 the AFL created the Pan-American Federation of Labor (PAFL), which the leader of the Puerto Rican trade union movement called the 'instrumentality through which constructive trade unionism can gain ascendancy in Latin America, thus saving the American trade union movement from a continuing battle at its back door with a most destructive and revolutionary labor movement.'[10] The PAFL consistently and openly supported US policy against the national interests of Latin America.[11]

In 1945, America's stated foreign policy in Latin America advocated lower tariffs in South America and unimpeded US investment in the agricultural and extractive industries, with a free flow of US-manufactured goods into the region. American unions favoured this policy because they viewed it as beneficial to their members in the industries affected.

More recently, support for US business interests is ensured through labour participation in such organizations as the Office of Inter-American Affairs headed by Nelson Rockefeller and the American Institute for Free Labor Development (AIFLD). The AIFLD provides the clearest evidence of US labour's support for American imperialist objectives. Founded by the AFL in 1961, it brings together the representatives of the major US corporations in Latin America, of the US government, and of the international unions. The CIA provides large sums to aid in financing the Institute's activities. Thousands of Latin American recruits are trained by the Institute to work for American interests in their home countries.[12] Moreover, where US interests have been threatened or where they might be advanced in Latin America, the AFL has done its best to promote these interests.[13]

In Latin America, the role of US labour as an agent of the empire is clearly visible because over a long period of time an indigenous and nationalist labour movement has resisted American incursions. AFL-CIO-backed unions have often been forced into the role of dual unions, thereby increasing their 'visibility.' The higher level of struggle for national determination also has forced the United States to show its hand to a greater extent.

The differences between Canada and Latin America are not great. The Office of Inter-American Affairs has its parallel in the Canadian-American Committee, with business, government, and labour representatives making sure that the colony remains 'pacified.' And the international unions, although more directly infused into the Canadian scene, play the same role as their AFL-CIO equivalents to the south. From the Spanish-American War to the Vietnam war, the role of the US labour leadership has remained the same: 'partners in progress' of the American empire.

By the close of the nineteenth century, penetration of Canada by American unions had become more deliberate in its design, and by 1902 it had fully blossomed.

A congress of Canadian unions – which, in 1886, became the Trades and Labor Congress – had been established in 1873, thirteen years before the founding of the AFL. The *Ironmoulders Journal* in the US greeted the Canadian initiative, and declared: 'The objects sought can only be obtained by such an organization. The Industrial Congress of the United States would be value-less to our Canada brothers, as most of the wrongs sought to be redressed must be redressed by the Canadian parliament, and a demand from an Industrial Congress composed largely of delegates from the United States would be laughed at by the parliament.'[14]

Thus American unions, before the founding of the AFL, recognized the existence of national differences that required separate national organizations. Significantly, this was also prior to definite shaping of American imperialist interests, and concern for the availability of Canadian natural resources. Until 1897 – when the first AFL delegate appeared at a TLC convention – labour in the two countries followed independent paths on most questions.

The AFL started out as an organization based on principles of exclusion, and was bitterly opposed to industrial unionism, especially as it was represented by the Knights of Labor. All organizations failing to abide by AFL edicts were classed as 'dual unions.' In contrast, the Canadian Congress took no part in jurisdictional disputes, but chose to organize workers regardless of craft or industry, accepting in affiliation both forms of organization; and it encouraged ties with socialist groups. Both of these aspects of TLC organization were rigorously fought against in the AFL.

Antagonism developed[15] and the AFL appointed John Flett as their paid organizer in Canada, charging him with responsibility for quenching the flames of revolt. At the TLC Convention of 1901, President Ralph Smith dealt with the growing crisis, saying: 'I think it is of vast importance that this Congress should adopt some method of increasing its own usefulness. There ought to be a Canadian Federation, for, while I believe that unionism ought to be international in its methods to meet the necessity of combatting common foes, this usefulness is only assured by the strength of national unions. A federation of American unions represented by a national union, each working with the other in special cases, would be a great advantage over having local unions in Canada connected with the national unions of America.'[16]

The pro-internationals element was at a disadvantage at the 1901 convention. To avoid defeat on the issue, they adopted the tactic of tabling Smith's recommendations for an independent Canadian federation until the Berlin (Kitchener), Ontario, convention scheduled for 1902. This gave AFL organizer Flett and his colleagues another year to mobilize support.

Following his report on anti-AFL sentiment in Canada, P.M. Draper, general secretary of the TLC, appealed to the 1901 AFL convention for additional funds to be assigned to Flett, and warned that 'a very strong feeling' in favour of national unions was growing in Canada.[17] The convention delegates responded by voting $300 to finance Flett's activities, and a convention committee commented, 'It is to be regretted that ... there seems to be a tendency toward severance among our Canadian brothers.'

Flett and others busily whipped delegates into line for the 1902 convention, while international executives put pressure on Canadian branches. J.H. Watson, BC vice-president of the Trades and Labor Congress, complained: 'what do we find? Canadian organizers paid by the American Federation of Labor organizing members of local unions and drawing their charter from a foreign country.'[18] But Flett's (and the AFL's) concerted and well-financed campaign proved unbeatable. Even Smith failed to get delegate nomination from his Nanaimo, BC, branch of the United Mine Workers, whose district he represented as a member of Parliament. Instead, he was delegated by a Vancouver local union.

A study of the 1902 convention proceedings suggests that the Canadian independence group realized that defeat awaited them. Only a token fight was offered; and, after a one-day debate, the delegates passed a constitutional amendment which shaped the destiny of the Canadian labour congress from then until the present. The amendment read: 'in no case shall any body of working-men belonging to any trade or calling at present having an international or national union be granted a charter. In the event of an international or national union of the trade or calling of the unions so chartered being formed, it shall be the duty of the proper officer of the Congress to see that the said union becomes a member of said international or national union. Provided that no national union shall be recognized where an international union exists.'[19]

That 'international' meant 'American' was made very clear in 1912, when British-affiliated unions were expelled. The congress elected the AFL organizer, John Flett, as president, and then went begging[20] to the American masters in a resolution: 'Resolved that as the Trades and Labor Congress of Canada has placed itself squarely in accord with the principles of international trade unions, and as such action will reveal the loss of revenues ... it is the opinion of the Congress ... all federal labor unions and central trades and labor councils should be under the jurisdiction and control of the Congress; and the incoming executive is instructed to take immediate steps to make such arrangements with the American Federation of Labor.'[21]

The question of charters was referred to the Executive Council, which met with Flett and Draper in Toronto on 25 April 1903. Council minutes show how these two colonials represented Canadian interests: 'President Flett and Secretary Draper said they were willing to concede the issuance of charters to the AFL.'[22] The request for the right to issue charters was withdrawn without even a reference to the Congress which had passed the resolution. The line of capitulation was clearly drawn, and from this point on a long list of American-supported functionaries would attack independent unions as dual organizations.

The evidence points to a deliberate plan of conquest plotted by the American unionists, and the record of the AFL in Latin America tends to support this thesis. Such a position is disputed by some theoreticians; Crispo, for example, says: 'There are several reasons why international unions operate in Canada. Except in one or two instances, these reasons tend to disprove that international unions were ever a conspiratorial part of the "American Manifest Destiny" school.'[23]

Where there is an identity of interests, there is little need for conspiratorial gatherings. Each of the parties 'knows' its individual tasks and fulfils them. The social and economic interests of American business unionists are linked to those of the imperialists and they perform their respective tasks with a degree of harmony. But meetings are held to discuss important issues: at gatherings of the Canadian-American Committee, founded in 1957, are found the Rockefellers, Morgans, Mellons, and DuPonts, along with leading international union officials. It performs in Canada functions similar to those performed by the Office of Inter-American Affairs and the American Institute for Free Labor Development. Stuart Jamieson, whom Crispo quotes, says of the internationals: 'A more important motivation among the predominantly American-controlled internationals is what might be called the "underlying dynamics of union growth". Most unions ... are dominated by the need to survive and grow. It is in the urge to grow, rather than in the search for "profit" as such, that the expanding American-controlled unions in Canada show many of the same motivations as the expanding American-controlled industries ... To ambitious union executives, like their counterparts in the ranks of management, Canada has seemed a logical extension of the American market.'[24]

The 'dynamics of growth,' as Jamieson and Crispo well know, could be fully satisfied at home. About 73 per cent of US workers and 70 per cent of Canadian workers are still unorganized. Here, indeed, is fertile soil on which the 'dynamics of growth' could flourish without causing international friction. This would be a worthy task for a labour movement to undertake. But this would increase internal economic pressures as a result of demands advanced by newly organized millions, and would not serve AFL and imperialist interests, which require the maintenance of Canada as a source of raw materials and as a market for US goods.

The only way to understand the aims of American unionists in Canada is through knowledge of their position on American foreign policy. How that position operates in practice has been demonstrated in Latin America and Southeast Asia. That it is less evident in Canada is not due to any desire on the part of internationals to treat Canadians more generously than they do others. When the anti-imperialist movement gains momentum, it will be clear where the labour-imperialists stand. Already it is evident on a small scale, in the fight against independent unions and in the placing of locals under trusteeship, what the future has in store for Canadians when the struggle sharpens.

INDEPENDENCE AND THE ONE BIG UNION

The most significant attempt to create an independent Canadian trade union movement was the organization of the One Big Union. It was called into existence during the upsurge of labour radicalism in 1919 and declined into insignificance by 1921-22. But during this short period of activity, the One Big Union raised some of the central issues involved in the development of an independent movement.

The impetus for the organization of the OBU arose from the dissatisfaction of the more radical union leaders (almost entirely Westerners) with the prevailing policies of the international labour movement. These dissatisfactions centred around two interrelated themes: class collaboration and trade union organization.

The issue of class collaboration came to a head when the conscription bill was introduced into the House of Commons on 1 June 1917, the day the US Congress adopted a draft conscription law. Prior to the war, the TLC had denounced the impending conflict as a struggle between the capitalist classes of various nations in which the working class had no stake.[25] Even after the declaration of hostilities and the shock of the disintegration of international labour solidarity, the TLC opposed conscription either completely or within the context of the demand for 'conscription of wealth' (i.e., nationalization of industry) if conscription of manpower were legislated. But with the passage of the conscription bill and the wholehearted support given to the war by the AFL, the leadership of the Canadian movement wavered.

At the TLC convention of 1917, the radicals proposed a national general strike to block conscription. But the TLC executive rejected this proposal on two grounds. First, it involved breaking the law of the land: 'Under our representative form of government, it is not deemed right or patriotic, or in the interests of the Dominion or of the labour classes, to say or do ought that might keep them [the government] from attaining all the results anticipated from enforcement of the law.'[26] Clearly, the executive was not willing to take the risks involved in opposing the government in Ottawa.

But the second major argument used for refusing to oppose conscription is the more interesting: 'It is just as well, at this time, that I should point out that the organized workers of Canada stand in a position that has no parallel in any other country of the world. This Congress can only exert its moral influence in the enforcement of decisions, and the economic power to support legislative demands is not vested in our movement, but is under the control of the international officers of our representative unions. When the executive council of the American Federation of Labor reaches a decision, members of that council, being heads of powerful international trade unions, can use their influence effectively. The same applies to the parliamentary committee of the British Trade Union Congress, but in Canada we cannot use our economic power without the sanction of the heads of our international unions ... In cases where our decisions are at variance with decisions taken by the American Federation of Labor regarding important national issues, it is difficult to secure that sympathy, that support in the exercise of our economic powers, as we otherwise would receive if the executive of the Congress were composed of heads of powerful economic organizations.'[27] As a delegate put it: 'President Gompers had committed the workers of the United States to conscription, therefore a general strike was not feasible.'[28]

This passive acquiescence to American domination meant that opponents of conscription were left to fight without the support of Canadian labour. As a result, the government was allowed to persecute a number of radical labour leaders under the provisions of the conscription bill and the War Measures Act. Class collaboration was reinforced when, as in the US, conservative labour leaders were appointed to various governmental bodies, the most significant being the appointment of Gideon Robertson, international vice-president of the Commercial Telegraphers Union, to the Senate of Canada.

The collaboration was opposed by the more radical Westerners at the 1918 TLC convention, when they moved that the Congress constitution be altered to ban from office all those who held posts with the government. They also raised the other major issue that would split the TLC in the following year, that of industrial versus craft unionism. The Winnipeg Trades and Labor Council moved that the Congress take 'a referendum vote on the question of organizing the Canadian Labour movement into a modern and scientific organization by industry instead of by craft.'[29] What this meant was a break with the internationals. As the Transcona Trades and Labor Council pointed out in their motion, joint strike action in Canada was impossible because it was 'necessary for each Craft to attain sanction from its International.'[30] Another resolution demanded the repeal of the 1912 amendment to the TLC constitution that banned bodies which were banned by the AFL.[31]

In addition, anticipating the unemployment crisis that would attend the end of the war, the Winnipeg Council proposed 'that the Trades and Labor Congress of Canada take cognizance of such an emergency and immediately take steps to promulgate a six hours [sic] day and a five day week for all Labour in the Dominion so as to assist in absorbing the surplus labour and safeguard against unemployment.'[32]

When these and other similar resolutions were defeated, the Western caucus decided to hold a Western Labour Conference in Calgary in March 1919. The BC Federation of Labor arranged to hold its convention a few days prior to the Congress, so that the BC delegates could attend both meetings.

The Western Labour Conference called for a referendum on a general strike to be held on 1 June for the following demands: the six-hour day; release of all political prisoners and restoration of complete freedom of speech; removal of all restrictions imposed upon working class organizations; immediate withdrawal of allied troops from Russia and Germany. The significant organizational resolutions advocated 'reorganization ... along industrial lines, so that by virtue of their industrial strength, the workers may be better prepared to enforce any demand they consider essential to their maintenance and well being,' and that the bodies represented sever their affiliation with their international organizations and co-operate in the formation of an industrial organization of all workers.

The form of organization that emerged was that of local units organized by industry where practicable, grouped geographically in central councils (in cities) or district boards (in larger areas), with the national general executive board delegated from the secondary units. The combination of industrial and geographic organization was meant to facilitate the co-ordination of actions of solidarity when a local unit was involved in a strike.

The final issue debated at the conference was that of political activity. Although it did not go as far as the IWW stand of rejecting all political activity, the conference did reject the narrow parliamentarian view of politics. In the words of one delegate: 'Power in politics is not found in Parliament but in the country prior to the election. Politics only exist where there are classes, and any action taken by a class in defense of its interest is political action. Hence you cannot define any particular action as political, but any action ... used to control political power in order to use it for the benefit of that class – that is political action, and it matters not what method it takes.'[32] The founders of the OBU considered on-going education in class consciousness to be more significant than occasional election campaigns and allocated one-third of its monthly dues to the general executive board for that purpose.

The labour organizations of Western Canada voted overwhelmingly to affiliate with the new organization, and the One Big Union became the major labour centre west of the Great Lakes. But before the OBU could get properly organized, events in Winnipeg led to the first test of labour solidarity based upon geographic organization. Although begun and carried through by locals of the old internationals, the Winnipeg general strike was coordinated by a general strike committee emerging from the Winnipeg Trades and Labor Council. Locals in the building and metal trades, who went on strike at the beginning of May 1919, appealed to the Council for support. In a referendum among the affiliated locals, a large majority voted for a general strike for the following demands: a living wage, the eight-hour day, the right to organize. Later the demand that all strikers must be reinstated without discrimination was added to the list. On 15 May 12,000 organized workers went out, followed by another 12,000 unorganized. In a few days 35,000 men and women were on strike and no public or private services were carried out in the city without the permission of the strike committee. This internal solidarity was maintained throughout, in spite of threats by municipal, provincial, and federal governments to dismiss postal, telephone, fire, and police workers if they did not go back to work. Such threats were carried out. Sympathy strikes spread throughout western Canada, and calls went out for a dominion strike committee.

To defeat the strike, two forces combined: the Canadian ruling class and its government, and the American Federation of Labor. On 29 May Gideon Robertson, Canada's first 'labour statesman' and the then Minister of Labour wrote to the AFL president, Samuel Gompers: 'In my opinion, the prestige and authority of the international unions whose local membership is participating in the strike ... should receive the rather serious consideration of the executives of the various organizations concerned ... The motives are undoubtedly in support of the One Big Union Movement.'[34] The internationals responded by advising their members to scab on the 'illegal' strike and by working to disrupt the crucial Toronto general strike scheduled for May 30. When the Toronto action partially failed, the momentum of the dominion-wide support movement broke down. With Winnipeg isolated, the governments were able to provoke the calling-in of troops and to arrest the leaders under hastily invoked legislation. These actions led to the defeat of the strike in Winnipeg.[35]

In Winnipeg, the internationals and the government also contributed to the strike's defeat. Senior railway running trades officials offered to mediate the strike but then carried on direct negotiations with the employers without keeping the strike committee properly informed. Labour Minister Robertson had a hand in these negotiations, and according to an inquiry conducted by the House of Commons in 1926: 'The Minister of Labour [Robertson] did on a whim of his own, and against the advice of his colleagues, prolong the strike by refusing to declare in favour of collective bargaining ... I think he said himself it was in the interests of the international unions ... The negotiations leading up to the riot were carried out in a manner to prevent it being settled.'[36]

The pattern of collusion between government, employers, and internationals was repeated in the subsequent campaign to destroy the OBU, the most notable example being the conflict in the Alberta and BC coalfields. The employers and government acted to force the workers back into the United Mine Workers in order to work at all.[37] The OBU might have been able to survive these attacks if it had been able to maintain internal solidarity. But this solidarity was seriously weakened by the policies of the newly formed Workers (later Communist) Party. Adopting the position of the US Communist leader William Z. Foster, they worked to get radicals back into the AFL in order to 'bore from within' and change the policies of the internationals from a position of internal strength. They felt that, by setting up 'ideal' revolutionary unions, the radicals divorced themselves from the 'mass of the working class.' But as OBU advocates pointed out, 'the mass of the working class' was unorganized and the membership of the internationals, because of their relatively privileged position and the collaborationist policies long held by the internationals, was least susceptible to radical programs. They also pointed out that getting 'revolutionaries' elected to office rarely had the desired effect: 'We workers in Western Canada have had our experience with "revolutionary" leaders before. We have placed them in responsible positions – and they are still there, and if we were to take these men today in the old craft unions, you will find them well-informed "revolutionaries." '[38] The Worker's Party, however, had the prestige of the Russian Revolution behind them. And as the labour historian Harold A. Logan put it in 1928, 'Doubtless the OBU has been considerably weakened by the subtle offer of an easier road to the goal of proletarian conquest.'[39]

This 'easier road' has been shown by history to be a dead end, both for the Communist Party and for the labour movement of Canada. The OBU, which posited the alternative of an independent and class-conscious movement, was destroyed before its potential strengths and weaknesses became clear. But the history of this attempt to create a radical labour movement in Canada contains important lessons for militants today. It deserves a more extensive study than our brief comments here.

LABOUR AND IDEOLOGY

It is clear that a total break, organizationally *and* ideologically, with the internationals is the necessary first step toward the building of a movement that will serve the real interests of Canadian workers.

If organizational change is not accompanied, or preceded, by ideological change, there will be no possibility of permanent transformation; for it is in the field of ideology – the policy of class collaboration – that labour and especially its 'left' section, suffers the greatest defeats.

Canadian unionists, as with most unionists in the US and Europe, do not have a clear notion or a general theory of capitalist society. They enter the field as bargainers in search of a satisfactory deal, having some idea of what the contract should yield in terms of their customary living standards and of future security. They are concerned not so much with the fact that the employer owns the means of production but with the extent of his bargaining advantage. It is in his power to threaten them with unfavourable legislation and with the use of competitive labour (such as strike breakers and 'cheap immigrant labour') that his advantage is seen to lie. Their impulse therefore is not to suppress the employer, but to deal with the recognized threats to their bargaining strength.

With political and class outlook thus restricted and distorted by the limitations of elementary trade union consciousness, the unionist is convinced that personal security and prosperity is fully dependent on the continuing prosperity of the capitalist system. This conviction is only slightly shaken by the exigencies of the collective bargaining process and, on balance, is strengthened by the conditions inherent in capitalism in the modern era of imperialism with its super-profits gained in exploitation of colonial peoples. Concerned with market control as a necessary adjunct to expansion of industrial production, union support is initially won for this particular aspect of the imperialist system, and kept alive through 'corruption' of top levels of skilled labour who receive minor rewards from the fruits of imperialist exploitation.

This economic, as distinct from class, interest in imperialism was accurately reflected by Gompers before the turn of the century when he shared with major corporate leaders the opinion that both industry and labour could share in the benefits of foreign expansion. He declared that the AFL 'did not oppose the development of our commerce, nor the power and influence which the United States may exert upon the destinies of the nations of the world.'[40]

A.W. Calhoun pointed out the unions' emphasis on productivity, and the labour leaders concern with 'ways and means of increasing output.'[41] He maintained there was no alternative within the bargaining process 'but for organized labor to go along with triumphant American imperialism in its conquest of the world. Better to be a side-partner to American business in its march towards the enslavement of the world, than to take poor chances in battle with the employers.' Calhoun contended that this could 'easily afford to hand out a continual stream of material benefits, so that social solidarity might be maintained in the face of an unfriendly foreign world.' He maintained that the corporate system could, and would, hand out tangible benefits to organized labour 'as the price of loyalty.'[42]

Canadian unionists are not materially or psychologically different from those in the United States. Captivated by the same concept of economism, they too equate personal security, present and future, with that of the existing social order, which means accepting United States domination of the economy, sharing with American workers concern for the stability of the American economic system, and as a direct consequence, domination of the Canadian union movement by the US representatives of business unionism. They believe implicitly the propaganda that says a break with the American system would reduce living standards by 25 per cent,[43] and cling the more tightly to American unions and the American system.[44]

The concept of economism has become more deeply rooted as a result of an extended era of relative prosperity which has allowed the unions to enlarge the scope of collective bargaining into decision-making areas hitherto viewed as the exclusive right of management. This venture into 'industrial democracy,' combined with an improved standard of living, imparts to unionists a sense of material affluence which permeates union philosophy, and the turbulence and idealism of labour's formative years recede ever farther into the background, to be replaced by a conservatism that clings increasingly to the existing capitalist system. Abandonment of the last vestiges of egalitarian principles is manifested in the striving of each union local to control a diminishing number of jobs and to surpass one another in wage rates and benefits. This, in turn, is transformed into competition between individual union members, at the ultimate cost of unity and solidarity.

The pursuit of what are essentially selfish goals, manifest in demands on behalf of the organized minority, creates a chasm that is advantageous to the employers and is not bridged by the many pious resolutions which are endorsed at union conventions but never acted on.

As at every critical juncture of the labour movement in the past, there is a marked increase in sentiment in favour of an independent Canadian union movement. Will such an endeavour result in any fundamental change in the trade union movement?

The struggle for an independent movement is a worthwhile effort. It mobilizes the unionists against the main concentration of union bureaucracy, centred in the 'international' and craft unions, the bureaucracy that is the mainstay of alien ideology. Moreover, Canadian workers must take control of their own destiny and accept responsibility for their own policies and actions, which they cannot do as long as they remain wards of the American unions. As a tiny minority in American unions, Canadian workers at present are restricted to the role of 'democratic opposition.'

But necessary as it is as a preliminary step in the direction of more important developments, the switch from international to independent Canadian unions will not, of itself, result in any fundamental transformation of the unions from organs of class compromise to weapons of revolutionary class struggle.

A socialist, commenting on the founding of the One Big Union in 1919, sounded a warning for revolutionary unionists that applies also to today's struggle for independent unions: 'The working class is not measurably nearer to emancipation simply by forming "One Big Union". Education was never more necessary than it is today in order to change that slave psychology and to enable the workers to view each and every question from their own class point of view.

'The struggles which are ahead of the labour movement must be regarded as training camps to prepare them for the final struggle and the duty of the socialist is to see to it that this is never lost sight of but is kept continually before the workers' eyes.

'The activities of the union, if it materializes, will be largely of a palliative nature; wage regulations, working conditions, etc.; all of which means a compromise with capitalism. The work of the socialist is to accelerate as much as possible the evolutionary trend, to disseminate the knowledge of revolutionary socialism and so establish that unity of thought which is a necessary prerequisite to unity of actions.'[45]

Today, despite their rhetoric and apparent enmity, the vanguard radicals, whose task it was, according to Lenin, to combat economism, and the right-winger meet on the common ground of economism in the trade unions. The rank and file is at least subconsciously aware of the fact, and is thoroughly disenchanted with the bleak prospect both parties present – a series of spiralling wage demands that no longer have any meaning, since every increase disappears in increased prices and increased taxes, sometimes even before the wage increase goes into effect. The average unionist is aware that the left is no more proficient than the right at bargaining, or vice versa. When one is elevated to office, it is simply in order to strike down the other, not in any expectation of an improvement. Frustration and demoralization are clearly evident in union meetings, and most unions are run by an activist group consisting of about 3 to 5 per cent of the membership. The role of radicals should be to convince workers of the necessity to strive for higher objectives as the only solution to current problems.

The roots of the crisis in the union are internal, not external, and are embedded in the class-collaborationist policy pursued by the movement. This class-collaborationist policy is built securely into what has become the main activity, and proud achievement, of the labour movement – the union contract, the signing of which is a fundamental act of compromise with the class enemy. Capitalist employers yield ground on such relatively minor points as union security, seniority, and fringe benefits, and receive in return a tacit agreement that the unions will safeguard the essential structure of the capitalist system. This acceptance of capitalist values stamps its imprint on the unions. Opportunism and self-interest permeate the entire movement. The union machine is integrated into the capitalist structure and union leaders extol its virtues. Any challenge to capitalism is abhorred, denounced, and generally prohibited in a variety of anti-communist clauses in union constitutions. The results are reinforcement of the foundations of capitalism and failure to strive for basic objectives that are in the interests of the working class. Unions derive their strength as much from employer co-operation as they do from services rendered the members. Dues check-off and compulsory membership – defended as sacred working-class principles under the misnomer of union security – are points on which employers co-operate with opportunistic union functionaries.

The illusion of equality with the employer generated by the collective agreement creates an imaginary balance of democratic privileges between exploiter and exploited. Enamoured of the fancied prestige of an illusory equality with management, sidetracked in the routine activity around petty demands, the worker loses sight of the struggle required for complete emancipation. Many of the best elements in the movement are forced to conclude that their efforts are futile, because what is hailed as a vital act of social regeneration – the union contract – turns out to be no more than a shoddy deal, founded on a coexistence pact between labour and capital.

Union meetings, once the scene of lively and spirited debates and the regular meeting-place of opponents of the *status quo*, are now, for the most part, respectable forums of conservative opinions that would be at home in a Chamber of Commerce or Rotary Club. Organizations that once were fertile ground for the development of new and challenging ideas are now intellectual deserts. If some other critical ailment fails to kill them first, the unions may well die of boredom.

CONCLUSION

If the above analysis is correct, what should be the role of the socialist left in working movements? Various leftist groups have assumed it is their task to emancipate the working class. To that end they have attached themselves to the trade union movement, in particular, and also to other working class organizations.

It is not the role of socialists to emancipate the working class. Only the people themselves can achieve their own liberation. The left can only point the way to liberation by explaining the necessity for radical social change to solve in a fundamental way the problems that have been raised in the context of the people's struggle. As Mao Tse-tung wrote in 1943: '"From the Masses to the Masses." This means: take the ideas of the masses (scattered and unsystematic ideas) and concentrate them (through study turn them into concentrated and systematic ideas), then go to the masses and propagate these ideas until the masses embrace them as their own, hold fast to them and translate them into action, and test the correctness of these ideas in such action.'[46] People accept revolutionary solutions only when it is clear that they provide real answers to concrete problems. The articulation of the demands raised in people's struggles and the formulation of effective solutions is the fundamental role that the left must play. It is not the role of socialists to draw up intermediate programs 'to take to the people'; rather, it is to take up the problems that emerge, to articulate them, to give them political content and to use them to educate workers as to the nature of the major contradiction facing the working class: capitalist ownership of the means of production.

The socialist left has but one program: to overthrow capitalism, to establish working class rule, and to build a truly free, socialist society. To this end their efforts must be concentrated on developing a revolutionary socialist consciousness in the working class.

Within the union movement it is not the role of socialists and communists to manoeuvre for positions of 'leadership' within the bureaucracy. Rather, it is to combat class collaboration by working for an independent movement that will break with the present limitations of trade union actions and goals.

It would also be a serious mistake to equate the union movement with the working class. The bulk of the working population is not in the organized union movement. In fact, that sector which is organized is often the most privileged and least open to revolutionary solutions. The simple-minded equating of union movement with working class has led all Canada's 'vanguard parties' into policies of economism and opportunism.

The development of a Canadian revolutionary movement means the organization of the working class in its broadest sense. This means especially the most oppressed sectors; the unorganized, unemployed, welfare-recipients, women, native people, youth, and students. In each of these areas of struggle, socialists must work for a revolutionary perspective around which all oppressed people can unite and liberate themselves.

NOTES

1 M. Mackintosh, *An Outline of Trade Union History in Great Britain, Canada and the United States* (Ottawa 1938), 7.
2 Canada, Department of Labour, *Labour Organizations in Canada, 1965* (Ottawa 1966), Table 3.
3 *International Unionism: A Study in Canadian-American Relations* (Toronto 1967), 31.
4 John L. Lewis claimed the UMW of America poured $1,124,000 into Nova Scotia up to 1920. Quoted in H.A. Logan, *The History of Trade Union Organization in Canada* (Chicago 1928), 202. Although no definite figures are available, the forty-year fight of the BRC against the CBRT and the USWA twenty-year battle with Mine-Hill (which had, in effect, become a Canadian union) must have cost several million dollars. These are just three of scores of similar cases.
5 B. Mandel, *Samuel Gompers: A Biography* (Yellow Springs 1963), 242.
6 *Ibid.,* 242-9.
7 Samuel Gompers, *American Federationist* (Sept. 1898), 239.
8 With the US occupation of the Philippines and Puerto Rico, and with the rise of American direct investment in Canada, in the late 1800s, the international career of the AFL began. In all the above countries, special commissioners were sent or hired to organize 'pure and simple' AFL-type unions in opposition to an already existing union movement.
   In the Philippines and Puerto Rico, the indigenous labour movement had fought against the Spanish and wanted independence. See R. Radosh, *American Labor and United States Foreign Policy* (New York 1969), chap. 11. In the case of Canada, the Trades and Labor Congress was on the verge of becoming a national union movement when the AFL appeared and began the process of balkanization of the trade union movement in Canada. See R.H. Babcock, 'The AFL in Canada, 1896-1908: A Study in American Labour Imperialism,' unpublished PHD thesis, Duke University.
9 Mandel, *Gompers,* 364-97. But the greatest price the workers had to pay was the war itself. There was widespread opposition to US involvement in what was essentially an imperialist war. And in spite of a great deal of rhetoric about 'defending democracy,' large sectors of the working and farming population saw no sense in involvement. An organization called the American Alliance for Labor and Democracy was formed to overcome this opposition. Gompers was named chairman, but the organization was actually run by George Crell, chief of the government's committee on 'public information.' The Alliance was financed by contributions from a secret presidential fund and from wealthy individuals. Later in the war the appalling slaughter led to increasing grass-roots pressure for peace among European workers. At this juncture Samuel Gompers and other AFL leaders became America's first 'labor statesmen,' touring the allied nations to bolster morale. Their special mission was to ensure that allied labour and socialist leaders did not contact representatives of 'enemy labor' to organize pressure for an early negotiated peace. See Radosh, *American Labor,* chaps. 2, 4, 5, 6.
10 Santiago Iglesias, 'The Child of the A.F. of L.,' *American Federationist,* XXXII (1925), 928. Iglesias, the president of the Free Federation of Workmen of Puerto Rico, a socialist and nationalist organization, was jailed by the American authorities under the Spanish anti-union code. The AFL secured his release and brought him to the US where he was converted to AFL-style 'non-political' unionism. He later returned to Puerto Rico and was successful in bringing the FFW into the AFL.

11   Radosh, *American Labor,* 350-6.
12   *Ibid.,* chaps. 13, 14.
13   When the Arbenz government in Guatemala began expropriating US property as part of
     a land reform, the AFL attempted to organize a dual union in order to build an opposi-
     tion. The CIA-sponsored 'Liberation Army' that invaded Guatemala and toppled the gov-
     ernment included members of this AFL-ORIT (Inter-American Regional Organization of
     Workers) union who planned to organize a respectable 'anti-communist' union movement.
     In fact the reactionary dictatorship that resulted destroyed the labour movement and agri-
     cultural workers were brought back to conditions that approached slavery. See Radosh,
     American Labor, 383-93.
          During the Cuban Revolution, US labour consistently backed the corrupt leadership of
     the CTC and through it the Batista dictatorship. After the Revolution when the Cuban
     movement withdrew from ORIT, the AFL-CIO officially declared Castro's policies 'a well-
     planned strategy designed to make Cuba an advanced outpost of the Soviet Union's drive
     to infiltrate the New World.' The AFL-CIO thus became one of the first groups recom-
     mending US government sanctions against Cuba. See *ibid.,* 375-83.
          In an operation similar to the one in Guatemala, also backed by the CIA, US-supported
     unions fomented labour and racial strife which led to the fall of Cheddi Jagan's national-
     ist government in Guyana. Finally the AFL-CIO-supported labour movement in the Do-
     minican Republic (CONTRAL) accepted the US invasion as 'necessary to prevent another
     Cuba,' exactly the position of the State Department. This led to its demise as the major
     representative of Dominican labour.
14   31 Aug. 1873.
15   Friction developed as a result of several issues: first, the question of bureaucratic tenden-
     cies in the unions, a source of conflict aggravated by foreign control; second, the question
     of a per-capita tax going to the AFL (taxation without representation), while the Canadian
     national organization was in dire need of finances; third, a direct assault on the material
     interests of the Canadian unionist, that is, his access to the US labour market was inhi-
     bited by the 'Alien Labour Law' supported by the AFL.
16   TLC, Sixteenth Annual Convention, Proceedings, 8-9.
17   American Federation of Labor, 1901 Convention, Proceedings, 116.
18   A letter in the Victoria *Daily Colonist,* 2 Feb. 1902.
19   *Labour Gazette,* IV, 421.
20   TLC officers, having placed themselves at the mercy of the AFL and the international
     unions, were now compelled to come to the American unions, hat in hand, with an appeal
     for continued financial assistance. In fact, the Canadian delegate was appealing to the AFL
     to pay the salary of the man who had just been elected President of the Dominion Con-
     gress, when he said: 'That its [the TLC] value has also been recognized for your body is
     evidenced by your repeated financial assistance. I trust you will not doubt our gratitude
     if we, like Oliver, ask for more ... We would have you still continue in maintaining and
     keeping in the Canadian field organizer John A. Flett, a gentleman evidently fitted for
     the work.' (1902 AFL Convention Proceedings) In response to the mendicant's plea,
     Gompers proposed a committee to study and report on the situation. The members sub-
     sequently reported: 'We also congratulate the ... [Canadian] Congress in their clearcut
     declaration along the lines of international organization ... We recommend that ... we con-
     tinue to maintain the services of a general organizer and to secure as many volunteer or-
     ganizers as may be determined by the president of the American Federation of Labor ...
     We ... believe that the granting of charters by the Labor Congress of Canada to federal
     labor unions would have a tendency to divide.' *Ibid.*
21   *Labour Gazette,* III, 229.
22   Minutes of Executive Council, *American Federationist,* 10, no. 6 (June 1903), 506.
23   *The Role of International Unionism in Canada* (Canadian-American Committee, spon-
     sored by the National Planning Association [USA] and the Private Planning Association
     of Canada, 1967), 11.

24 In *International Unionism*, 21.
25 Convention proceedings of the Trades and Labor Congress of Canada up until 1914 indicate virtual unanimity in opposition to war. After the outbreak of hostilities, opposition passed from war itself to conscription, with the Western delegates providing the main opposition force. Opposing stands on conscription was an important issue leading to the split between east and west. Convention proceedings, *Labour Gazette,* and Congress Journal, 1912-1918.
26 Quoted in C. Lipton, *The Trade Union Movement of Canada, 1827-1959* (Montreal 1966), 176.
27 *Ibid.,* 177.
28 *Ibid.*
29 TLC, Thirty-fourth Annual Convention, Proceedings, 129. The complete resolution read as follows: 'Whereas, in the past the Capitalist class have used every means at their disposal to defeat the workers in their attempt to ameliorate the conditions under which they work; and, whereas, the present form of Craft organization leaves us in the position whereby the Capitalist class can successfully defeat us in any attempt we may make; therefore, be it resolved, that we call upon the Trades and Labor Congress of Canada to take a referendum vote on the question of organizing the Canadian Labour movement into a modern and scientific organization by Industry instead of by Craft.'
30 *Ibid.* The International Association of Machinists in Winnipeg moved the same resolution, as did several other locals (lodges) of the same union. In part the resolution read: 'whereas, to successfully conduct a strike all crafts in an Industry must act together and realizing that the present organization in Craft unions, whereby it is necessary for each Craft to secure sanction from its International, tends to defeat this object a successful strike, therefore be it resolved, that the Executive of the Trades Congress be instructed to take a referendum vote of all Crafts affiliated on the following question: are you in favour of reorganizing the workers of Canada in a modern and scientific manner, that of organization by industries instead of by Craft?'
31 *Ibid.,* 130.
32 *Ibid.,* 140.
33 In Logan, *Trade Union Organization,* 383.
34 In Lipton, *Trade Union Movement,* 209.
35 *Ibid.,* 208-11.
36 *Ibid.,* 211, quoting Peter Heenan, a subsequent Minister of Labour.
37 Logan, *Trade Union Organization,* 404-5.
38 *One Big Union Bulletin,* 30 Aug. 1923, 1.
39 Logan, *Trade Union Organization,* 411.
40 See Gomper's speech on United States foreign policy, *American Federationist* (Sept. 1898).
41 'Labor's New Economic Policy,' in *American Labor Dynamics,* J.B.S. Hardman, ed. (New York 1928), 320.
42 *Ibid.,* 320-8.
43 See *Toronto Star,* 4 Jan. 1972.
44 Lead articles in journals of most craft, and some industrial, unions reflect this viewpoint; the recent pulp and paper union request re Nixon's 10 per cent surcharge is a case in point.
45 *The Camp Worker,* Vancouver, 17 May 1919.
46 Mao Tse-Tung, *Quotations,* 128-9.

R.B. Morris

a pseudonym for a teacher at the University of Saskatchewan

The reverter clause and break-aways in Canada

IN RECENT YEARS, a number of Canadian local unions have successfully seceded from internationals.[1] Secession from the International Brotherhood of Pulp, Sulphite and Paper Mill Workers resulted in the formation of the independent Pulp and Paper Workers of Canada in British Columbia; the Canadian Union of Operating Engineers in Ontario came into existence after breaking from the International Union of Operating Engineers; the Canadian Concrete Forming Union in Toronto, now affiliated with the Canadian Union of Construction Workers, also came into being after a successful secessionist movement. The Canadian Association of Industrial, Mechanical and Allied Workers (CAIMAW) was formed from a local formerly affiliated with the International Molders and Allied Workers Union in Winnipeg.

More recently, on 24 May 1970, fifteen locals of the Saskatchewan Joint Board of the international Retail, Wholesale and Department Store Union successfully disaffiliated. And in 1971, breakaway locals from the Retail Clerks International Association formed the Canadian Merchandising Employees Union.

There already exists a federation called the Council of Canadian Unions (CCU) for independent locals, should they wish to affiliate. The CCU is an all-Canadian body whose primary purpose is to offer a home for break-aways and newly formed independent organizations. Since its membership is small – about 10,000 – the CCU presents little threat to the Canadian Labour Congress.

Ed Finn, Research Director of the Canadian Brotherhood of Railway, Transport and General Workers Union, noted recently that there is a growing awareness of a 'nationalist sentiment among Canadian unionists.' Finn further added that recent break-aways 'are only the first stirrings of the nationalist ferment now bubbling up within Canadian labour. Unless the internationals heed these incipient rumblings and grant effective self-government to their branches in this country, the next decade could see a titanic – and ultimately successful – struggle for Canadian union emancipation.'[2]

Finn's article suggest that these break-aways are a response to the bureaucracy of international unions. This is very different from the secessionist movements and break-aways of the 1920s and 1930s, which were strongly influenced and instigated by the ideology of the left. Today's break-aways appear to be non-ideological, although non-ideological revolts may very well be led by 'leftists'; for it is extremely difficult to challenge union bureaucracy, and the ideologue tends to have the stomach or temperament for fighting what appears from the outset to be a lost cause.

One of the difficulties faced by secessionists is the existence of the reverter clause which controls the disposition of money and other property of a local union or intermediate body. If the local, for any reason, severs its affiliation with the parent body, or international union, under this clause all monies, books, and property revert to the parent body upon disaffiliation. The reverter clause is found in all international union constitutions except those of the Retail, Wholesale and Department Store Union, the Bricklayers, Masons and Plasterer's International Union, and United Glass and Ceramics Workers of North America.[3]

The 1968 constitution of the International Union of Operating Engineers contains a typical reverter clause: 'If at any time a Local Union or other subdivision shall withdraw, lapse, dissolve, be suspended, placed under supervision or expelled from the International Union, or shall have its charter revoked, all of its real and personal property, paraphernalia, books, charter, seal, records, card indexes and funds shall immediately revert to the International Union and the General President shall at once, in person or by deputy, take possession of such property, paraphernalia, books, charter, seal, records, card indexes and funds of said Local Union or other subdivision.'[4]

The courts in North America view the constitution of a union as a contract binding upon the international, the local, and the members. Thus, a local union whose members are dissatisfied with their international is faced with the prospect of either remaining subject to the parent body or losing its assets by judicial enforcement of the reverter clause.

In *Lakeman and Barrett* v. *Bruce,*[5] the British Columbia Court of Appeals held that a minority of the local could claim the property of the local against the majority who wished to become a local of a rival union. The minimum number of members required to retain affiliation with the parent body is specified in each constitution.

For example, the Canadian constitution of the International Union of Mine, Mill and Smelter Workers (1963) states that a local union shall not withdraw from 'the Union or dissolve so long as at least ten (10) members in good standing object thereto.'[6] Thus, when a majority of workers belonging to Local 637 of Mine-Mill wished to change its affiliation, the Ontario High Court denied them the right to do so as long as ten members remained loyal to the union.[7]

Sometimes the courts do grant exceptions to the formal contract theory, when they see fit. They have held that a local can secede without surrendering properties if it can prove fiduciary irresponsibility on the part of the parent body.[8] And United States judges have suspended the reverter clause on behalf of locals seeking disaffiliation from left-wing and corrupt internationals.[9]

It is nonetheless apparent that, once a local is chartered by an international or national union, the reverter clause has the effect of thereafter minimizing the worker's free choice of his bargaining agent at the local level. In his comprehensive *International Unionism: A Study in Canadian-American Relations,* John Crispo notes that: 'In the early 1940's ... the Marine Workers Federation broke away from the old CIO Industrial Union of Marine and Shipbuilding Workers of America, without any ill will on either side. However, this is an exception to the general rule. *Normally, international unions resist with all the resources at their command any attempt by one of their constituent parts to sever the link.* As a result, it is usually very difficult for any such group to secede.'[10]

Stuart Jamieson further points out that 'If the central executive of all internationals ... exerted to the full powers and prerogatives allowed them under most union constitutions, most of them could, legally, have complete control over the Canadian branches and "American domination" would be a fact.'[11] There can be no doubt that degrees of control differ from union to union; but when secession is the issue, international union leaders greatly desire to keep what they have and are inclined to use whatever means are available to maintain their ties with subordinate bodies.

Other obstacles impeding secession are the possible loss of the contributions to benefit plans, and the fear of loss of bargaining rights.[12] The nature of the bargaining unit also can be crucial; a multi-plant or multi-employer bargaining unit tends to increase the risk of failure of a dissident movement. But despite the slim chance of success and the stigma attached to secession, break-aways do occur. It appears that they become possible only when conditions between the subordinate body and the parent have so deteriorated that disaffiliation is seen as the only solution. Thus, secession becomes the ultimate weapon used by activists as a check on union bureaucracy.

Even after successful secession from the parent body, the leaders of break-aways continue to pay a high price for their independence; for once a local or subordinate body secedes from a national or international union affiliated to the Canadian Labour Congress (CLC), it is subject to raiding by other affiliates.

The problem of raiding has existed since the early days of labour organization. Indeed, one of the primary reasons for the merger of the AFL and the CIO in 1955 was to stop the intense rivalry between the craft and industrial unions in the United States. The most bitter years of raiding were between 1935 and 1941; and from 1945 to the merger in 1955, there was a proliferation of bilateral no-raiding agreements among unions. The AFL adopted a no-raiding policy among its affiliates, as did the CIO; and in some cases, no-raiding pacts existed between AFL and CIO affiliates. This made the marriage between the two federations possible.[13] Now the constitutions of both the AFL-CIO and the CLC[14] contain a no-raiding provision.

Regardless of the circumstances or reasons, any break-away is subject to raiding as a 'punishment' for committing the cardinal trade union sin of secession and disunity. Once the break-away succeeds, the CLC will not admit the independent back into the federation, unless it reaffiliates with an already existing affiliate to the Congress. Such reaffiliation usually occurs with the permission of the parent union from which the subordinate body seceded.[15]

THE RWDSU BREAK-AWAY

This was the case when fifteen locals seceded from the international Retail, Wholesale and Department Store Union in Saskatchewan in 1970. These locals were able to break away with relative ease from the international RWDSU because it is the only international union in North America that has in its constitution what might be called a non-reverter clause. The RWDSU constitution specifically states that: 'Upon disaffiliation ... the local union shall have no claims for monies paid to the International Union and the International Union shall have no claim upon the assets, funds, contracts or other properties of the local union.'[16]

The RWDSU was organized primarily by the coming together of many large locals that were already established. Its unique non-reverter is a result of the refusal of many 'progressive' district council leaders to surrender their right of disaffiliation to the international and subsequently to frustrate their freedom of choice. The constitution further states that: 'Affiliation of local unions with the International Union is voluntary and the right of local unions to disaffiliate from the International at any time shall be inviolate, irrespective of any other provision of this Constitution.'[17]

The main complaint against the international on the part of the secessionist leaders was its failure to take any serious steps towards establishing a distinctive Canadian structure within the RWDSU. Len Wallace, secretary-treasurer of the Saskatchewan Joint Board of the RWDSU, publicly stated that he was opposed, not to the concept of international unions, but to the international RWDSU's failure to establish a Canadian District Council.[18] Prior to the break-away, the Canadian director of the RWDSU was appointed by the international president.

In a newsletter distributed by the Saskatchewan Joint Board of the RWDSU, the secessionists wrote that: 'The RWDSU began organizing in Saskatchewan in 1946. As more Locals were established and we learned more about Unions, we began to seek reforms in the make-up of the International Union. For example, in 1952, 1954, 1958 and 1962, the years in which International Conventions were held, we submitted resolutions and Constitutional amendments calling for a distinct Canadian Structure within the International Union. The record will show that these many proposals were ignored completely by the top brass. In fact, they were never printed or made available to the several hundred Delegates attending these Conventions.'[19]

The secessionists further argued that in October 1955 a convention was held in Toronto to establish a Canadian council, but that the 'Convention opened and closed within minutes' after the present Ontario director of the RWDSU moved 'That a Canadian District Council with a formal Constitution is superfluous.'[20] Other grievances were levelled against the international's refusal to publish detailed financial reports and to establish a Canadian research and education department. The international, they maintained, also ignored the Saskatchewan Joint Board's proposal for mergers with other unions in similar jurisdictions.

Because of these long-standing grievances against the international, the executive of the Saskatchewan Joint Board adopted a resolution on 10 December 1969 to commence disaffiliation proceedings. Under the RWDSU constitution, after a waiting period of 90 days, a vote can be taken of a majority of the bargaining unit; and of the ballots cast, a majority must be in favour of disaffiliating.

The strategy of the secessionists was to take all votes on the issue prior to the international union's convention in June. The need for this was spelled out in the first issue of the secessionists newspaper. They claimed that the 'International Secretary-Treasurer, at a meeting with the Joint Board Executive on December 9 stated he intended to make every effort to remove this freedom of disaffiliation at the International Convention in June. Therefore, for us to disaffiliate according to the rules of the Constitution and to ensure that our funds and contracts are protected, WE MUST DO IT NOW.'[21]

It appears that senior officers of the international planned to tighten up on its non-reverter clause as a result of the disaffiliation of its largest component, District 65 with 30,000 members in New York City, in early 1969.[22] To the Saskatchewan secessionists, the introduction of a reverter clause was all the more possible without District 65 being represented at the June convention; for this local had always been in favour of the existing non-reverter clause. When they learned of the movement in Saskatchewan, leaders of the international attempted to persuade the locals to withdraw their disaffiliation notices.[23] The secessionists resisted these attempts, however, and by the end of May all votes had been taken and they won a majority in all locals.[24]

Subsequently, at the Special Joint Board Convention on 24 May the members resolved to open discussions with the Canadian Labour Congress concerning affiliation of the new union with the Congress. In accordance with CLC policy, however, the RWDSU as an independent union had to seek affiliation with an existing CLC affiliate in order to be admitted to the Congress. Indeed, the CLC had already suggested that the independent RWDSU transfer to the Canadian Food and Allied Workers, the Canadian section of the Amalgamated Meat Cutters. But since the Meat Cutters constitution has a typical reverter clause, affiliation of the Saskatchewan group with this union was clearly unacceptable.

The leaders of the independent union cast about for a union that might be a suitable affiliate, but in all cases their basic expectations were frustrated: 'We have done some exploring to the extent of carefully reading the constitutions of several unions, all international unions incidentally, and we find quite a number of areas that give rise to concern. For instance, none appear to contain a procedure for voluntary disaffiliation. It appears once you are in, you stay in and all funds, books and property becomes the property of the international. Moreover, although a provision permitting the establishment of a Canadian organization appears to be rather common, the rights and power of such an organization are stated in rather vague terms.'[25] Rather than accept a compromise of its requirements, the RWDSU chose to remain unaffiliated. Thus, although by disaffiliating from the international it did not violate the RWDSU constitution, the union has been unable to gain admission to the CLC.[26]

Since the RWDSU break-away, no attempts have been made to raid the union. In the first place, the evident loyalty of its members tends to discourage such attempts. Second, a raiding campaign would be very costly, because the locals are widely dispersed throughout the province. And perhaps most important, the RWDSU leadership has a good relationship with most union leaders and affiliates in Saskatchewan. The independent RWDSU could still be viewed as a threat, however, and the possibility of raiding is always present.

The break-away had a significant effect on the international RWDSU. For example, early in 1971 a Canadian district council of the international RWDSU was set up[27] – the kind of structure which the secessionists were calling for prior to their break-away. Its establishment appears to be a response by the international to the successful break-away in Saskatchewan and a reaction to growing nationalist sentiment and concern for increased Canadian autonomy among its active rank-and-file members.[28]

BREAK-AWAYS AND NATIONALISM

The successful large break-aways tend to promote Canadian unionism and Canadian nationalism when organizing new locals or when competing with affiliated ones. Their newspapers carry articles on such matters as other secessions, the conservatism of the AFL-CIO leadership, the higher amount of per capita tax leaving Canadian local unions to US headquarters than monies returned, the Viet Nam War and US imperialism, foreign ownership of the Canadian economy, and international union interference against what they consider the best interests of Canadian workers.[29]

Ed Finn states that 'it is now apparent that growing numbers of these activists are no longer satisfied with the degree of autonomy their internationals
allow,' and that a 'nationalist sentiment is on the upsurge among Canadian
union members.'[30] Finn cites as an example the refusal of delegates to a special convention of Canadian Brotherhood of Railway, Transport and General
Workers to authorize their leaders to negotiate a merger agreement with an
American union.[31]

Also, at its May 1970 biennial convention, the CLC leadership recommended
the following standards to the delegates on Canadian autonomy: (1) election
of Canadian officers by Canadians; (2) the authority of these officers to speak
for the union in Canada; and (3) the lifting of international union constitutional restrictions on political activities in Canada. Although these are guide-
lines, and are not binding on the affiliates to the Congress, they indicate the
administration's awareness of the growing demand for more autonomy for
Canadian sections of US based international unions.

In short, a major barrier to the success of Canadian break-aways is the reverter clause in American union constitutions. When secession does occur it
tends to promote Canadian unionism and Canadian nationalism. The very
existence of these independent locals or federations (CNTU[32] or CCU) gener-
ates increased debate on the whole question of international unionism and
Canadian autonomy. A break-away movement might well be a factor in re-
vitalizing trade unionism at the local level.

CONCLUSION

Unity has been the shibboleth of trade union leaders since the early formation
of workers' organizations, and students of industrial relations believe unity
essential for industrial stability. At present, industrial stability has become
synonymous with industrial peace, which in effect means no work stoppages,
uniformity in negotiations and in management industrial relations, centralized
bargaining units, fewer union elections and contract negotiations.

Unions, moreover, have become bureaucratic and oligarchical. The result
has been the discouragement of opposition caucuses, conformity among full-
time paid staff, and increasing intolerance of criticism. In this context, rank-
and-file revolts represent a force for expanding democracy and disaffiliation
becomes the ultimate weapon available for opposition caucuses.

Break-away leaders are, nonetheless, accused of fostering dual unionism and
factionalism within the labour movement. But there is no labour 'movement'
in North America. In the past, the principal source of energy for much of what
has been most creative and promising has been supplied by rival unionism.[33]
Since the merger of the major federations in Canada (1956) and in the United

States (1955), this important source of vitality in social unionism has been greatly inhibited. Today, radicals need to define the purposes of trade unions in terms of a long-range political program for socialism and independence in Canada. In so doing, they ought to explore those conditions most favourable for the revitalization of left-wing activism in the unions.

Clearly, there are limits to break-aways and rival unionism in those industries where the concern of the union is with jobs and not with men. Consequently, the competition is over jobs and not for the workers themselves. Examples of this would be the building trades (with some exceptions), Maritime industry and local market industries where the hiring hall is crucial – especially where labour is casual. It is extremely difficult to set up a rival organization in these industries where jurisdiction is so heavily observed.[34] It costs more to attack than to defend when rivalry exists.

Although one cannot make a universal general statement about the value of such competition since it depends on each concrete situation, discussion of this supposed anathema is essential for the development of a socialist strategy for labour in Canada. Rivalry, however, could produce the following advantages:

1 It presents to members a consistent and frequent set of genuine alternatives to the accepted limits of trade unionism. It may directly or indirectly affect collective bargaining.

2 The relationship between the leaders and rank and file comes under attack. Democracy increases. Trade union staff recruitment is quite different during 'normal' times as compared to times of stress. During 'normal' times seniority and reliability become prime requisites in staff selection; in other words, 'loyalty' is the main concern of the leaders when promoting or hiring full-time paid staff for the union 'machine.' Rival unions do not assume members are apathetic.

3 Dissemination of information becomes a virtue instead of a vice.

4 Opposition exposes faults of incumbents and discourages collusion.

5 It spurs new organizing. During the most intense period of rivalry between the AFL and CIO, trade union membership had its greatest growth. Activists tend to 'come to life' as they are cultivated by the competing unions.

6 The penalty of defeat is not fatal in cases of rank-and-file revolts. The existence of dissatisfaction within a local is the major justification of raiding. Consequently, rank-and-file activists who are suppressed by the incumbents have an alternative when a rival federation exists. Rank and file movements not only provide a training ground for new leaders (in the past it was left-wing political parties), but increase the opportunities for meaningful debate among the trade union membership. It should be remembered by radicals that the suppression of opposition within trade unions are not offences by the 'trade

union movement' but against it. Radicals today should not only protect the right of dissent, but to create the opportunities for dissent.

At the present time, break-aways and rival unionism are seen as wasteful and destructive by labour leaders and their 'intellectual' spokesmen. But radicals today do not have to accept their unexplored assumptions condemning all secessionist and rival movements within Canada. On the contrary, what needs to be explored is their efficiency in activating the rank and file at the grass-roots level, and in transforming the democratic and independence struggle into the socialist struggle.

NOTES

1 This article will deal with those recent break-aways which are large enough to afford full-time staff to service the break-away locals. These break-aways are not locals which have disaffiliated from an international by voting 'no union' as a result of a Labour Relations Board election, nor are they considered to be 'company unions.' According to the Department of Labour, there were 124 independent local organizations with a membership of 56,414 as of 1969. This comprised 2.7 per cent of Canadian organized labour. As of 1967, 64 per cent of all organized workers in Canada were members of locals chartered by US-based unions. Corporation and Labour Unions Returns Act, *Annual Report.*
2 'The Struggle for Canadian Labour Autonomy,' *Labour Gazette,* Nov. 1970, 767.
3 The constitutions of the Bricklayers and the Glass and Ceramic Workers are silent on reverter. In contrast, the RWDSU has what could be called a non-reverter clause, which clearly specifies the right of the break-away to keep its assets.
4 Art. XIV, sec. 8(b), 45-6.
5 (1949) 3 DLR 527 (BCCA). See also (1950) 3 DLR 146 (BC).
6 Art. 24, sec. 3.
7 International Nickel Company of Canada Ltd., *Shedden* v *Kopinak* (1950) 1 DLR 381 (Ont. HC).
8 *Woodell* v *Potter* (1929) 64 OLR 484.
9 When the left-led United Electrical Workers Union (UE) was expelled from the CIO the court allowed the UE locals to keep its books, money, and property. See NLRBU, Highland Park Mfg. Co. 19 Labor Cases, par. 66, 327, 341 US322 (1951). In the United States the reverter clause has not been forcefully applied in cases resulting from locals seeking disaffiliation from expelled communist-dominated unions. There, patriotism prevailed over precedent in the interpretation of the reverter clause in union constitutions.
10 (Toronto 1967), 84. Italics added.
11 Stuart Jamieson, *Industrial Relations in Canada* (Ithaca, NY 1957), 69.
12 Crispo, *International Unionism* (Toronto, 1967), 85-6.
13 Rivalry declined during the war years. Between 1946 and 1959, rapid bargaining changes took place which tended to minimize rivalry. From 1951 to 1955, no-raiding pacts were common.
14 The Trades and Labor Congress and the Canadian Congress of Labour merged to form the CLC in 1956.
15 The Canadian Labour Congress grants charters of affiliation by a two-thirds vote of its executive council. This is different from AFL-CIO policy, which allows any affiliate to veto an application for membership if the affiliate has a legitimate stake in the jurisdiction claimed by the union seeking affiliation. The reason behind the CLC's move in this direction was to permit the Congress to take in independents (i.e., BC Telephone Employees' Association, Loblaw's Workers Council, etc.). It must be remembered however,

that 25 out of 30 executive officers of the Congress are representatives of American-based unions; and two-thirds of all CLC revenues are from affiliates of international unions. In effect, break-aways wishing to become directly chartered by the Congress must obtain the permission of leaders of American-based unions.

16 1966, Art. XVI, sec. E, 51.
17 Art. XVI, sec. 1.
18 *Saskatoon Star-Phoenix,* 28 Jan. 1970.
19 *Defender,* no. 1 (Feb. 1970) (published by the Saskatchewan Joint Board RWDSU), 3.
20 *Ibid.*
21 'Why We Must Get Out Now,' *ibid.,* 3.
22 *John Herling's Labour Letter* (19 April 1969), 4. District 65 has affiliated with the United Auto Workers and the Teamsters in their Alliance for Labour Action, District 65 has set up a new union called the National Council of Distributive Workers of America. David Livingston, president of District 65, charged that the international RWDSU and the AFL-CIO had failed 'to provide aggressive and progressive leadership' for Negro and Puerto Rican workers. He also predicted that other RWDSU locals in other parts of the country would also disaffiliate from the international.
23 This was a clever tactic on the part of the international. If any notice were withdrawn and re-issued prior to the June convention, the locals would have to wait another 90 days before an election, and this would bring them past the convention date. Thus, if a reverter were introduced into a constitution at the convention, the locals, being bound by it, would be able to disaffiliate only at the cost of forfeiting all their monies, books, and properties to the international. In the face of such a penalty, the secessionist movement likely would die out. (In the event, the international convention produced no change in the non-reverter clause.)
24 The results were reported in the *Defender,* no. 3 (June 1970), 2.
25 *Ibid.* (Nov. 1970), 2.
26 The United Fishermen and Allied Workers Union have found themselves in the same position. The Fishermen were expelled from the TLC in 1953 and subsequently raided by the Seafarers International Union. The Fishermen withstood the raid. At the 1970 CLC Convention, the Fishermen sought direct affiliation with the Congress, but this was denied. As in the case of the Saskatchewan RWDSU, the Congress urged the Fishermen to enter through the Canadian Food and Allied Workers Union (Meat Cutters). Both organizations rejected this precondition. Recently, the Fishermen were raided by the Meat Cutters. The Saskatchewan RWDSU contends that there is no all-Canadian national food worker's union in Canada, maintaining that the Canadian Food and Allied Workers is essentially part of the Amalgamated Meat Cutters and Butcher Workmen of North America, an American-based union.
27 RWDSU *Record,* 18, no. 2 (31 Jan. 1971).
28 It should be noted that the international is still keeping a tight rein on its locals. There is no provision for the election of Canadian leadership, and the present steering committees for conference-planning is composed entirely of international representatives.
29 For example, the *Leaflet* published by the independent Pulp and Paper Workers of Canada (PPWC) has carried stories on all of the above items.
30 'Nationalist Feeling Is Growing among Canadian Unions,' *Canadian Dimension,* 6, no. 3 & 4 (Aug.-Sept. 1969), 4, 5.
31 *Ibid.*
32 The Confederation of National Trade Unions (CNTU) with approximately 250,000 members in Quebec is a rival independent federation to the Quebec Federation of Labour (QFL). The QFL is the provincial federation of the CLC. Both federations have engaged in rivalry, although there is little rivalry now at the federation level. Representatives from both these federations claim that the existence of both the CNTU and QFL in Quebec has enabled local leaders to get out of a union with which they are dissatisfied. Consequently, there is increased worker choice in determining their bargaining agent. This has

made both federations 'more alert' regarding their respective local affiliates. During recent political events in Quebec, the CNTU and QFL have co-operated with one another. Both representatives said that the present situation in Quebec of having two equally powerful federations results in both being more 'leftist' than they might otherwise be.

33 The 'left' in organized labour has never been allowed to develop in an orderly fashion because of recurrent intervention by the State to crush left tendencies ostensibly in the cause of national unity, 'industrial peace,' and objectively in order to drain militant progressive rank and file movements of their vitality and to entrench the trade union leadership which is both self-serving and has acted to serve the interests of ruling class.

34 This is not the case with industrial unions. The merger of the AFL and CIO put an end to the AFL craft philosophy of each man in his respective jurisdiction, since the CIO unions were not going to give up those craftsmen organized to the AFL unions. Neither were the craft unions going to return the industrial production workers to the respective CIO union in that industry. Therefore, jurisdiction gave way to 'established bargaining relationship.' In other words, whenver a union signs an agreement for a unit or local of workers, that thereafter becomes their property and no union can raid this group without violating the AFL-CIO constitution.

Charles Lipton

author of *The Trade Union Movement of Canada, 1826-1959*; he is currently preparing a volume on contemporary problems in the labour movement in Canada

Canadian unionism

EDITOR'S NOTE: This article was to be a chapter in Charles Lipton's book, *The Trade Union Movement of Canada, 1827-1959.* In deciding to make the book solely a text of history, he omitted this article and planned to include it in a subsequent volume on contemporary problems facing Canadian unionism. It appears here substantially as it was written in 1966. The argument he presents has become even more pertinent to Canadian labour in the intervening years.

CANADA'S labour history has been marked by a continuing fight for a sovereign trade union movement. How stands that fight today? The answer of the Canadian Labour Congress leadership is simple. They say the fight is just about won. In support of this contention they point to the Congress itself, which, they insist, is a sovereign centre. But against this cherubic outlook stand two massive facts. First, Canada's unions are mostly international unions, and it is they who are the main components of the Congress. Second, the Congress was founded during the Cold War when the bases of Canadian unionism in the chemical, textile, lumber, and other industries had been destroyed. It was founded, not as the product of the fight for Canadian autonomy, which reached a high point in the TLC Victoria convention of 1948, but as a sequel to the defeat and betrayal of that cause. Moreover, not content with the practical domination they had established, the international unions wrote that domination into the Congress constitution: a clause provides that, where jurisdiction is affected, present affiliates to the Congress, which means mainly the international unions, can vote the affiliation of new bodies. This is a clause which gives US headquarters virtual power of decision on the admission of the CNTU and independent unions like Mine-Mill and United Electrical Workers. Of course, a Congress convention could decide on their admission; yet weighing constantly on the Congress is the threat of dismemberment, the threat that international unions will 'pull out' and organize perhaps a dual centre.[1]

The degree of sovereignty held by the CLC may be debatable, but there are objective standards by which the freedom of Canadian members of international unions can be measured:

1 Constitutional powers: the powers of the Canadian membership under the constitution as compared with powers of international headquarters.

2 Operative powers: the power to strike, control over funds, appointment of staff in Canada.

3 Canadian organs of control: their efficacy and effectiveness.

4 Violations of Canadian rights: their number and quality.

5 Freedom of action of the Canadian membership: in politics and foreign policy.

We shall deal with each of these in turn.

CONSTITUTIONAL POWERS

The constitutions of international unions grant considerable powers to general officers. These include: approval of collective agreements; discipline of locals; granting or rejection of requests for financial aid; revocation of charters; putting of locals into receivership and seizure of their funds; installing of an international officer to run the local. Given such powers, given that the bulk of the membership is located in the United States, given that Canadians seldom constitute more than 10 per cent of total international membership, it follows that Canadians stand in a relationship of subordination to parent bodies in the US. The point is not that international officers possess powers, for that is inherent in the constitution of any organization; nor is it the type of powers they possess. The point is that these international officers are not subject to membership in Canada, but are subject primarily to membership in the United States. That is to say, the presence of international unions in Canada is in its very nature a denial of Canadian sovereignty, and beyond that it is a denial of something even more precious – sovereignty of the Canadian working class.

It has been suggested that amends can be made for such a situation by inserting in the international constitutions clauses under which certain powers are non-operative in Canada. But for such clauses to have their maximum effect, they would have to provide for the complete right of self-government by the Canadian membership, including the right of seceding from the international union; and in turn, for such rights to be effective, the Canadian membership must have its own organization, its own elected officers, and its own finances. But even in such a situation – the most ideal possible under an international union – and even where there was a dedicated progressive leadership in the United States prepared to do its utmost to uphold the right of the Canadian membership, the element of servitude would remain, for all these Canadian powers would still be subject to the will of people in another country. Therefore, the only sure basis for Canadian self-government in union matters is the sovereign Canadian union, as distinct from the international union. Of course, it is inherent in the very fact of a sovereign Canadian union that it could decide to enter into a relationship with a union in the United States and that it could decide also to terminate that relationship.

So much for the formal rights of the Canadian membership in international unions. In practice, the situation varies from local to local and from union to union. It is determined by such factors as the general level of development of the membership in given situations, their degree of mass participation, the relative weight of progressive and reactionary trends among them. It is determined also by the policies which prevail in the international union. A change takes place in the situation in the United States – a change in leadership, new pressure from courts, Congress, the National Labour Board, the Department of Labour, the President – and the results may soon be felt in Canada. The winds shift in the US, and all too often the House of Labour in Canada gets blown down.

OPERATIVE POWERS

A typical operative power is the power to strike. As of 1958, most Canadian locals of international unions did not have that power, not completely.[2]

Against this, the argument has been advanced – as in the Report of the Royal Commission on Canada's Economic Prospects, 1956 – that 'approval by International Headquarters is typically formal and granted as a matter of course.' That is not true, for there are many cases where approval is not granted – for example, the Halifax building trades strike of 1952. But it is not just that the contention is factually false. It is also intrinsically false. For, if the strike fund is located in the United States, if the power to ratify or vote a strike decision is located in the United States, then approval can scarce be merely 'formal.' The day will never come when the man who has the cash stands in a merely formal relation to the man who needs the cash.

So much for the power to strike. There are other operative powers. They include control over money and appointment of staff. As far as money is concerned, a good part of the union dues goes as per capita to US headquarters and Canadians cannot decide how it will be spent. As far as staff – always a prime lever of US domination – is concerned, the top officials in Canada are appointed and their salaries decided by the American officers. Of course, a chief appointee in Canada may be, and usually is, a Canadian, though sometimes he is an American who has taken up residence in Canada, as in the case of Harold Daoust of the Textile Workers Union of America and H.C. Banks of the Seafarers International Union. But the nationality of the leading union officer in Canada is not the main thing, any more than the nationality of a company executive is the main thing. Decisive is ownership and control. In 1948, at the Victoria Convention of the Trades and Labor Congress, Frank Hall, Canadian representative of the Brotherhood of Railway and Steamship Clerks said, 'I am not responsible to this Congress ... When you leave this Convention, Brothers and delegates, regardless of what disposition is made of this question, I shall still be Vice-President of the Brotherhood of Railroad and Steamship Clerks.' Hall did not say, but he could have said, that he was also not responsible to his own membership in Canada, for he owed his appointment to international headquarters.

CANADIAN ORGANIZATION:
ITS EXTENT AND CHARACTER

A basic unit of Canadian organization in the international union is the local. It has two sides. It is a Canadian body, but it is a Canadian body connected with a union, most of whose locals are in the United States. Now, for the US locals, an international union can fulfil the function of a general union. Constitutionally, at least, the US locals can determine the policy and leadership of their organization. But that is not the case for the Canadian locals. They are often isolated from each other and so the more dependent on their links with international headquarters. And even when they are grouped in a province-wide or Canada-wide organization, they cannot determine the policies of the international union. So Canadians pay for a general union but don't get it. They are told that through the international unions they get 'big organization,' when in fact they get the opposite – the reinforced tendency to local isolation. A Canadian Auto Workers Union of 60,000 members, a sovereign Canadian Steel Workers Union of 80,000 members, a Canadian Railway Workers Union of 150,000 members, a sovereign Canadian Teamsters Union of 40,000 members – such bodies for Canadian purposes would be so much more powerful than their present international union counterparts, that their sheer coming into being would entail a substantial change in the relation of forces of organized labour and capital in Canada.

With Canadian union feeling rising in recent years, a tendency has developed for a closer knitting of international union locals in Canada. Provincial districts and Canadian districts have been set up. But even where there are such districts, though they serve as levers for expansion of Canadian autonomy, they may also serve as a lever for tightening the grip on Canadian locals, for centralizing US control of Canadian locals behind the facade of Canadian district organization; and in any case, the predominant tendency remains of comparatively isolated locals confronted by the power of the international union. This is particularly true for craft unions like the Plumbers, Carpenters, Electricians, Machinists, and Printing Trades. The problem is illustrated by three events which occurred in the period 1954-1958.

In 1954, when the Bookbinders asked for an elected vice-president, they were told that this would be tantamount to a state body in the United States asking for such a privilege.[3]

In 1955, many United Auto Workers members in Canada were demanding that a Canadian director be elected in Canada instead of at the international convention, where, it was said, Canadian delegates were subject to the pressure of the organization in the United States. That demand was rejected.

In 1956, the BC Provincial Council of the United Brotherhood of Carpenters and Joiners (UBCJ) demanded that a Canada-wide section of the union be established. As of 1964, there was no Canada-wide organization of the Carpenters.

What about the Canadian district? In 1957, of ninety-three international unions, only six had a Canadian district and a Canadian director. That covered about a fifth of the total Canadian membership of international unions. Moreover, where there is a Canadian district, that does not necessarily mean real autonomy. Is that district truly free? Does it have its own national convention of local delegates to decide policy and also leadership? Does it have its own treasury and strike fund? Does it get the bulk of the union dues spent from what stays in the locals? As of 1964, there were scarcely any international unions in Canada which could pass such a test, save a few progressively led international unions – a special and exceptional case to be considered below.

VIOLATIONS OF CANADIAN RIGHTS

What is the record of violations? Between 1950 and 1962, receiverships were clamped on locals, local elections voided, strikes broken or denied assistance, whole unions destroyed – the period is full of these events, involving Carpenters, Teamsters, Plumbers, Bridge and Iron Workers, Textile Workers, and many other unions – all in all, a considerable proportion of trade union membership in Canada.

Here are a few examples:

1950, Chemical Workers. International ICWU headquarters dismisses its Canadian staff and violates the right of its Toronto local at Consumers Gas to appoint its own business agent.

1950, Rubber Workers. International headquarters of URWA dismisses entire Canadian staff.

1951, Lumber and Sawmill Workers, Ontario. International headquarters of UBCJ seizes the treasury of certain locals of this body – one of its affiliates in Canada – and lifts their powers.

1952, Canadian Textile Council. International headquarters of UTWA dismisses the entire Canadian staff of this body, its affiliate in Canada.

1953, Teamsters. International headquarters dismisses the Canadian director, MacArthur, and also Neil MacDonald, business agent-elect of Montreal local 106. It clamps a trusteeship on that local, and somewhat later it imposes trusteeships also on other locals, such as local 938 at Toronto.

1954, Plumbers, Montreal. International officers of the United Association of Plumbers and Steam Fitters negotiate an agreement with certain oil companies against which the members of Montreal local 144 are on strike. They do this behind the backs of the membership, and when the membership wishes to continue the strike, international headquarters denies it strike benefits. All this is a stab in the back, not just to the Montreal local, but to Quebec labour unity, for involved in that strike as well is the Plumbers union of the CNTU.

1956, International Brotherhood of Electrical Workers, BC. International headquarters of IBEW dismiss the business agent of their Vancouver local. They despatch to Canada a phoney board of enquiry into communist tendencies among Canadian members.

1957, International Alliance of Theatrical Stage Employees and Moving Picture Machine Operators of the United States and Canada (IATSE), Toronto. Local union protests infringements of its rights by New York headquarters. Its chief steward at the CBC charges that the local union has 'no say whatsoever in contract negotiations.' It is charged too that $3 dues are being deducted and sent to New York with the local seeing scarcely a dime.

1959, IATSE, Montréal. US interferency by the IATSE reaches the point of strike-breaking during the CBC Montreal strike. Members of that union in Montreal are ordered to remove their picket lines from the CBC. The orders come from a Canadian source – Hugh Sedgewick of Hamilton, IATSE chief representative in Canada – but he said he got them from New York.

1959-60, Plumbers, Montreal. International headquarters strikes at local 144's autonomy once again. It lifts the local's power to hold meetings and conduct business for a period of almost a year.

1960, Bridge, Structural and Iron Workers, Vancouver. International headquarters dismisses the local union's elected officers and cancels its right to conduct its own business.

1960, United Auto Workers. Paul Siren, a UAW organizer in Canada, on the staff of that union practically since its inception in the 1930s, makes so bold as to support for office a candidate for the Canadian vice-presidency running in opposition to George Burt, the candidate supported by the Reuther administration. Not long after, Siren is peremptorily dismissed.

1962, International Union of Electrical Workers. At a convention of Canadian IUEW locals held in Toronto, international president James B. Carey ousts the Canadian IUEW president C. Hutchens and puts the eleven Canadian staff members under his personal control. One delegate protested 'we live in Canada, a democracy!' Another said, 'You can sell that stuff in the US [but] you can't sell it here.' But Carey got away with it.

The list of violations above is far from complete. Nor would a complete and updated list tell the tale; for what must be taken into account also are those further violations initiated by international headquarters in the United States but carried through within Canada by Canadian districts, central councils, provincial federations, and the Canadian Labour Congress.

These violations are but the surface expression of the deeper wrong, as with accidents and crimes. A constant conformism to avert such reprisals – that is the greatest violation of all. Canadian members fear loss of conditions, contracts, certificates, loss of pensions and other accumulated union benefits; they fear disruption and raids from the United States, if they do what they have to do to free themselves. That does not mean they cannot do it; and sometimes not to do it may be worse than to do it. But generally caution and careful preparation are needed, and preferably co-ordination and multiple action.

The number of overt violations of Canadian rights is diminished, not just by fear-induced conformity, but also by non-conformity. For the fight for Canadian rights goes on constantly, with some gains and some losses, some benefits and some sacrifices; every so often US headquarters forces a general flare-up. The result is an equilibrium between Canadian freedom and US domination. But this is not the placid harmony depicted by Claude Jodoin and E.A. Forsey. It is rather the equilibrium of struggle, the battle for Canadian unionism fought but not yet won.

FOREIGN POLICY AND POLITICAL ACTION

Since the Cold War began, there has been an identity of foreign policy between the Canadian Labour Congress (and its antecedent centres) and the AFL-CIO. More recently that identity has diminished, but in broad lines it still persists. Has US domination of Canada's unions played a part in producing this identity? Dr Forsey of the Canadian Labour Congress has said 'No.' He says that the identity is due rather to a coincidence of attitude between the free trade union movements of the United States and Canada. But what coincidence produced the coincidence? And how free is Canada's free trade union movement? What about the eleven years (1947-1962) of reprisals against Canadian union members who challenged the chief tenets of State Department policy? Of course, Jodoin and Forsey are 'free' – free to agree with Washington. But those who disagree are not so free.

Consider now political action. The kind of problem encountered is illustrated by what happened at the 1959 International Convention of the Brotherhood of Railroad and Steamship Clerks. A Canadian local submitted a resolution asking that the constitution be amended to enable locals in Canada to participate in party politics. Speaking in support of that proposal, a BRSC delegate from Winnipeg (Baatable) said that the present constitutional ban on political action should not be 'applicable to Canadian lodges and members.' This the international president, George Harrison, flatly opposed. So did the resolutions committee, and the reason it gave was typically US imperialist. It said the amendment 'would be a violation of [US] state and federal laws.'

It is certain that policies of this kind have slowed down labour political progress in Canada. It is certain that they have played their part in producing the situation which prevailed on the eve of the 1962 federal election, where scarcely a sixth of total union membership in Canada had affiliated with the New Democratic party, although that party had been initiated by the Canadian Labour Congress with a membership of over a million; and even where union affiliation had taken place, as in the United Steel Workers of American and the United Auto Workers, opposition of international officers to such a course was bound to bulwark those elements in the Canadian membership who for one reason or another did not want to support the New Democratic party. This was the trade union organizational reality underlying the parliamentary electoral reality, and this reality continued to operate in the 1963 federal election, when the number of successful New Democratic party candidates declined. Here we have an inkling, at least, of what international unionism means to labour's political progress in Canada.

What has the CLC leadership been doing about it? In 1962, the Canadian Labour Congress vice-president, William Dodge, went to the United States to ask those international unions whose constitutions contained bans on political action to free Canadian organizations from these bans. That was a noble mission, but one he could not press to victory because he linked to it a lie, and that lie was contained in his suggestion that these bans represented the last survival of Canadian labour subordination to the United States. But how could that be true when he was there in a foreign country asking foreigners to do for Canadians what Canadians should be able to do for themselves? The outcome was that some international unions lifted the bans, while others did not; and even in the case of those that did, that was not necessarily the final solution, for there are bans which persist in life long after they have been dropped from constitution. Where there is power, where there is control over paycheques, a wink and a nod may suffice.[4]

CANADIAN UNIONISM AND PROGRESSIVE UNIONISM

So far we have dealt with international unionism and its relationship to Canadian unions. But there is a superior starting point: Canadian unionism – the total trade union movement of Canada. Beyond that, it is the fight to free that movement from servitude to the United States, the fight for a sovereign Canadian movement. An advanced expression of that fight is the completely Canadian union. Examples are the unions of the Confederation of National Trade Unions (CNTU), the Canadian Brotherhood of Railway, Transport and General Workers (CBRT), the National Union of Public Employees (now incorporated in Canadian Union of Public Employees), the United Fisherman and Allied Workers Union (UFAWU), the Canadian Textile Council's directly chartered locals in the CLC, and CNTU independent locals, such as the Vancouver Outside Workers. In addition, bodies like the Mine-Mill Canada and the UE Canadian Council, though connected with the US, fulfil, at least in some decisive respects, the function of Canadian unions.

The percentage of Canadian-union membership to the total union membership is a decisive index of Canadian labour progress. Its range of variation through the last half-century is shown by the following statistics: in 1911, it stood at 10.8 per cent – a low connected with a decade of hatchet work by international unions on Canadian unions after the 1902 split in the Trades and Labor Congress; in 1935, it stood at 48.8 per cent – nearly half;[5] in 1955, it stood at 29.5 per cent. These figures do not include UE and Mine-Mill. In 1963, the total of members in such unions was 430,137, *including* UE and Mine-Mill, as compared with a total membership of 1,449,181, or 29.6 per cent of the total.

There is Canadian unionism and there is progressive unionism. The two are distinct, but they are also closely connected. The whole history of the movement attests to this. For example, those international unions which provide the greatest degree of autonomy for the Canadian membership tend to be the progressively led international unions. Conversely, those international unions which refuse autonomy tend to be the more reactionary unions. Those unions that are completely Canadian or virtually Canadian – bodies such as the CNTU, the CTC, the UFAWU, the International Union of Mine-Mill and the Smelter Workers, UE, and the CBRT – tend to be more progressive than the average international union. Many of the unions which in 1963 were not in the CLC were Canadian unions, for example those in the CNTU and the CTC; or they were unions fulfilling the functions of Canadian unions, for instance the UE and Mine-Mill; or they were international unions which had fallen out with the AFL-CIO in the US such as the Teamsters.

It might be useful here to summarize the experience of some progressive unions, and take a brief look at one reactionary union.

The UE has been virtually autonomous in Canada ever since it was founded here in the late 1930s. In 1956, this autonomy was given constitutional recognition by the UE international convention. In the late 1950s, the international Longshoremen and Warehousemen's Union took similar action. An example of the most advanced Canadian autonomy within the international unions is that of Mine-Mill. In 1953, its international convention amended the constitution to provide for its existence in Canada as a distinct Canadian entity. Subsequently, Mine-Mill Canada was established, and this was approved by a referendum vote of the Canadian membership. It is noteworthy that all three unions linked these decisions to the struggle for Canadian independence from US imperialism, the common struggle of Canadian and US workers against their common foe, US imperialism.

But more typical is the case of a reactionary international union which took a negative stand to Canadian rights, despite the energetic measures the Canadian membership took to uphold its rights. In the years 1942-52 in Canada, the United Textile Workers of America grew into an organization of 12,000 members grouped in twenty locals in Ontario, Quebec, and the Maritimes. All this work was done by Canadians. The Canadian membership struggled constantly to expand its autonomy. To this end, it set up a Canadian district which held annual conventions, elected Canadian leadership, and had its own treasury and strike fund based on per capita paid direct from the Canadian locals to the Canadian district headquarters. By 1950, a level of autonomy had been attained in the UTWA unsurpassed by any other international union. All this was the work of the Canadian district and its officers. Part of the general pattern then prevailing in the UTWA of Canada were vigorous negotiations, a constant effort to organize the unorganized and improve conditions, hard-fought struggles for trade union rights, and struggles against raiding by the rival Textile Workers Union of America. This pattern of progressivism and Canadian unionism the headquarters of international UTWA resented and feared, and in 1950 it moved to destroy the Canadian district's autonomy. This challenge the Canadian district met by establishing itself as a distinct Canadian organization called the Canadian Textile Council, while it retained its affiliation with the international union. In 1952, when the CTC was locked in battle with the Dominion Textile Company in Quebec in a major strike, international headquarters decided its time had come. It moved in on the Canadian organization and dismissed the entire staff. The CTC response was to sever all connections with the international union, thereby becoming a sovereign Canadian union in the textile industry. The years that followed have brought their toll of company attacks and raids by US unions; but meanwhile, if only on an exceedingly modest scale, the CTC has persisted as an advanced base of progressivism and Canadian unionism in the textile industry.

BIG BUSINESS AND INTERNATIONAL UNIONS

Historically, it is clear that big business has tended to support international unionism where the alternative was a militant Canadian union. There is the evidence of the 1920s and 1930s: the One Big Union versus the international unions; Nova Scotia Coal Miners versus United Mine Workers of America international headquarters. There is the evidence of the 1940s and 1950s; the Canadian Seamen's Union versus the Seafarers' International Union; the Canadian Textile Council versus the United Textile Workers of America and the Textile Workers Union of America; the International Union of Mine, Mill and Smelter Workers versus the United Steelworkers of America. In all these struggles, the companies swung their weight behind the international unions.

Why does big business prefer international unions? One reason is that the companies look to the stand-pat leadership of the average international union to put a curb on the Canadian membership. Consider David Dubinsky, international president of the International Ladies Garment Workers Union: at the 1962 international convention of his union, he charged that peace marchers were, wittingly or otherwise, tools of Moscow. Capitalists in Canada see the point in maintaining connection with a person such as this: they can use reactionary leaders in the United States as a counterweight to the Canadian working class' efforts for peace. Hence at Drummondville, Quebec, in the mid-1950s, the Canadian Celanese Company blocked a CNTU bid at organization, but did not shut the door tight on the United Textile Workers of America.

In a brief submitted to the Royal Commission on Canada's Economic Prospects in 1957, two federal government experts, I. Brecher and S.S. Riesman, stated: 'Headquarters officials sometimes participate directly in Canadian negotiations ... with an observable bias towards moderation and restraint ... To the limited extent that intervention from headquarters has occurred, the influence has characteristically been in a moderating direction. There are good reasons ... The top executive is frequently a well-paid group ... they would quite naturally be expected to have much the same respect for conservatism as can be attributed to any high-income managerial group occupying a position of substantial authority.'

Another reason why big business in Canada may prefer international unions is the physical and organizational distance between the Canadian membership and international headquarters in Chicago, Cleveland, Washington, or New York. This facilitates top-level manoeuvring between management and high-placed union officers behind the backs of the Canadian membership. Here are three examples: In 1946, the president of the Dominion Textile Company, Blair Gordon, wrote a letter to the United Textile Workers of America international headquarters at Washington, in which he asked the Americans to provide a Canadian leadership more to the liking of the company. In 1949, there was a coincidence of activities involving the US State Department, the federal Liberal government, and the executive councils of the American Federation of Labor and Trades and Labor Congress, whose combined result was the expulsion of the Canadian Seamen's Union from the Trades and Labor Congress, the smashing of the strike conducted by the union, and finally the smashing of the union itself. In 1959, the Dominion Bridge Company in British Columbia and the international headquarters of the Bridge, Structural and Iron Workers Union conducted negotiations behind the backs of the union membership then on strike.

It should be remembered, above all, that many of the companies are American and that their parent companies in the United States have already established relations with international unions in the US. Sometimes master agreements are negotiated in the United States and extended, with comparative ease, into Canada.

We have listed above some of the reasons why big business in Canada prefers international unions. The ultimate preference of big business, of course, is no union at all. Hence, when an international union in Canada does get involved in a struggle, big business will not hesitate to fight that union, and in that fight it may turn against the union that very quality which in the first place it found attractive – its international character. This helps explain the recurrent big business cry of 'foreign union.' Two examples in recent years are declarations by N.R. Crump of the CPR and Fox of St Lawrence Paper. Attacks such as these would harness Canadianism to anti-labour purposes. They are attacks in force because they are aimed at a genuine weakness in the labour movement. The way to defeat them is to win the given struggle, whether it be conducted by a Canadian or international union, but beyond that to move as swiftly as possible to a completely Canadian trade union movement.

International unionism is a key link in the system of US domination of Canada. We need only look at the trade union movement and monopoly capital in the United States to see a union movement that has been more class collaborationist, less inclined to fight the foreign and domestic policies of its ruling class, more committed to capitalism than the trade union movement of any other important capitalist country. Monopoly capital in the United States is more powerful than monopoly capital in any other important capitalist country. The result is an abnormally unfavourable balance of forces between capital and labour in the United States as compared with most other developed capitalist countries. This unfavourable balance of forces tends to be transmitted to Canada by the system of international unionism. There is a constant export of labour conservatism to Canada. It has been going on for sixty years. It has played its part in producing in Canada a labour movement of a special kind, one which in some ways is more disunited and more backward than is the labour movement of any other advanced capitalist country: one which correspondingly has failed to grasp the magnificent opportunity presented to it in the 1960s when US imperialism became weaker on a world scale while the movement for Canadian independence became stronger.[6]

The export of labour conservatism manifests itself in various ways, sometimes directly through the international unions themselves, sometimes from the harassing activities of employer and government agencies in the United States. The unions in the United States are under constant pressure from such legislation, as the Taft-Hartley and Landrum-Griffin acts. In terms of practical politics, an international union which did not act to keep its locals in Canada 'clean' would be in the black books of anti-labour circles in the US; and when the US labour leaders are dealing with these anti-labour circles, even when they are trying to fight them, generally it is not the rights of the Canadian membership which stand uppermost; on the contrary, these rights may well be deemed expendable.

Through such chains of connections, international unions become a major link in US economic aggression on Canada. A right-wing clique dominates the US trade union movement, a clique centred in the leadership of the Building

Trade unions, the International Ladies' Garment Workers Union, the Brother-hood of Railroad and Steamship Clerks, and several other unions. It is signifi-cant that the leaders of these same unions constitute also the hard core of the right-wing in the Canadian Labour Congress. It is also significant that this Ca-nadian clique is most fanatical in its support of US foreign policy, is most vicious in opposing Canadian autonomy and Canadian unionism, is most prone to ride roughshod over the rights of its membership in Canada, is most ready to use the Canadian Labour Congress for its own aims as it used the antece-dent centres in the past, and is most ready to threaten the Congress with dis-memberment, with the formation of a dual centre when, under pressure from the Canadian membership, the CLC begins to show a bit of opposition to US designs.

In Canada international unionism and class collaborationism through right-wing union leadership form an intermeshed, interacting combination which historically has dominated the trade union movement. This interconnection shows in the arguments used by right-wing labour leaders in Canada to justify international unionism. 'International unions for international business' was the slogan advanced by the executive council of the Canadian Labour Con-gress in 1960. It said that international unions provided an example of 'good international relations' which had 'paid off.' Just as many companies operat-ing in Canada are American, similar close ties between trade unions members of these countries should be maintained. But what is the so-called interna-tional structure of the North American economy, if not a euphemism for US domination of the Canadian economy? And, given that domination, is it not true that the kind of labour movement this country needs is one which is sov-ereign and not subject to pressure from the base imperialist country?

Not 'international unions for international business' but 'Canadian unions for international business; Canadian unions to combat international business' should be the operative slogan of the Canadian labour movement.[7]

A FIGHT ON TWO FRONTS

It is tragic that during the Cold War years, in the midst of growing US in-roads in Canada, the issue of Canadian unionism was brought more to the fore. When the matter came up at trade union conventions in the 1950s and early 1960s, often it was for defensive reasons – some new assault by international headquarters, some new chopping of heads, some new barrier to political ac-tion, some new challenge to an independent foreign policy for Canada. The issue of Canadian unionism as such has not been recognized enough as a prin-cipled question, as a principle, a passion, deeply imbedded in the reality, needs, and aspirations of the workers, one which must find its creative solution. More than ever, the continuation of the rotten system of international unionism in Canada becomes a decisive internal weakness of the organized labour movement, an impediment to its forward progress on the front of conditions, peace, and Canadian independence. Let this be recognized, and it follows that the trade union struggle in Canada cannot be conducted on one front alone but on two fronts. The fight for militancy is inseparable from the fight for Canadian unionism, and vice versa. The fight should be conducted on both fronts, and the danger which constantly assails progressives in Canada – that of intervention from the US – will begin to diminish and their prospects for victory will begin to increase. And, as the fight develops on both fronts, it will become increasingly clear that the system of international unionism in Canada is not just a weak link in the chain of Canadian organized labour, but is also a weak link in the chain of American capitalism and its dominion over Canada; and this because international unionism is one of those links in the system of US domination of Canada which is most within reach of the organized workers in this country, once they decide firmly to be masters in their own house, masters of their own movement.

We say then that, given this truth, this reality, and the basic attitude of the workers, it is tragic that in recent years there have been no serious sustained, massive battles on these issues. There have been skirmishes: for example, the debate at the Canadian Congress of Labour convention of 1955. At that convention, progressives demanded that the Congress take a stand for Canadian unionism in view of Canada's growing domination by the United States. They asked why there should be a situation where the United Mine Workers of America in Canada should not be in the Canadian Congress of Labour simply because its parent body in the United States had decided to withhold per capita tax. 'Why should we consider ourselves as children when it comes to running our own affairs in the trade union movement?' asked Sam Jankins of the BC Marine and Shipyard Workers Union. This was a sensible question to ask of a trade union centre founded in the name of a Canadian movement.

It will be recalled that the Canadian Congress of Labour was established in 1940 as a merger of the All-Canadian Congress of Labour and the CIO unions expelled from the Trades and Labour Congress on US orders. Between the CCL's militant Canadian origins and the right-wing clique which had come to dominate it in Cold War years, however, the gap was great indeed. The administration's response to these all-too-modest proposals of the progressives was negative. There was dark talk about people who followed 'that particular line.' More sophisticated reasons were also advanced, reasons to placate the majority which demanded something better than red-baiting. George Burt, UAW director in Canada, said Canadians were members of international unions 'because of the power we derive from membership in the international unions.'

Surely the source of the UAW's strength in Canada is not the US membership at Detroit, but the Canadian membership at Windsor, Oshawa, and St Catharines. Canadian auto workers are the only auto workers in the world who have an international union. Auto workers in France, Britain, Italy, the Soviet Union, the United States itself (for there the UAW fulfils the function of a national union) have national unions, not international unions, and are none the weaker for it.

George Burt referred to premier Hepburn's attack against the internationals in 1937. It is true that Hepburn in the 1930s, like Smallwood in the 1950s, was prepared to pin the US label on the union he was fighting, but his real target was the process of self-organization by Canada's industrial workers then going on in auto, steel, electrical industries, and hard-rock mining. For that matter, if we go back to the founding years of the USWA in the 1930s, it may well be asked whether we would not have been further ahead if we had established merely working co-operation with the CIO while maintaining a completely independent organization in Canada. Certain it is, however, that the auto workers at the time, and the Left which was influential among them, decided otherwise. So Burt was turning on the very people who, rightly or wrongly but, generally speaking, sincerely, had helped bring the CIO into Canada and had helped advance him to leadership. At the 1956 CCL convention, J.K. Bell of the Nova Scotia Marine and Shipyard Workers Union reminded Burt about this, but he also added: 'It might have been all right [in the 1930s] but I think Canadians have since developed and want their own labour movement.'

How then, shall we sum up the place of international unionism in Canadian labour history? In the final decade of the nineteenth century contradictions began to develop between the *substance* Canadian unionism, and the *mode* international unionism, so that the central contradiction began to be posed: *Canadian unionism versus international unionism.* This contradiction developed through the first five decades of the twentieth century. It gave rise to new centres, such as the National Trades and Labour Congress, the One Big Union, the Confederation of National Trade Unions, the All-Canadian Congress of Labour, and the Workers Unity League. It also expressed itself within the Trades and Labor Congress of Canada, the Canadian Congress of Labour, and its successor, the Canadian Labour Congress.

There is much that is positive in labour's history. Many a union battle in Canada, however, has been fought under the banner of the international unions; and there has been constant solidarity between Canadian and US organized workers' movements in Canada and the United States. Yet unions would have been built in Canada, and relations of solidarity would have been established between US and Canadian workers, had there been a sovereign movement in Canada and a sovereign movement in the United States. What is positive in international unionism then is not the *appearance* or the *mode* - international unionism, but the *essence* or the *substance* - Canadian unionism.

International unionism has also meant strike-breaking, jurisdictional chaos imposed on Canada's workers, repeated disruption of Canadian labour unity, and persistence of archaic craft structures as opposed to a scientific plan of industrial unionism.

International unionism has imposed balkanization on Canada's organized workers. It has frustrated development of a system of Canada-wide industrial unions - general unions proper, such as exist in Britain, Australia, France, Italy, the Soviet Union, indeed, in practically every country.

Beyond that, international unionism has meant the reinforcing of the tendency to local isolation in Canada. The constituting of central organs (trade union centres, provincial federations, city central councils) or even the constituting of a central political party such as the New Democratic party could not compensate for this lack of structural identity at the base. The result has been to hold back unification of Canada's workers for economic, legislative, and political action; and to impede the development of the kind of labour movement in Canada which could begin in a serious way to undertake central class objectives such as the shorter work day, total organization of the unorganized, Canadian independence, and peace.

The negative effects of international unionism apply also on the country as a whole. International unionism has been a major link in the system of US domination of Canada, has provided US imperialism with a base in Canada, one worth more to it than outright acquisition of a province or outright ownership of a number of major industries. Again and again, in central crises of the class struggle in Canada - in the conscription crisis of 1917, in the Winnipeg general strike of 1919, in the fight for unity and peace during the 1930s, in the momentous struggles of the Cold War era - the system of international unionism has operated as a major reserve of reaction to defeat the working class. It has converted Canada into a guinea pig for labour imperialism, the labour front of US imperialism; the kind of labour imperialism which, during the Cold War years, the reactionary US labour leaders, the Dubinskys, Meanys, and Harrisons, tried to impose on the peoples of Latin America, Western Europe, Asia, and Africa.

Again, international unionism has served as a vital link in the system of class collaborationism, the system of capital domination of labour from within. Again and again, the right wings in Canada and in the United States combined their forces and provided each other with a reserve of strength to prop up their domination of the unions. The result has been bad, not just for Canada's organized workers, but also for US organized workers.

The conclusion is clear. The winning of a sovereign trade union movement – a sovereign Canadian union for each industry, a sovereign movement for the country as a whole – stands as a central class objective for Canada's organized workers. The prime objective should be, not autonomy within the international union, but a system of sovereign Canadian unions:[8] Where direct action to break links is not possible, the struggle should be conducted for Canadian autonomy within the international union. But that must mean, not just the facade of autonomy, but the content: a Canadian district, a Canadian constitution, a Canadian leadership elected by the Canadian membership, a Canadian treasury, a Canadian strike fund, and the right of the Canadian membership to secession. And even where such autonomy has been established, it should be regarded as but a second best, a transition link to the form which is proper and classical for Canada – the sovereign Canadian union: a body which will be master in its own house, but will also be free to establish such links of solidarity as it sees fit with organized workers in the United States or anywhere else.

This is what can prevail by the will of Canada's workers.

NOTES

1 This threat was heard in 1962-63 in connection with a dispute between the Carpenters (United Brotherhood of Carpenters and Joiners) and the International Woodworkers of America. The Carpenters walked out of the 1962 convention on that issue, and subsequently they suspended payment of per capita to the Congress. At the time, it was said that the Carpenters and some other international unions were considering the organization of a rival centre.
2 In 1958, in fifty-three of seventy international unions, permission was required from headquarters before a local could strike with full support of the union.
3 In 1960, Donald Secord, CBRT secretary-treasurer, cited a similar case. Canadian members in one international who were demanding additional rights were told that if this demand were granted, the next thing would be that Catholics and Protestants would put forward similar requests, not to speak of the people of Alaska.
4 A further indication of the policy pursued by the CLC leadership is Dodge's address to the 1961 international convention of the United Brewery Flour, Cereal, Soft Drink and Distillery Workers of America at Baltimore, Maryland. There he defined 'legislative program, political action ... foreign trade and International affairs' as those areas where there should be autonomy, and he went on to say that 'in administrative, financial and constitutional matters, autonomy is not as important.' *Canadian Labour* (Oct. 1961.)
5 This underlines the significance of the decision by communists and progressives in the late 1930s to dissolve or merge the Canadian unions established in the late 1920s and early 1930s into international unions of the CIO and AFL. That was probably a mistake, though it had its positive side, and was connected with the circumstances of the day. It is a fact, however, that from its inception in 1922 until 1964, the Communist party of Canada, though performing yeoman's work in the fight for Canadian unionism both as a party and through its adherents, has never clearly understood this struggle – and this is one big reason for the setbacks it has suffered.

6   The use of international fraternal organizations by US imperialism in its conquest of Canada is not confined to the labour movement. It involves also various religious bodies and fraternal organizations such as Jehovah's Witnesses, the Zionists, Rotary International, the Shriners. Revealing was this incident at the University of Toronto in 1960 involving a coloured woman student who was denied membership in a fraternity. It turned out that the US headquarters of the fraternity had advised the officers of the Toronto chapter that admission of a coloured person would involve the organization in difficulties with its chapters located in the Southern United States.

7   Further evidence revealing the interconnection between class collaborationism and international unionism is the joint TLC-CCL brief submitted in 1957 to the Royal Commission on Canada's Economic Prospects. In upholding international unions, this brief advances arguments more palatable to management than to labour. It speaks about the 'moderation' of international unions. It considers ten objections to international unions. Of these, eight are employer-type objections, and only two are worker-type objections. It deals with the problem of strikes – that is to say, the right of Canadian members of international unions to strike, not from the standpoint of the Canadians' right to strike, but rather their *right not to strike.* That is an employer-tilted approach; for, as far as the employers are concerned, the freer the workers are *not* to strike, the better they (the employers) like it. But as far as the workers are concerned, the freer they (the workers) are to strike (implicit in which is the right *not* to strike), the better they (the workers) like it.

8   The Communist party of Canada, which should be a leader in this field, has confined itself in practice to the 'Canadian autonomy' slogan. This has been one important factor holding up progress to building a Canadian trade union movement.

H.E. Bronson

teaches in the Department of Economics and Political Science at the

University of Saskatchewan

Continentalism and Canadian agriculture

MOST ASPECTS of the current crisis in Canadian agriculture[1] have been widely analysed, including the problems of export markets, interprovincial trade, the cost-price squeeze, and the defence of the family farm. But there has been a tendency to neglect or minimize the impact of continentalism, which inevitably affects the other problems and in some cases may be the major factor involved.

More attention to continentalism has become particularly necessary since the Federal Task Force on Agriculture endorsed it in the following terms: 'The Task Force emphasizes the desirability of Canada taking the initiative in attempting to create a continental market with the United States for grains, oil seeds, potatoes and livestock. Such a development would emphasize the importance of efficiency at three levels: by farmers; by agribusiness (both in supplying inputs and in processing, packaging and promoting); by governments in providing the desirable climate for informed decision-making by farmers and agribusiness. Another implication of a common continental market is that all inputs by agribusiness and farmers should be tariff-free.'[2]

The purpose of this study is to bring the effects of continentalism into better perspective by showing, as far as available information permits, how it is involved in the present Canadian farm crisis. It is not possible to analyse in detail the extent to which the continental market has affected agriculture in the past, because the necessary data are not available.

Early in 1971, the National Farmers' Union (NFU) asked the Dominion Bureau of Statistics to compile data concerning the degree of farm land ownership by foreign individuals and corporations in Canada, but these figures were not readily forthcoming. Detailed information also was sought with respect to the trends and proportions of foreign ownership and control in agribusiness, again without result.

From the facts which are known, it appears that many of the adversities now suffered by Canadian farmers are attributable to the developing influence of continentalism, an influence which the Task Force endorses as essential for future efficiency in agriculture. The Report, however, neglects the negative features of the continental market with respect to land ownership and agribusiness. Even more significant is its failure to deal adequately with the adverse effects of continentalism on the cost of Canadian farmers' equipment and supplies and on the prices received for their products.

In both of these areas, Canadian farmers readily recognize their long and continuing history of exploitation by corporate agribusiness. A major difference between farmers and other owners of capital is that nearly all farmers are workers. Their incomes do not represent 'returns' to capital because they do not provide enough, in most cases, to constitute fair wages for the operator and for the working members of his family.

Their low average income per working hour, which results from the price squeeze imposed by their suppliers and buyers, actually makes them self-supervised employees of agribusiness. And these corporations, like those which exploit direct wage earners, are increasingly dominated by cartels based in the United States. Their operations are being recognized as the means by which American imperialism penetrates the economy of its norther colony.

Under these circumstances, the Task Force's promotion of a continental market is even more questionable. Is it more concerned with integration of the Canadian and American economies than with the welfare of Canadian farmers? And since it seems to reflect or inspire the views of the federal government, must farmers take political action to change policies in their favour?

In attempting to answer these questions, this study will outline the difficulties which currently exist in the major sectors of the Canadian farm economy,[3] and will try to show the impact of both the production and marketing features of continentalism.[4]

THE CRISIS IN CANADIAN AGRICULTURE

During the late 1960s and the early 1970s, the Canadian farm economy slumped under the pressure of heavy 'surpluses' and sharply reduced net income. The Canadian wheat carry-over reached a record one billion bushels on 30 July 1970. Diversification into hog production cut the prices of that product, by April 1971, by more than 50 per cent from prices obtained 18 months earlier.

'Excess' poultry and egg production led to the 'chicken-and-egg war' as some provinces tried to close their borders to imports from other provinces. Milk producers chose to dump surplus product into the fields rather than to sell it at the world market price.[5]

Faced with crises of this nature throughout the farm economy, the Canadian government increasingly insisted on allowing the market to 'rationalize' agriculture.[6] And as noted above, the Task Force Report concluded that the market is decreeing more dependence on the United States as a buyer and investor.

This consignment of farmers to the mercies of a controlled and manipulated market supports the view that Canadian governments have always been the servants of major business and financial interests, and have helped farmers only when agricultural development was required by these dominant interests.[7] By controlling prices, agribusiness firms have always been able to skim off any extra income allotted to farmers.

In many cases, world markets for farm products are controlled and manipulated by cartels and governments working together. For example, Canada has been adversely affected by the decline of West European sales as the European Economic Community has expanded,[8] and future prospects in this area appear to be worse. The important Japanese, East European, Soviet and Chinese markets are also uncertain. Purchases by these countries tend to be restricted by Canadian resistance to their imports, which have generally been far below the volume needed to balance trade.[9]

Most important in a world where two-thirds of the people are inadequately fed is the inability of these people to convert their needs into effective demand. Regardless of how the responsibility for these conditions may be diagnosed, it is evident that starvation combined with food 'surpluses' will not be tolerated indefinitely.

The Task Force Report, however, seems to assume that the hungry world will remain hungry during the next two decades. Instead of being concerned with developing food products and trade to meet the needs of deprived nations, the Report expects Canadian farmers to adjust to the needs of an expanding American market, which already takes over 40 per cent of Canadian farm exports other than wheat.[10]

Meanwhile, in 1970, the Lower Inventories for Tomorrow (LIFT) program was put into effect by the federal government, with the primary objective of diverting farm output from wheat production to commodities which the US market might more readily accept. As a result, prairie wheat acreage was cut from 24.4 million in 1969 to 12 million in 1970. Later that year, the federal government modified the LIFT program to take account of the setbacks which had occurred in world wheat and corn yields. But the basic objective remained – to divert farm production away from wheat.

Many of the problems which the Task Force Report and the LIFT program sought to solve had been building up for years. The Report noted that from 1946 to 1967, the farm labour force declined by 55 per cent, indicating agriculture's 'relative unattractiveness.' In fact, the pressure on farmers has been mainly economic, and is usually identified in terms of the 'cost-price squeeze.' Here lies the reason for the decline in the number of farmers.

The squeeze is apparent in a comparison of trends in farm receipts and costs between 1958-62 and 1969. Total cash receipts increased by 45 per cent over this period, while total operating and depreciation costs rose by 70 per cent. The squeeze was worse on the prairies, where cash receipts increased by only 32 per cent over the same period, while operating and depreciation costs were up 76 per cent.[11]

Conditions deteriorated sharply in 1970. Accrued net farm income[12] received by farm operators in Canada fell to 19 per cent below income in 1969, which itself showed a 3 per cent decline relative to 1968.[13] Assuming that there were 400,000 farm operators in Canada in 1970,[14] the average net income per farm was $66 a week, as compared with the composite industrial wage and salary average of $126.77.

The low farm average income meant that many farmers had net losses rather than net income. Assuming a 'poverty line' of $3000 annual income, the Task Force Report estimated that one-third of Canadian farmers were below that line, and observed further, with little basis for contradiction, that the 'line' would have to be raised higher than $3000.[15] The Report offered only a few brief phrases of encouragement to those being driven off the farms. Training programs and income supplements were mentioned, together with the hope of non-farm employment.

But it was emphasized that farmers seeking extra work would face still competition from the unemployed and from the 200,000 workers joining the labour force each year. Furthermore: 'there can be no thought that incentive grants or any government programs have the power to put industry wherever there are farm and other rural people in need of employment ... it is unlikely that off-farm employment can draw off large numbers of farmers from the poverty category.'[16]

Such prospects understandably have done little to reduce farmers' concern over declining incomes and possible termination of their operations. The injustice of the situation has been further emphasized by the fact that, during the post-war period, agricultural productivity increased by approximately 6 per cent annually, compared with 2½ per cent for the rest of the economy.[17] Additional tension has resulted from the growing realization among farmers that their adversities can often be related to exploitation by agribusiness and to neglect or mismanagement by government. And the fact that both agribusiness and government are increasingly dominated by American interests makes the problem even more formidable.

Having attributed these conditions and trends in agriculture to market forces, the Task Force argued that these forces should be allowed to continue the same process of 'rationalization.' The Report, moreover, accepted the prospect of further reductions in the number of people on farms over the next two decades. Of the 430,000 farms in Canada in 1966, the Report estimated that 'only a third or so are large enough, by today's standards, for long-run viability.'[18]

Those who still remain on the farms have been faced by federal government demands for drastic changes in output, with emphasis on the reduction of wheat and milk. The outlook for wheat has remained poor despite some easing in the build-up of unsold world supplies. Acreage limitation in the United States and drought in Argentina and Australia were major factors leading to reduced world production in 1970-71.

In Canada, the LIFT program reduced the 1970 harvest by more than 300 million bushels compared with 1969, although yields per acre were higher.

Such reductions, however, do not significantly affect world production, nor do they solve the 'surplus' problem, which is based on the 2293 million bushels held by the five main exporting countries at the beginning of the 1970-71 crop year.[19]

For grain growers, rapeseed and feed grains – especially barley – seemed to offer the best alternative to wheat on Canadian farms. Rapeseed, which doubled in acreage between 1969 and 1970, accounted for four million acres on the prairies. But Otto E. Lang, speaking for the Canadian Wheat Board, warned that 'the quantity that can successfully be marketed has not yet been established. Aggressive selling and increased substitution of rapeseed oil for soybean oil will be required to market the crop.'[20] As the main world producer of soybeans, the United States was expected to expand output in 1971, thereby contributing to an over-supply of edible oils.

Projected new demand for barley was also far from guaranteed. Exports had expanded from a low of 15 million bushels in 1962-63 to 82 million in 1969-70, with higher volumes predicted.[21] Lang called for an increase in barley acreage from the 9 million of 1969-70 to 16 million for 1971-72. Nevertheless, he reminded producers that 'to retain consistent substantial export volumes of feed barley requires that the price of Canadian barley on world markets be consistently competitive with other feed grains, in particular with US corn.'[22]

In fact, Canadian farmers were forced to face this problem immediately. Their bumper barley crop of 1971 coincided with a record US corn crop and with a general world 'over-production' of feed grains. The question arose: 'Will we now need a LIFT plan for barley as we did for wheat?' The continental and world market systems obviously were not going to solve the problem of food 'surpluses' in a hungry world.

In both feed grains and oilseeds, Lang emphasized the need for annual evaluation of the costs and benefits, with particular reference to the world market. And he went on to promote expansion in another area which also had been given priority in the Task Force Report. The western farmer, he argued, 'should be encouraged to participate aggressively in the expanding livestock sector of the industry.'[23]

This was in full accord with the high priority given earlier by the Task Force to the expansion of Canadian feeder cattle exports to the United States – with the price reductions which that country would require. 'Governments and producers should accept as a target the export of 500,000 feeder cattle per year by 1980 and the production of enough beef and veal to meet Canadian consumption demands in full ... Canada should initiate discussions to remove *all* tariffs on cattle and beef in order to achieve a completely free continental market.'[24]

The price reduction required to achieve this level of exports was estimated at $1 to $2 per hundredweight relative to American prices. With this adjustment, 'the export market would be unlimited up to the capacity of Canadians to produce feeders.'[25] In other words, the United States was expected to accept all the unfinished Canadian cattle likely to be produced as a result of emphasizing that product instead of wheat.

Thus, according to the Task Force Report, 'wheat will no longer be king on the prairies; cattle will have exceeded it.'[26] In fact, cattle dethroned wheat as a prairie cash-earner in 1969; but the expansion of cattle production to meet the prospective annual export of half a million feeders[27] would mean a decisive lead for cattle as a farm cash-earner if wheat output continued to be restricted by inadequate world markets.

The inadequacy of world demand for Canadian wheat has been clearly related to American production and marketing policies. And these policies seem certain to persist and even intensify as the United States struggles to solve its balance of payment crises. The Task Force Report apparently recognized this situation. 'The year 1966 marked a series of major changes in US wheat policy, all of which affected Canada adversely. The US wheat acreage allotment was increased by about 30 per cent, a modified two-price system was introduced using domestic milling certificates, and aggressive selling in commercial markets supplanted much of the earlier emphasis on food aid.'[28] From this the Report concluded that Canada could lose even more of the world wheat market to the United States unless Canadian wheat exports are made 'fully competitive' in price, credit conditions, and quality.

The 1966 changes in American wheat policy were followed in 1967-68 by the declaration of a 'free year' in wheat marketing, with accompanying price reductions. At the same time the Canadian Wheat Board was trying to maintain price levels consistent with the International Grains Arrangement which had been negotiated to come into effect in the following year.

With its 'free year' pricing, the United States was able to increase its wheat exports by 2 per cent to 761 million bushels, while world exports declined by 15 per cent and Canadian exports fell by almost 40 per cent to 336 million bushels. As a result, Canada was left with over one-half of the total wheat stock held by the four leading wheat exporters. The same condition prevailed at the end of the 1968-69 crop year,[29] when world production (excluding China) rose to a record 11.3 billion bushels and the world carry-over reached 2374 million bushels.[30]

The world situation worsened in 1969-70. Crop yield was 8 per cent below that of the previous year, but carry-over stocks in the hands of the five main exporters increased by another 200 to 300 million bushels. Furthermore, the International Grains Arrangement failed to prevent a price war in 1970, during which the price of wheat was forced down to more than 10 per cent below the IGA minimum.[31]

When exports improved late in 1970, the Canadian government was still recommending wheat acreages well below the 29.4 million acres seeded in 1968. Although the Task Force called for improved market research and more aggressive selling, it was evident that government policy-makers saw little hope of prevailing against American selling tactics.

The projections accepted by the Task Force for 1975 wheat exports from Canada to the 'developing' areas (i.e. Africa, Latin America, and Asia excluding China) were based on the assumption that production would increase by 35 to 85 per cent in those countries, compared with 1961-63 averages. Over the same period, increased consumption by a population growing at an estimated 2.3 per cent annually would add 50 per cent to their anticipated effective demand for wheat.

This would mean little chance for increased exports to those areas, although the projected 1975 consumption of 71.2 to 73.9 million metric tons by this 52 per cent of the world's population would indicate that their effective demand per capita was still far below their real need. (By 1975, the remaining 48 per cent, including the USSR and China, were expected to consume 189 million metric tons.) In other words, the 'developing' but hungry nations, including over half of the world's population, would be consuming only 28 per cent of the world's wheat. On a per capita basis, this can hardly be described as an improvement over the comparable 23 per cent for 1961-63.[32]

TOWARDS A CONTINENTAL MARKET

In view of the assumption that little or no improvement can be expected in the hungry world's effective demand for Canadian wheat, the Task Force's interest in the future requirements of the American market is understandable. The Task Force recognized that in food as in most other commodities, the US would seek unfinished products to be processed in that country. But the Report failed to warn that this trend would further increase the advantages which Americans have already gained in employment, terms of trade, and value of production, by using Canada as a source of raw materials.

In fact, the Report clearly recommended that Canadian agriculture should cater to American interests with any farm product which would be acceptable. The federal government was urged to take 'strong initiatives toward serious discussions of free trade for a further group of vegetables and fruits in which Canada has a comparative advantage, including carrots, onions, cole crops, turnips and strawberries.'

There was no comment on the fact that although 'apples are virtually on a free trade basis now,' the marketing problems for that commodity remained unsolved. Instead, the Task Force recommended a greater sales effort in the American market by the apple industry. No mention was made of attempting to build such sales in the form of processed or finished apple products, but a major obstacle to that procedure was indicated. 'Research for the Task Force estimates that over 70 per cent of the pack of fruits and vegetables is processed in American-owned plants. The parent company of some of these Canadian firms appears reluctant to use in Canada the advanced machinery and technology used in its American plants. The American investors may have good private reasons for such practices but such a policy means that technology in Canada advances more slowly than would otherwise be the case.'[33]

It is significant that despite this rare recognition of the penalties of continentalism, the Task Force omitted any remedial suggestions, which presumably were inhibited by its commitment to more complete continentalism. Meanwhile, under the conditions existing early in 1971, Nova Scotia apple growers were faced with a one-third decline in the prices of apples used for processing. According to a NFU report, this meant that 'very soon a painful decision will have to be made as to removing a large percentage of trees from production.'

Spokesmen for the 12,000 apple growers in Canada denounced 'unfair trade advantages granted other countries' as a cause of their problems. They demanded prohibition of apple and apple-product imports from 'countries which have closed their markets to apples from Canada.'[34] As the Nixon administration subsequently moved toward a much greater degree of protectionism, the apple growers' recommendations obviously gained in acceptability relative to the Task Force's hopes for free trade.

As noted above, the major export promoted by the Task Force, on the basis of free trade and adaptation to the American market, was feeder cattle. The Report specifically discounted the chances for expanding sales of finished cattle or dairy products. Even with feeder cattle, it was recognized that possible over-production in the US might lead to lower prices, and to import quotas.

Thus with these export products, as with apples, the development of secondary industry was clearly down-graded in favour of advancing and maintaining the primary industry level, despite the fact that this means fewer jobs and lower national income than secondary industry would provide. In the case of the recommended expansion of feeder cattle exports, the Task Force accepted the income loss from an anticipated price reduction of $2.00 per hundredweight, or more, relative to American prices.[35]

Perhaps as compensation, the Report expressed hope that if the Americans conceded a completely tariff-free continental market for cattle and beef, cattle exporters would gain $1.50 per hundred on finished animals and $2.50 on feeders. But Nixon's protectionist bombshell of August 1971 left little hope for anything substantial in the way of tariff reductions.

Even with lower prices for feeder cattle exports, the Task Force regarded a maximum effort in this category as the most viable alternative to the problems of a congested grain market. In further support of the cattle exports, the Report urged a shift from dairy products (for which higher American demand seemed unlikely) to beef cattle. Its recommendations to the dairy industry were consistent with its general approach.

The Canadian Dairy Adjustment Commission (named to replace the present Canadian Dairy Commission) would be expected to help milk producers to develop profitable enterprises without 'extensive subsidies.' Otherwise it would help them 'to phase out of milk production.' 'The CDAC and provincial regulatory bodies must provide the kind of economic climate for processors and others involved in the dairy industry so that marketing efficiency may be improved. Such measures include: (a) programs to bring about more stable milk production, especially seasonally, (b) ending those regulations that inhibit the expansion and merger of processors and distributors.'[36]

Thus for both farming and agribusiness, the Task Force seemed to be relying, with persistent faith, on the market's mythical power to promote efficiency, and on the power of free trade to work for the benefit of all. Farmers and others who have learned by experience to ridicule such assumptions must now decide whether government policy makers are suffering from illusions or are trying to rationalize the foreign corporate take-over of Canadian agriculture.

Whatever its motives, the Task Force evidently was promoting government intervention only to assure those adjustments necessary for a smooth transition to further integration of farming and agribusiness.[37] This seemed to be regarded as the best alternative to the present situation, where highly competitive farmers find themselves at a bargaining disadvantage in 'buying from and selling to sectors with only a few large firms.'[38] But the Report failed to explain how farmers could expect less exploitation as employees or minor partners of large corporate conglomerates.

In any event, the integration process inevitably means fewer and larger farms, the decline of rural life, and a continuation of the population drift from the country to a precarious and often destitute existence in large urban centres. For those remaining on the fewer and larger farms, the Task Force's recommendations to the dairy industry are of interest.

Faced with large surpluses of milk powder in the hands of the Canadian Dairy Commission, the Task Force approved drastic reductions in the number of milk cows in Canada.[39] As for the surplus of milk powder, it said: 'In order to bring powder supplies into balance with demand, milk production would have to decline by as much as 2.5 billion pounds ... We continue to buy powder at 20 cents per pound, store and transport it and sell it to non-Canadian users at five to eight cents per pound. With production of 380 million pounds and consumption of 160 million, the outlook is indeed serious and deteriorating.'[40] This 'deteriorating' outlook was directly related to the fact that 'per capita consumption of milk in all of its forms has been falling for many years, and there appears to be no likely developments which would reverse that trend.'[41] Here again, the Task Force appeared to be accepting a continuation of the widely inequitable income distribution which has prevailed even in an expanding Canadian economy. Extensive poverty has undoubtedly been responsible for declining per capita consumption of milk[42] and other relatively expensive foods as prices have risen.

With its projected declining market for milk and an increasing American demand for feeder cattle, the Report logically proceeded to recommend sale of surplus milk powder to feed the cattle. Prices, of course, would have to be greatly reduced, and provision was made to prevent the cheaper milk powder from being diverted to human use. 'The CDC, which has been buying skim milk powder at 20 cents per pound and exporting it at five to eight cents, should make powder available to livestock feeders at prices competitive with substitute ingredients. Presumably the CDAC would have to denature the powder by using a harmless vegetable dye and thereafter might sell it at prices close to those net prices currently received in export markets.' The CDAC would also be expected to use some of the funds now available to the CDC 'to provide positive encouragement for dairy farmers who wish to enter beef cattle production.'[43] This recommendation was part of the Task Force's general view that the best allocation of government subsidies is that which help to direct production toward markets where expanding demand is anticipated. Here, as with other products, the demand was expected to be American.

The Report made no attempt to defend this recommendation in terms of equitable distribution of world food surpluses. Instead, it discussed two sets of policies to be implemented, assuming that improved productivity would result from more emphasis on feeder cattle output at the expense of milk and wheat production. First, price supports, subsidies, and other policies 'must be amended to reduce the relative attractiveness of producing milk and wheat. Second, new policies must be developed to provide positive encouragement to beef feeder production.'[44] It was these recommendations which led the NFU to advise its members that 'Canadian agriculture is to be diverted from milk and grain for hungry people to meat products for affluent Americans.'[45]

Some members of the Task Force felt that the meat requirements of American consumers could provide an important export outlet for Canadian pork products. The dominant view, however, was that such exports could not expand significantly unless Canadian prices fell by 'about $5.00 per hundred-weight below the relationship they "normally" have with US prices.'[46]

Evidently, this was another case in which prospects for the export of finished products were regarded with pessimism. In agriculture, as in most other industries, the development of continental trade seems to require extension of Canada's role as a supplier of raw materials or unfinished products to the United States. As in other industries, this procedure would likely mean further integration of Canadian farm production with the supplying and processing plants of American-controlled agribusiness. Consequently, the proportion of feeds, fertilizers, machinery, and other supplies provided directly by American firms could be expected to increase. This would bring more unemployment to Canadian industries and services, thereby adding to the disintegration of Canadian towns and villages which depend mainly on farming. Acceptance of integration with American agribusiness would also bring further loss of Canadian control over the output and prices of farm supplies.

An important example of this appeared in the Barber Royal Commission Report on farm machinery, in which tractor prices on the North American continent were observed 'to be set by the two firms with the largest share of the market, International Harvester and Deere,'[47] both American firms. With this structure, the 1967 net wholesale prices of tractors 'averaged from 17 to 38 per cent lower in Britain than they did in Canada,' and by 1968 the spread had widened to between 30 and 45 per cent. These prices, dictated by the two dominant American firms, represent large profit margins above costs which are also unnecessarily high because of excess capacity in the farm machinery industry. The Commission Report estimated that 'between five and ten firms of efficient size could easily produce all the tractors currently sold in the non-Communist world. In fact, some 20 to 30 firms are now producing tractors in significant volume.' Commission figures indicated further that if the number of firms were reduced so that a firm now producing 20,000 units annually could attain a volume of 120,000 units or more, the unit costs for an average-size tractor could be reduced by over 25 per cent.[48]

Under existing circumstances, however, prices paid by farmers must cover both the unnecessary costs and the high profits maintained by the American-dominated cartel. The Task Force Report entirely neglected this problem of cartels in the continental market. The Barber Report urged discussions and negotiations with parent companies, international action against combines, and investigation of low-cost imports of machinery not currently represented on the Canadian market.[49]

As might be expected from commissions which reflect the class bias of the federal government, neither Report admitted any basic flaws in the monopoly capitalist system. Similarly, there was no recognition of the certainty that pro-capitalist governments can never be depended on to take effective action against the influence of international cartels, or the injustices of the 'markets' controlled by these cartels. Until these problems are solved, it will not be possible to feed Canadian farm surpluses to a hungry world; or to revive the Canadian rural economy; or to prevent an American take-over of both agribusiness and the land itself.

CONTINENTALISM AND CORPORATE FARMING

As already indicated, economic integration with the United States means not only the adaptation of Canadian output to American demand, but also the provision of outlets in Canada for surplus American capital. In view of the accelerating trend toward large-scale, assembly-line production in agriculture, corporate farming has become a major attraction for American investors. Continuation of the corporate trend was anticipated in the Task Force Report: 'It may become impossible eventually for the individual farmer to accumulate sufficient savings during his lifetime to develop an efficient size of business and own a debt-free farm by the time of retirement ... A corporate form of farming with hired management and equity financing through the stock market may eventually evolve out of the far-reaching changes which are certain to occur in agriculture during the next two or three decades.'[50]

An important and controversial example of attempted penetration by corporation farming from the United States occurred in Nova Scotia in 1970. Cattle operators from Ohio, Montana, and Florida proposed an investment of $2.4 million in a 'Canadian corporation' which would set up a 20,000-head beef cattle complex. Following the familiar pattern of expecting Canadian taxpayers to provide most of the money, the group planned to obtain the remainder of the $6 million initial investment from the provincial government.

Although the scheme had the support of the Nova Scotia Department of Agriculture, it was delayed by strong farmer protest. The NFU presented a brief to the Department, pointing out that corporate farming of this type 'is a vehicle which invites wholesale take-over of the last resource (farm land) by US investors and/or control by US business.' The brief referred to a prediction that the project, beginning on a scale comparable to the largest of Canadian cattle feedlots,[51] would, 'within a very few years, control a third of Nova Scotia's beef production.'

Noting the plan for an initial importation of 10,000 head of American cattle to start the feeding complex, the NFU warned that this process could exert pricing pressure against local producers, who would be justified 'in viewing a government loan to this enterprise as using their own tax money to put them out of business.'[52] The union saw 'more justice and less risk if the government will impose in its own people the confidence it appears to have in these foreign entrepreneurs.'

Provincial governments, searching for more investment, tend to support such ventures into corporate farming without full consideration of the consequences. Such was the case when Ogilvie Flour Mills, a subsidiary of John Labatt Ltd.,[53] announced plans in 1971 for a feed mill and hog breeding operation in Manitoba. In its original welcome of the plan, the Manitoba government mentioned an investment of $5 million and an output of 60,000 hogs annually in three to five years. This meant that the government was prepared to endorse a project which would be producing 8 per cent of Manitoba's normal hog output.[54] (Later, the actual plan was reported to involve an investment of only $1 million.) The prospect of 60,000 hogs a year from one integrated enterprise brought widespread protests from the farmers and from the NFU. The union's regional co-ordinator for Manitoba, Phil Schwarz, called for laws against corporate farming. He warned that corporate control over agriculture was growing at 'an unprecedented rate.'[55] Furthermore, this form of organization attracts American investment and control to Canadian agriculture.

Schwarz became especially concerned with the growth of this control in dairying. He noted that four major American chains – Kraftco,[56] Borden, Beatrice Foods, and Carnation – are rapidly extending their holdings in Canada. By the end of 1970, these firms controlled approximately forty dairies in Ontario alone. Beatrice officials described their Canadian take-overs as part of 'an overall international expansion.'[57]

Another example of such expansion is the Simplot organization of Idaho, which extended its potato processing into Alberta and Manitoba. In 1968 these two plants, together with four in the United States, were processing 60 carloads of potatoes daily on a year-round basis.[58] Supplies came from 80,000 acres whose owners delivered their entire output under contract. The Simplot conglomerate, which includes fertilizers, mines, lumber, feeds and frozen food processing, has been continuing its expansion into other provinces.

Smaller corporate units have been active in expanding direct farmland ownership in Canada. Additional land purchases by Americans are frequently reported. One recent article described the impact of 40,000 American immigrants in the ranchland of central British Columbia.[59] Seeking a new farm frontier, these Americans generally wish to retain their citizenship, and expect to send their children back for the military draft. This attitude has aroused considerable resentment among Canadians in the area. Young local farmers trying to get a start must also contend with the higher land prices bid by Americans.

Higher prices for land and the trend toward integrated, corporate agriculture thus give concentrated American capital an increasing advantage over

Canadians who are trying to develop or maintain viable farm units. The Task Force on Agriculture accepted this 'increasing formal and informal integration' together with farm mergers and consolidation, 'not primarily for increased production efficiency, but to structure units that are large enough to afford better management.' And further: 'As the size of units increases, financial requirements multiply and operating problems increase in complexity, ease of entry into commercial farming will be drastically cut allowing much greater rationalization of supply-demand relationships.'[60]

The Report was thus accepting the development of commercial farming, where fewer and larger units would be integrated with agribusiness. As in other industries, fewer and larger firms would mean more effective barriers against new entrants, and greater control over prices and output – to the disadvantage of both farmers and consumers. This concentration and control would not only inhibit 'free market' supply-demand relationships, but also would facilitate the transfer of ownership to large-scale American enterprises.

Under the improved management visualized by the Task Force, a 'high and rising proportion' of present farm operators would become 'employees working for salaries and wages.' Some family farms would survive, but like the corporate farms, they would be 'rationally managed, profit-oriented businesses.'[61] With such an orientation, they would inevitably pursue continental markets and control.

In resisting these trends, the NFU has emphasized as a principle, 'that the more the individual farmer's bargaining power can be harnessed collectively, the greater will be the farmer's bargaining power.'[62] Attempting to exercise this power at the November 1970 agricultural conference in Ottawa, NFU president Roy Atkinson insisted that government 'has no right to legislate people off farms ... why should a man with 10 cows and three pigs be jack-knifed into the asphalt jungle of Toronto because of government policy?'[63]

AN ANTI-CONTINENTALIST APPROACH

Immediate realities oblige farm organizations to strive for some form of effective bargaining power against the exploiting class represented by agribusiness and government. But it is unrealistic to assume that any farm union can exercise enough lobbying power to bring about legislation which will place farmers' interests ahead of business and financial interests. The NFU has already pursued this method to the extent that little remains but its announced threat of a nation-wide non-delivery strike. If this is tried, farmers across Canada may learn by experience that governments are not neutral, but are servants of the investing class. Such governments must be replaced, and this requires political action, against which farm unions have developed deeply ingrained opposition.

Apart from the difficulties of organizing the majority of farmers politically, there is, as the Task Force pointed out, 'the political reality that Canadian voters are divided 92% non-farmer and 8% farmer.' And the government 'must give primary attention to the views of the urban population.'[64]

Such an attempt to align the farmers against the urban people neglects the fact that most of the latter are wage and salary earners, and that the prosperity of one group depends on that of the other.[65] Furthermore, while the farmer and the worker are essential in any economic system, the private middleman is totally unnecessary for the attainment of full employment and improved living standards. In fact, it can be safely asserted that the achievement of these goals is impossible where private entrepreneurs, and particularly, foreign ones, are in a position to impose their erratic, profit-seeking policies on the economy and on the government.

Under these circumstances, there is a solid basis for mobilizing a majority of Canadians in support of a farmer-labour government. This does not necessarily imply support for the New Democratic party. The Manitoba government's enthusiasm for the proposed Ogilvie Flour Mill conglomerate shows that an NDP administration cannot escape the priorities which must dominate any party as long as it depends primarily on the private entrepreneur for investment. The NDP faces what the Toronto *Star* described as Mr Blakeney's big gamble 'when he begins to legislate the salvation of the family farm in the face of a continental trend to large units and "agribusiness."'

The Saskatchewan NDP's farm program included the control of unnecessary duplication in farm services; a guaranteed net income per acre; the restriction of corporate ownership to family farms and groups of families farming co-operatively; and the retention of farm ownership in Canadian hands. Of major importance among these desirable planks was a proposal for a Land Bank commission[66] which would purchase land 'offered voluntarily on the market at competitive prices and lease this land, guaranteeing tenure, on the basis of need, with option to buy.'

The NDP, like the Task Force, was thus relying basically on the 'market at competitive prices,' combined with a rejection of proposals for public ownership of agribusiness. As a result, its general program seemed likely to end up more as words than deeds. The Waffle movement strongly objected to inclusion of the phrase 'with option to buy' in the Land Bank program, arguing that this was against convention policy and was conducive to the development of large private estates. Reliance on 'competitive prices' also indicated acceptance of an advantage for the wealthier 'competitors.'

And if agribusiness pricing and quality remains under the control of foreign cartels, a guaranteed income per acre could become a gold mine for these industries at the expense of the taxpayers. A farmer labour government would have to recognize that the Task Force Report is correct in pointing out that acceptance of the market as it now operates means acceptance of a continentalist agribusiness which functions as an instrument of American imperialist expansion.

Such a government, on the prairies or in Ottawa, would have to recognize that an end to the exploitation of Canadian farmers and workers requires top priority to breaking the grip of continentalist market manipulators. It would need to abandon the fantasy that anything resembling a free market now exists, or would be desirable if it did exist.

In this initial anti-continentalist struggle, which already seems to have wide support among Canadians, a farmer-labour movement would gain the experience and support needed to proceed toward a more rational economy. Such a system would include an attempt to establish more equitable trading relations with those billions of people who need food. It would guarantee employment for all Canadians able to work, including those who may leave the farms. It would plan the development of villages and towns as suppliers of the farm economy.

These achievements would provide the basis for abolishing the exploitation of workers, farmers, and consumers by private investors, both domestic and foreign. And this would mean that governments had at last begun to rely on the farmers and workers of Canada with the confidence which is now placed in foreign entrepreneurs.

NOTES

1 According to the Federal Task Force Report, the term 'agriculture' includes both agribusiness and farming. See *Canadian Agriculture in the Seventies* (Ottawa 1970). The report defines agribusiness as 'those firms which provide farm supplies and certain direct services to farmers as well as those firms which market farm-produced commodities.' Apart from Task Force references, this study will equate agriculture with farming operations.
2 *Ibid.,* 250-1.
3 Attention will be confined mainly to grains, oilseeds, hogs, dairy products, and cattle, which together provided three-quarters of farm cash income in 1970. It will become evident, however, that producers of other farm products face similar problems.
4 Readers wishing to acquaint themselves with other aspects of the farm crisis will find most of them elaborated in the references cited.
5 *Union Farmer,* April 1971.
6 The federal government's farm income stabilization plan, introduced in the fall of 1970, has been denounced by farmers as a plan to stabilize their incomes below the cost of production. According to NFU president Roy Atkinson, 'when one considers phasing out of the Temporary Wheat Reserves Act, probable elimination of FAA, no commitment by government to support initial prices established by the Canadian Wheat Board, it would appear that the government is moving toward even less support for farmers.'
7 See V.C. Fowke, *Canadian Agricultural Policy* (Toronto 1947), 272-5.

8 Europe's imports of Canadian farm products have declined by 25 per cent during the last
   five years and are expected to shrink further as the Common Market's integrated agricultural policies develop. See John Schreiner, 'Our Farm Exports Look to US – Maybe
   Vainly,' *Financial Post,* 28 Nov. 1970.
9 Average annual imports for the three years 1965-67 were $262.7 million from Japan,
   while exports to Japan averaged $427.4 million. For the same period, annual imports
   from the People's Republic of China averaged $20.0 million, compared with exports of
   $125.8 million. From East Europe, including the USSR, comparable imports were $61.2
   million and exports were $298.6 million.
10 Department of Agriculture, *Proceedings of the 1970 Canadian Agricultural Outlook
   Conference,* 17. Hereafter cited as *Outlook.*
11 *Ibid.,* 137-56. See also *Canadian Agriculture in the Seventies,* 17-18.
12 Includes value of physical change in farm inventories, and value of home-grown produce
   consumed by farmers.
13 *Canadian Statistical Review,* May 1971, 20.
14 The Task Force reported 430,000 farms in Canada in 1966, and predicted 'the disappearance of approximately 40,000 small farm operators in the next five years.'
   Agriculture in the Seventies, 409-11. (Actually, more than 64,000 disappeared during
   that five years, according to figures released in April, 1972.)
15 *Ibid.,* 7.
16 *Ibid.,* 414.
17 Economic Council of Canada, *Fifth Annual Review,* chap. 5, and *Agriculture in the
   Seventies,* 5-9.
18 *Ibid.,* 409.
19 *Outlook,* 1.
20 Proposals for a Production and Grain Receipts Policy for the Western Grains Industry
   (Ottawa, Oct. 1970) (hereafter cited as the Lang Proposals), 5-6.
21 Barley sales were expected to account for 4 per cent of total Canadian farm cash receipts.
   In 1970, wheat accounted for 13 per cent, cattle 24 per cent, dairy products 18 per cent,
   and hogs 12 per cent. *Outlook,* 155.
22 Lang Proposals, 7.
23 Lang Proposals, 8. Lang estimated that increased livestock numbers 'could provide demand for the production from an additional three to four million acres of forage over
   the next three years.' The 1970 prairie forage crop acreage was about 12 million.
24 *Agriculture in the Seventies,* 177.
25 *Ibid.,* 163.
26 *Ibid.,* 254.
27 Canada's annual average export of cattle to the US over 1965-69 was 192,000 head. See
   Situation '70, 149.
28 *Agriculture in the Seventies,* 87-8.
29 *Ibid.,* 88.
30 *Situation '70,* 1, 25.
31 Following the increase in the value of the Canadian dollar in June 1970, the price of No.
   1 Northern (in store Thunder Bay) immediately declined by another 6 cents per bushel.
   By the first week of August, the price reached as low as $1.72, which can be compared
   with the average of $1.95 for the year 1968-69. See *ibid.,* 6. The final payment for No. 1
   Northern delivered in the 1970-71 crop year, after deduction of wheat board expenses,
   brought the final total price received by farmers for that grade to $1.67.
32 *Agriculture in the Seventies,* 89.
33 *Ibid.,* 235.
34 *Union Farmer,* April 1971.
35 In mid-1970, the Canadian government's decision to unpeg the Canadian dollar led to an
   increase in its value relative to the US dollar. As a result, export prices for Canadian cattle
   declined by at least $1.50 per hundred relative to American prices.
36 *Agriculture in the Seventies,* 203.

37 The Report did concede that other industries benefit from tax concessions, subsidies, loans, grants and 'a host of other activities which result in incomes very different from those which would have been determined by the free play of market forces.' *Ibid.*, 24. Farmers, presumably, would be expected to see themselves participating in these benefits by integration, i.e. by entering into contracts with agribusiness buyers or suppliers or perhaps incorporating and merging with these firms.

38 *Ibid.*, 18.

39 The total number was projected to decline from 3,006,000 for 1957-61 to 1,677,000 in 1980. *Ibid.*, 202.

40 *Ibid.*, 198.

41 *Ibid.*, 196. Between 1964-66 and 1980, per capita milk consumption was projected to decline by 15 per cent (252).

42 The Economic Council of Canada observed that the amount spent on food by poor families was only 67 per cent of the food expenditures by non-poor families. (*Sixth Annual Review*, 116.) The Council also estimated that in 1961, 4.2 million non-farm people and 550,000 on farms were living on incomes below the poverty level. *Fifth Annual Review*, 108-9.

43 *Agriculture in the Seventies*, 204.

44 *Ibid.*, 165. In January 1972 the federal government announced a two-price system for wheat, whereby the top grade sold for human consumption would bring farmers $3.00 a bushel (basis Thunder Bay). It was not immediately clear whether this move was designed to revive wheat production or to prevent further Liberal losses in the impending federal election. But the promise of higher returns was undoubtedly one of the factors which led Canadian farmers to plan a wheat acreage of 21.4 million for 1972, an increase of 11 per cent over 1971.

45 *NFU Reveals Task Force Objectives*, Saskatoon (July 1970).

46 *Agriculture in the Seventies*, 172. The economics of hog processing and transportation is such that the export of pork greatly exceeds that of live hogs.

47 Royal Commission on Farm Machinery, *Special Report on Prices* (Ottawa 1969), 92.

48 *Ibid.*, 61-2, 198-9.

49 *Ibid.*, 96-7.

50 *Agriculture in the Seventies*, 335.

51 One of the largest is a 25,000-head feedlot near Brooks, Alberta, which is already integrated with a $500,000 feed mill, and is now expanding into slaughtering and meat packing.

52 This observation, of course, could be applied to most other farming operations in Canada.

53 John Labatt is reported to be controlled by International Utilities in the United States.

54 There has been a rapid general trend toward larger size in livestock units. Between 1952 and 1967, the average number of hogs per farm in Canada tripled; the size of cattle herds more than doubled, while the size of the average turkey flock became almost ten times greater. See Economic Council of Canada, *Fifth Annual Review*, 96.

55 *Union Farmer*, Feb. 1971, and *Free Press Weekly*, 6 Feb. 1971.

56 In September 1971, the NFU organized a national boycott of Kraftco products with the objective of forcing this 'largest dairy monopoly in North America' to pay better prices for milk.

57 'US Food Giant "Creams" Dairies,' *Financial Post*, 2 Jan. 1971.

58 Maritime farmers and their potato marketing agencies were advised by the Task Force to 'proceed with a vast re-structuring of the industry' since 'only eight per cent of the growers ... having more than three acres of potatoes actually grew more than 67 acres.' *Agriculture in the Seventies*, 221. Furthermore, 'horticulturists and prominent growers consider acreages from 100 to 200 and upward per farm are required to realize an efficient use of modern technology.'

59 Don Newlands, 'The Americans Are Coming, the Americans Are Coming,' *Canadian Magazine*, 3 April 1971.

60 *Agriculture in the Seventies*, 9.

61 *Ibid.*
62 NFU Policy Statement, First Annual Convention, Dec. 1970.
63 Canadian Press, 27 Nov. 1970.
64 *Agriculture in the Seventies,* 274. With reference to this ratio, the Report did not distinguish between actual and eligible voters. But since it has not been shown that the proportion of non-voting farmers generally varies greatly from that of non-voting urban dwellers, the distinction is not important. More significant may be the Report's reminder that rural-urban representation in the House of Commons 'is of the order of one-third *versus* two-thirds.'
65 The argument that wages push up farm costs is rapidly losing credibility. According to the DBS Census of Manufactures, the wage element in farm machinery costs dropped from 32.1 per cent in 1957 to 20.0 per cent in 1967, while the 'profit and other' proportion rose from 17.6 per cent to 23.2. Cost of materials rose from 50.3 to 56.8 per cent.
66 At the first full session of the Saskatchewan legislature under the Blakeney government, Land Bank legislation provided a fund of $10 million to purchase land. The executive-secretary of the Saskatchewan Federation of Agriculture estimated that 800 farms (about one per cent of the province's total) might be purchased with this amount. Jack McCloy, an executive member of the NFU, criticized the fund as 'inadequate.' Saskatoon *Star Phoenix,* 15 March 1972.

Leo A. Johnson

teaches in the Department of History at the University of Waterloo

The development of class in Canada in the twentieth century

THERE IS, in all likelihood, no greater point of division between non-Marxist and Marxist intellectuals in North America than that which arises over the definition, importance, and purpose of the study of class. Primary to this division is the degree to which the non-Marxist (or 'liberal') intellectual depends upon the measurement of the subjective attitudes of individuals as his basis of analysis. In contrast, the Marxist measures or defines his categories by the objective relations of those studied. Thus, the liberal when dealing with class uses the subjective perceptions of individuals as his primary conceptual framework, and tends to downgrade or dismiss external objective criteria; while the Marxist, beginning with his objective criteria for class, assumes a direct relationship between the objective condition of individuals and their conscious understanding and activity – an expectation which, in the short run at least, is frequently disappointed. While it can be argued that neither basis for analysis automatically creates a distorted or useless perspective, it is important to recognize that serious misconceptions about the development of class in Canada have occurred in the conclusions of both groups and that these are the result of weaknesses in their methodological approach.

Class, to the North American liberal intellectual, relates primarily to the subjective rank-recognition of an individual's status held by his peers.[1] Thus the categories that have been developed within this framework (essentially, upper, middle and lower class) offer little basis for the analysis of problems which reach beyond the world of ideas, attitudes, and ideology. The liberal scholar is likely to be little concerned with long-range understanding of why certain social or economic phenomena (such as revolutions) occur, but rather contents himself with the investigation of short-term activities of groups (for example, voting), to which investigations of the consciousness or attitudes of individuals in them has generally provided satisfactory answers. Where more profound or searching questions are raised, the liberal intellectual's response traditionally has been to examine the correlations between material conditions and personal attributes of individuals (especially attitudes towards work) and to assume that the latter have caused the former. Only occasionally has this view been seriously challenged by radical scholars such as C. Wright Mills and Gabriel Kolko.[2]

Moreover, concentration on the consciousness of individuals has tended to create a strong emphasis on 'culture' as a causative factor in social behaviour. Since in North America there exists a great degree of superficial cultural homogeneity at least at the level of the consumption of, and a general conditioned desire for, mass-produced material goods, social analyses which incorporate as a primary input such generally shared subjective characteristics naturally fail to find significant class differentiations among social groups or individuals; and class as an analytical tool, therefore, has had little intellectual, social, or political value.

To a Marxist scholar, however, class carries a precise definition which relates, not to the attitudes of individuals, but to their external material relationships centred on those created by the productive process. Thus class definitions and relations differ between societies where the means and modes of production are different.[3] In a capitalist society, it is argued, three fundamental relationships to the means of production exist: the capitalist class or bourgeoisie, who own the means of production and purchase the labour power of others to operate it; the petite bourgeoisie or independent commodity producers, such as farmers and craftsmen, who both own and operate their means of production; and the proletariat who do not own their means of production and therefore are required to sell their capacity to work – that is, their labour power – in the market place. Marx recognized that in any society such divisions are never so clear cut or all-inclusive. Thus special-interest and functional social groupings which cut across class lines or existed in an adjunct or parasitic relationship to the main classes (such as white collar 'clients' of the bourgeoisie, or the demoralized 'lumpen-proletariat') were deemed worthy of analysis as well.[4] Moreover, Marxists have always recognized that while an individual may objectively belong to one class, subjectively he may suffer from 'false consciousness' and behave as though he belonged to another and therefore act in ways which in fact injure himself and his class peers.

This concentration on the individual's relationship to the means of production stems from the Marxist idea that the farther a worker is from control of his means of production, the greater is his alienation, and consequently the greater will be his potential for revolution and the attainment of the socialist state. Moreover, Marx's studies concluded that in a capitalist society there were certain inherent class antagonisms and relationships which made the ultimate collapse of the capitalist system a certainty. What must be emphasized, however, and what has frequently been forgotten by leftists, is that Marx concerned himself with the general analysis of the process of change and revolution within capitalist society, and not with the description or prediction of particular historical developments or the individual strategies that revolutionary groups would be required to undertake to meet the unique social and political formations of their own society.

The development of Marxist theory occurred within the context of what was perhaps the most vigorous intellectual debate of the nineteenth century. No scholar investigating the development of Marxist thought can fail to be impressed by the diversity of approach, concern for sources, factual accuracy, and scientific approach, and the spirited and self-critical debate which hammered out the central themes of Marxist thought over the four decades prior to the publication of *Capital*.[5] Unfortunately, when one looks back over Canada's political and intellectual history there is little evidence on the Canadian left of the deep concern for factual accuracy, indigenous theoretical elaboration, and insight into the unique circumstances of national class development which has characterized European Marxist thought. In most cases the little intellectual work that has been undertaken is devoted almost entirely to polemics rather than analysis.[6]

The failure of Canadian Marxists to recognize fundamental differences in the origins and development of class and class relations in Canada from those in Europe (and more recently Asia) has resulted in serious errors in both analysis and political leadership. In particular, lack of indigenous analysis has led to a failure of the left's 'time sense'; that is, even when Canadian developments have paralleled classical models, the left has failed to recognize the precise degree or stage in the development of the paradigm. As a result of these failures, political leadership of Canadian Marxists has been almost uniformly disastrous – indeed, for the most part it has consisted of little more than seizing upon any spontaneous unrest that may arise, proclaiming it 'the Revolution,' and leading it into direct conflict or confrontation with the dominant social forces where it either has been crushed or has collapsed when the short-term conditions have been alleviated. As a result, left leadership is generally and rightfully distrusted in Canada by the very classes whose interests it desires to serve. In this circumstance, most Marxists in Canada have betrayed the first principle of the Marxist intellectual tradition – to be 'scientific': to know the facts, and to understand events within the particular historical context of their occurrence.

A second serious consequence of the left's neglect of analysis is the lack of a firm basis from which to criticize the various faddish and superficial theories that appear in the academic community. Thus we are confronted with 'youth as class,' 'worker as an objectively reactionary force,' 'the sexually repressed middle class as proto-fascists,' and simple-minded responses, pro and con, on the question of Canadian nationalism. Since the main questions regarding class in Canada have seldom been asked, let alone answered, the left in Canada has become the victim, just as liberal intellectuals have, of a situation where all ideas about class are equally plausible, and where statements about class are reduced either to the level of opinions and ideology, or to facile applications of analytical models drawn from foreign and historically different circumstances.

This article is both a response to the situation and a challenge to other socialists and Marxists to begin the process of indigenous analysis and criticism which has proved so fruitful in the development of correct analysis and successful political strategy elsewhere. Since the investigation is in its initial stages, few comments about political strategy will be offered, although the facts themselves suggest major criticisms of both 'new' and 'old' left positions.

The reader should be aware of two considerations relating to the statistics cited in the pages that follow. First, the Dominion Bureau of Statistics and the Taxation Department (the two main sources) do not use the same definitions of occupation, and consequently disparities in numbers exist in reference sources. Since the purpose of this work is to establish historical tendencies rather than absolute conditions, the discrepancy between sources provides no serious problem – particularly since both sources yield results showing identical tendencies. Secondly, it must be remembered that a study covering forty years embraces two generations. To the casual reader processes of impoverishment or proletarianization occurring over that long a period may seem to occur with great rapidity and drama, whereas in real life the process may be so slow (1 or 2 per cent per year) that the individual being impoverished may experience no more than a growing malaise, a sense of uneasiness, or a feeling of helplessness.

Finally, it must be remembered that the political activist who draws his knowledge of impoverishment and exploitation and his perception of the need for major social change from statistics rather than from the direct experience of those processes runs the risk of describing them in a language of such force, drama, and sweeping importance that the very people of whom he is talking fail to recognize their own lives and life experiences in his words. The finest analysis is pointless if it is not faithfully presented to and fully understood by those whom it was designed to benefit.

THE PETITE BOURGEOISIE

In Canada, historically, the petite bourgeoisie has been comprised of two groups, the independent commodity producers such as farmers, fishermen, and craftsworkers, and the small bourgeois businessmen, such as retailers, independent salesmen, and rentiers.

Social and political history

During the early part of the nineteenth century, Canada's history was dominated by the struggles of the farmers and small businessmen – the classical petite bourgeoisie – against the domination of aristocratic elements such as the Family Compact and Château Clique. By 1848 with the granting of responsible government and the introduction of elective local government, most of the ideals of these groups had been achieved. Of course, the landless agricultural workers were still disenfranchised, as were the poorer proletarian urban elements, but the more prosperous crafts workers and skilled tradesmen –

in the words of the period, those who had 'a stake in society' – had been accommodated.

While certain 'radical' elements such as the Clear Grit and Rouge parties continued to argue for universal or household franchise, such an ideal was clearly opposed to the interests of the petite bourgeoisie and labour aristocracy, and was strongly rejected for many years by all enfranchised groups.

By the 1870s, however, a cloud had begun to cover their peaceful horizon. The development of a capitalist mode of production and distribution with the resultant destruction of the small local manufacturing and distribution centres, and the growing tendency towards monopoly control of prices, tariffs, freight and interest rates, began to force the independent commodity producers to find means of defending their interests against the growing power of the large capitalists.

At the same time, the crafts workers also were coming under attack by the new capitalist mode of production. By 1872, consciousness of their own interests produced the first major concerted effort to win better working terms by the creation of organizations such as the Toronto Trades Assembly and the Nine Hours League, as well as Canada's first labour-oriented newspaper.[7] By the 1880s, the capitalist mode of production, which utilized large amounts of unskilled labour, had begun to make significant inroads in the ranks of skilled crafts workers, and ancient and respected crafts such as shoemakers (the Sons of St Crispin as they styled themselves) were in serious decay.[8]

As might be expected, the two groups most affected by the new capitalism discovered that they shared a common interest in combining against monopoly, centralization of production and distribution, and the competition of cheap labour. As a result of their common problems and their similar position in the economic structure, which at least provided them with common enemies, the monopolists and bankers, from 1870 to the present there is a recurring pattern of alliances between farmers and better paid workers, either as third party movements or as advanced wings of one of the 'old' parties. In the nineteenth century these groups tended to support the Macdonald Conservative party and, in the twentieth, the King Liberals.

Since both old parties generally placed the interests of capitalists and big businessmen ahead of those of the farmers and workers, the latter found themselves forced at times of extreme stress to undertake a long series of third party and extra-parliamentary strategies. Surprisingly, the literature concerning these groups almost entirely fails to recognize both the continuity of leadership between them, and the fact that the central issues which spurred their creation stemmed from a single problem – the deterioration of their status in the developing capitalist economy. Thus, the Nine Hours movement, the Grange, Patrons of Industry, the progressive farm-labour alliances of the 1920s, and the Social Credit and CCF parties in 1930s and 1940s represented the interests of farmers and workers as they attempted to defend themselves against the erosion of their position.

Over the years, as the two old parties competed with each other and the third party groups for support, considerable concessions were made to working class elements, who gradually were granted the franchise and a degree of protection from the grosser sorts of exploitation and poverty in exchange for their votes.

Since the purpose of these concessions was to win working class support for existing economic, political, and ideological positions, they were usually made before demands for improved social justice by working class elements had lead to the growth of class consciousness. Only in the First World War and the depression did exploitation and hardship develop to the point where consciousness of the working class emerged – only to be undermined by Mackenzie King's recognition of the dangers it presented, by his introduction of social legislation designed to reduce tension, and the vigorous repression of radical leadership.

As a result of these historical social and political developments working class elements traditionally have entered the political arena on terms and conditions set by the on-going struggle between the petite bourgeois and capitalist classes. It would appear that so long as this struggle holds centre stage, and no great political or economic errors are made by the capitalist protagonists, the growth of working class consciousness will be slow – particularly when a minority of strongly unionized and highly paid workers enjoy a standard of living conducive to property ownership, a high standard of commodity consumption, and the attainment of other externals of petit bourgeois status. It is in the light of these understandings that one should consider the significance of the current stage of decline of the petite bourgeoisie.

Over the past forty years, the petite bourgeoisie has come under more extreme pressure. As a result they have declined both in income and numbers relative to the general population. Statistics provided by the Department of National Revenue single out five groups of petite bourgeois which provide an insight into the rapidity of their decline as a significant class. As Table 1 points out, these groups in 1968 (farmers, fishermen, independent businessmen, investors, and self-employed salesmen) not only realized little income from their capital investment, but their earned income was below average as well. As a result of their decline in prosperity relative to that of the general society their numbers have shown a marked decline in relative numbers from 14.7 per cent of income earners in 1948 to 10.9 per cent of earners in 1968 – a loss of over 25 per cent in just twenty years.

TABLE 1

The independent petite bourgeoisie, 1948-68[9]

	1948	1958	1968
Total income earners	3662,030	5530,496	8495,184
Total petite bourgeoisie	559,480	731,481	928,713
Petite bourgeoisie as a percentage of all earners	14.7%	13.3%	10.9%
Average income: all earners	$2091.30	$3299.75	$4918.00
Average income: petite bourgeoisie	2518.80	3659.20	4601.90
Petite bourgeoisie income (1949 dollars)	2596.70	2925.00	2965.10
Petite bourgeoisie income as a percentage of average	120%	111%	94%

The independent commodity producers

Among the independent commodity producers, the farmers have been particularly hard hit. The decline in numbers of independent farmers is not, of course, a new story. While the number of occupied farm units in Canada increased in Canada as a whole between 1901 and 1941, this increase came almost entirely from the expansion of agriculture into unsettled areas of the Prairies and British Columbia. In the long-settled areas, a decline in number of farm units was already under way as early as 1901-11 in the Atlantic region.[10] Over the years the decline has accelerated as competition and the rapid expansion of capital investment in agriculture have forced the weak or undercapitalized farm out of business.

One cause of the reduction in the number of occupied farms is the rapid growth in size of farm units. This increase in size of units has occurred in all areas, but has been especially pronounced in the prairies. But farmers in the Atlantic region experienced great changes in the 1951-61 period, when the number of occupied farms dropped by 47.6 per cent while average size increased from 112 to 168 acres.[11]

Along with decline in numbers and increase in farm size, significant changes in patterns of ownership have occurred also. In the areas under greatest economic stress, the Atlantic and Prairie regions, absentee ownership, generally corporate, has made significant inroads. By 1961, fully 42 per cent of all Prairie farms were absentee-owned. In contrast in Quebec, Ontario, and British Columbia owner-occupied farms remained a high proportion of all units.[12]

Related directly to the rapid decrease in numbers of farm units and increase in unit size is a rapid increase in capitalization and decrease in farm employ-

TABLE 2

Farm income, 1948-68[13]

	1948	1958	1968
Number of farmers	190,090	205,331	291,553
Farmers as a percentage of all earners	5.19%	3.71%	3.43%
Average income of farmers	$1619.81	$2234.13	$3244.36
Farmer income (1949 dollars)	1669.91	1785.88	2090.44
Farm income as a percentage of average	78%	68%	66%

ment. Thus while there has been only a slight increase in acreage cultivated between 1931 and 1961, farm capitalization has increased by almost 450 per cent. At the same time the farm labour force has declined by almost 50 per cent. With the over-all growth in the labour force, the agricultural sector has declined drastically from 28.79 per cent in 1931 to 10.23 per cent in 1961.[14]

Over the years, economists and government officials have justified the decimation of agricultural workers and farm owners on the grounds that higher capitalization and larger farms would lead to increased productivity and a higher standard of living for farmers. As Table 2 demonstrates, farmers have responded by increasing capitalization from 4 billion dollars in 1931 to more than 19 billion in 1961. Moreover, farm productivity, measured in persons supplied with food and fibre per farm worker has tripled in the same period, from 11 per farm worker in 1935 to 31 in 1962.[15] Despite this enormously increased investment and productivity, farm incomes are falling farther below average. Although the per capita purchasing power of farmers increased by about 20 per cent between 1948 and 1968, this increase was less than one-half the average gain of other income earners. As Table 2 points out, farm incomes declined from 78 per cent to 66 per cent of average. Thus, while productivity increased by 60 per cent between 1948 and 1958, income increased by only 5 per cent.

Moreover, farmers as well as consumers are exploited by the monopoly situation which exists in the food processing and distribution industry. As a result, an increasing share of the consumer's dollar is going to the agribusiness middlemen. Because the farmer is economically vulnerable in comparison to the corporate giants who buy his products, he continues to fall farther and farther behind other sectors in income, despite increased investment and productivity.[16]

A major result of the abandonment and consolidation of farm units and the rise of absentee agribusiness has been the creation of an underclass of dispos-

TABLE 3

Source of income of farmers, 1948-68[17]
(percentages)

	Farmers with taxable incomes		Farmers with non-taxable incomes	
	Farming	Wages & salaries	Farming	Wages & salaries
1948	91.1	4.3	90.6	5.1
1958	82.3	8.5	83.1	8.9
1968	76.2	11.0	64.6	20.0

sessed rural dwellers. The rural dispossessed (those who have been forced off their farms) now make up one-third of the population of the Maritimes.[18] Moreover, not only are the non-farm rural Maritime residents maintained through additions from the farm sector, but their average age is declining rapidly, indicating that they are likely to be a permanent feature of maritime society and economy.[19] While economists have attempted to justify the forced reduction in size of farm numbers by their economic claims of increased income for those farmers remaining, they have ignored entirely the hardships experienced by those forced from the land who are either incapable of making the transition to urban living, or who, because of their lack of skills, are incapable of being absorbed in the urban economy. Thus, just as nineteenth-century government policy created a labouring class in Canada, so twentieth century policies have helped bring into existence an under-class of dispossessed farmers.[20]

Not only have the remaining farmers undergone a process of relative impoverishment – and for those who are forced off the farms, proletarianization – but even those who have remained on the farm have experienced a severe erosion of status. As their income from farming falls farther and farther below average, farmers are forced to turn more and more to wage labour in an attempt to maintain their standard of living. Of course, as Table 3 demonstrates, the lower income farmers are subjected to this process to a greater degree than are those with higher incomes; however, both income groups are clearly undergoing the same process. Thus, even those farmers who retain ownership of their farms have lost much of their cherished independence.

Perhaps the most dramatic example of an independent commodity producing group who have declined to the level of the proletariat is provided by the recent strike of fishermen at Canso, Mulgrove and Petit de Grat, Nova Scotia. In spite of a long and historic tradition of rugged individualism, the rise to dominance of a few powerful fish processors and competition from floating foreign fish factories had so eroded the fishermen's independence, that by the 1960s, their legal and historical description of co-adventurers had become a mockery of their poverty. Working sixteen hours a day, twelve days in each two-week cycle, their incomes were as little as $2500 a year. Meanwhile, Nova Scotia's archaic labour laws continued to class them not as employees but as small entrepreneurs in partnership with the dominant companies and hence not eligible for the legal protection of union certification. Thus it became necessary for the fishermen and their families to fight a bitter seven-month strike in order to win the legal rights of other proletarianized groups.[21]

The independent petite bourgeoisie

Other independent sectors of the petite bourgeoisie are undergoing processes of impoverishment and proletarianization similar to those experienced by the farmers. As Tables 4 and 5 demonstrate, the process of relative impoverishment is not as far advanced among other sectors of the petite bourgeoisie as among the farmers. As Table 6 demonstrates, independent businessmen and salesmen are experiencing the same process of proletarianization that occurred among farmers still owning their independent means of production. With their numbers reduced from their numerical and political dominance of the 1850s to a mere 10.9 per cent of income earners in 1968, it is clear that the whole petite bourgeoisie is reaching the last stages of destruction. Little remains of their former power except their myths and ideals, which are perpetuated by the major capitalists and independent professionals as the first line of defence against those who would question the legitimacy of private ownership of the means of production.

It would be difficult to over-estimate the economic and historical significance of the destruction of the independent petite bourgeoisie and in particular of the independent commodity producers. For the past century, Canada's history has been shaped by their losing struggle against the maturing capitalist economy. During this period the consciousness of the emerging proletariat has been dominated by the 'progressive' and 'populist' idealism of the petite bourgeoisie, and has, again and again, been diverted from its own best interests into a struggle for goals appropriate only to a 'respectable' class of property owners. On the only two occasions when working class people acquired sufficient autonomy of vision to make their own demands and to undertake strategies which seemed to contain the possibility of the attainment of a classless society (in 1919 in the One Big Union and the general strike, and in the 1930s with the rise of the Communist party of Canada), the workers found their erstwhile allies, the petite bourgeoisie, lined up solidly with the capitalists against them in a strategy of state repression. Given the numerical predominance of the petite bourgeoisie at those points in time, as well as the high level of their conscious class self-interest, the likelihood of a working class triumph was very

TABLE 4

Business operators' incomes, 1948-68[22]

	1948	1958	1968
Total income earners	3662,030	5530,496	8495,184
Total business operators	241,770	301,070	351,621
Percentage of all income earners	6.6%	5.4%	4.1%
Average income of business operators	$2951.80	$4031.00	$5166.90
Average income (1949 dollars)	$3043.10	$3301.50	$3329.20
Average business operators' income as a percentage of average income	141%	129%	105%

TABLE 5

Independent salesmen's incomes, 1948-68[23]

	1948	1958	1968
Total income earners	3662,030	5530,496	8495,184
Total independent salesmen	29,010	63,323	25,274
Percentage of all income earners	0.8%	1.1%	0.3%
Average income of independent salesmen	$3291.90	$4674.10	$5957.80
Real average income (1949 dollars)	$3393.70	$3736.30	$3383.80
Average independent salesmen's income as a percentage of average income	157%	142%	121%

TABLE 6

Source of income: farmers and retail traders, 1948-68[24]
(percentages)

	Farmers		Retail traders	
	Farming	Wages & salaries	Business income	Wages & salaries
1948	90.9	4.6	—	—
1958	82.7	8.7	83.6	8.3
1968	73.4	12.8	78.5	12.0

small. Therefore a socialist strategy which drew its analysis from the European experience and concentrated on politics and confrontation tactics rather than social development would appear to have been badly timed, unless significant sectors of the petite bourgeoisie could have been persuaded to join the workers in a socialist revolution.

With the decline of the petite bourgeoisie, a completely new situation has arisen in Canada. First of all the triumph of the capitalist in this century-long struggle with the petite bourgeoisie means that the essential class composition of Canadian society has been greatly simplified. In a situation where some 83 per cent of Canadians depend upon wages and salaries for their income, the loyalty of the majority of the population to the principle of private ownership of the means of production must be greatly weakened. Thus, traditional appeals to the working class and classical strategies which were inappropriate in the Canadian class situation in 1920 or 1940 may now take on a new validity as the essential class conflict shifts to one between the working class and the capitalist owner.

Second, while the ideological remnants of the petite bourgeoisie – capitalist struggle are likely to linger on for some time to come (indeed, it is now to the advantage of the capitalist to confuse the situation by the perpetuation of populist and progressive ideals), the significant fact is that the petite bourgeoisie itself can no longer serve effectively as the first line of defence against a genuinely class-conscious working class. Finally, a disillusioned petite bourgeoisie itself can make significant contributions to a socialist revolution, particularly in the early stages. It can be argued, therefore, that the failure of the left in Canada in previous periods should not be explained simply as a failure of analysis and timing. Tactics and theoretical analysis which may be valid for a struggle between capital and labour should not be discarded out of hand simply because they failed at a time when the major conflict was occurring between the petite bourgeoisie and the capitalist class. Rather, they must be re-examined within the context of Canadian society and history and be accepted, modified, or rejected as they appear useful in the changing Canadian context.

THE CAPITALIST CLASS

The structure of capitalism in Canada

More than a decade ago, a brilliant husband-and-wife team, L.C. and F.W. Park, wrote a remarkable book, *The Anatomy of Big Business,* which has been entirely ignored by Canadian academics. Their work is a detailed, well-documented study of capitalism in Canada which points out the class relations and corporate ties that bind together the small group of big businessmen that control the Canadian economy.

Commenting on the importance of the concentration of ownership and control of the major means of production in Canada, the Parks argued that: 'The power of the [big businessmen] is a class power, that this group, the most important sector of the ruling class, own the means of production in Canada and their power is based on this ownership.

'Now the means of production are in fact owned by ... the handful of giant corporations, [but] corporations also have owners, and in the last analysis, after stripping away the holding companies that complicate the picture, the financial groups in control of the corporations control them on the basis of owning a controlling interest ...

'Those who own the controlling interest generally do not manage the corporations they control. Managers can be hired – and fired ... The fact that the controlling group may play a smaller role in active management does not mean that their power over the corporation and their managers is less. The power remains and is exercised whenever big decisions have to be made.'[25]

Over the years, a number of lists have been prepared naming the major capitalists in the country.[26] While authors have given lists of various lengths (from a high of 922 down to the proverbial 50), all authors agree that a very small group of men control the main components (industrial and financial) of the economy, and that they are linked together in complex patterns of intercorporate ownerships, cross directorships, and social relations.

In Canada, the central institutions of capitalist control are the network of banks, trust companies, and insurance companies which accumulate the savings of the ordinary citizen into vast pools of money which are made available to the industrial and investment interests of the bank directors and corporate owners. The largest of these networks, the Bank of Montreal–Royal Trust–Sun Life–CPR–Steel Company of Canada group,[27] controls assets of more than 20 billion dollars – an amount equal to more than one-fifth of Canada's annual gross national product.[28] As Ashley pointed out in 1957, the thirty directors of the Bank of Montreal held among them more than 220 corporate directorships. Similarly, the twenty directors of the Royal Bank held 240 corporate directorships including 12 in Montreal Trust; twenty-two directors of the Canadian Bank of Commerce held 225 directorships including 7 in National Trust; and twenty directors of the Bank of Nova Scotia held 220 directorships including 5 in Eastern Trust.[29]

A second method of approaching the activities and relations of the capitalist class is that used by John Porter. Porter's method consisted of an examination of the boards of directors of the 183 'dominant' corporations - those manufacturing establishments employing more than 500 workers in 1952.

According to this method of examination: 'The [Canadian] economic elite, then, consists of the 922 individuals who hold the 1,317 directorships. Of these, 203 individuals, about 22 percent, hold more than one directorship in the dominant corporations. Most of them of course hold directorships in other corporations which are not classified as dominant. The 203 who hold more than one directorship hold altogether 598 (or 45.3 percent) of all directorships. The largest number of directorships [in dominant corporations] is ten (E.P. Taylor).'[30]

Porter demonstrates the significance of banks and major insurance companies as central elements in the concentration of economic power. Especially striking are the large number of interconnections held by directors of the Bank of Montreal, Royal Bank, and the Bank of Commerce. They hold 200 of the 297 directorships on the dominant corporations and 34 of the 55 directorships on the largest Canadian insurance companies.[31]

Similarly, the Sun Life, Mutual Life, and Confederation Life insurance companies held central positions, their directors holding 107 of the 188 directorships in leading corporations held by directors of Canadian-owned insurance companies. Such a concentration of power in six financial corporations is made even more impressive when one remembers these corporate directors meet together on the boards of directors of their innumerable smaller industrial interests as well.[32]

These groupings are not accidental or impermanent. For example, an examination of the directorships held by the directors of the Bank of Montreal in 1968 shows that the degree of interconnection between the major components of the Bank of Montreal network has, if anything, increased. In addition, the network has been widened to include several other important corporations. A similar situation exists among the other banks.

Not only have the corporate networks spread, but their assets have greatly increased over the years. The values of assets of the major banks have grown enormously between 1951 and 1971.[33] This vast increase, in both greater concentration and asset value, has meant that greater and greater power over the economy has been acquired by the corporate directors.

A crucial element in the rapid growth of assets of the major capitalists has been the absence of a capital gains tax in Canada.[34] In Canada, the wealthy can escape the effects of high personal income tax by not paying corporate profits out of the treasury to the dividend holders. Thus a 'growth-oriented' bank like the Bank of Nova Scotia paid out only 50 per cent of its net profits after corporation taxes in 1971, while other banks tended to pay out about two-thirds of their profits.[35] By exploiting tax laws in this way, the Bank of Nova Scotia increased its assets by 711 per cent between 1951 and 1971, from $874,000,000 to $7,085,000,000.

TABLE 7

Percentage of all shares held by income level, 1948-68[36]

	Percentage of all shares		
	1948	1958	1968
Top 1% of all income earners	57	51	42
96th to 99th percentile of income earners	21	21	20
91st to 95th percentile of income earners	5	7	10
Total, top decile of income earners	83	79	72
9th decile of income earners	4.6	5.4	6.8
6th, 7th and 8th decile of income earners	1.9	4.9	11.4
Total, 6th-9th deciles	6.5	10.3	18.2
Bottom 50% of income earners	10.5	10.7	9.8

Over the past sixty years the vast growth of wealth and concentration of power in the capitalist class has been reflected in the enormous increase in economic power wielded by certain individuals. Whereas in 1913, the most significant capitalist was Senator Robert McKay who held directorships in corporations whose assets totalled $1,600,000,000, by 1957 standards he would not have ranked in the top 100. In that year the corporate director who ranked one hundredth on the list was Norman Dawes with directorships controlling assets of $2,200,000,000, while first place was held by Charles Dunning of the Bank of Montreal network with directorships of $10,800,000,000[37] - a total now surpassed by every director of Canada's three major banks.

Not only does corporate control rest in the hands of a very few powerful men, but the most ownership of shares, and the resultant benefits of dividends and capital gains go to a limited number of individuals as well. In 1968 for example, 1311 wealthy individuals owned among them $1,156,540,000 in shares, or about 9 per cent of all shares held in Canada - an amount equivalent to that owned by the 4,000,000 lowest income earners in the country.[38]

As Table 7 shows, over the past twenty years there has been a broadening of shareholding among upper income groups (in the 6th to 9th deciles) and a decline in the proportion of shares held by both the top ten per cent and bottom half of income earners. It would appear that, during a period when independent ownership has become less and less viable, those who would formerly have aspired to an independent petit bourgeois status have made an attempt to maintain an element of participation in the capitalist sector of the economy by acquisition of stock in the giant corporations. During a period of a shortage of technical and managerial skills when wages and salaries were high, this acquisition of shares undoubtedly gave them a sense of ownership and status otherwise denied to them. It should be noted that industrial giants such as Bell Telephone have taken great care to cater to these attitudes among its employees, hoping to improve employee performance by encouraging them to purchase a few shares each through salary deductions and incentives. Finally, it should be noted that only a very small proportion of Canadians own shares. In 1968, only 870,852 out of 8,495,184 income earners (10.3 per cent) possessed so much as one share.[39] Thus the vast majority of the benefits of capital gains go to the few wealthy shareholders.

In terms of power over the economy, the extreme concentration of share ownership in the top 1 per cent of income earners allows almost total control – not merely because of the huge proportion directly owned, but because a high degree of concentration in a few hands permits easy organization of those shares for decision-making purposes.

Canadian capitalism and imperialist development

No change in the state of the Canadian bourgeoisie has as much significance, or is likely to have such important long-range effects, as the take-over of the Canadian economy by the American-based multinational corporation. For the parent corporation the take-over of the Canadian means of production satisfied three main needs: the defence and expansion of the capitalist system; the creation of a stable corporate monopoly free from the uncertainties of the market place; and a field for profitable investment of capital.[40] By 1969 about 8700 Canadian concerns were controlled by non-residents, and foreign capital was invested directly or indirectly in some 12,000 Canadian concerns. In all, 74 per cent of petroleum and natural gas, 65 per cent of mining and smelting, and 57 per cent of manufacturing were foreign-controlled. In 1969, foreign residents owned assets in Canada valued at 46.9 billion dollars.[41] In the same year, total share capital held by Canadian private individuals was about 14.0 billion dollars.[42]

While it is perfectly understandable that foreign corporations would want to take over control of Canadian industry and natural resources, it is perhaps not so clear why Canadian businessmen would so eagerly co-operate in this process. It is not until one examines the corporate ideology of the Canadian businessman, the assumptions he accepts, and his economic interests that some understanding appears.

As the Parks said of the Canadian businessman: 'It is not in terms of their birth or citizenship that [they] are un-Canadian but in terms of their outlook ... The problem and source of danger to the future of Canada lie in the fact that those who control the key sectors of the economy have taken as their premise that US capital is and will be dominant, that Canadian development is necessarily subordinate to and dependent on ("integrated with") the drive of us groups for their own benefit.'[43] Even a casual glance through *Industrial Canada*, the monthly journal of the Canadian Manufacturers Association, is enough to convince oneself of the accuracy of the Parks' statement.

Gerard Filion, president of Marine Industries Ltd. (controlled by the Simard family of Quebec), vice-president of the General Investment Corporation of Quebec (the provincially funded development corporation), and 1971 president of the Canadian Manufacturers Association, demonstrated his complete acceptance of the dominance of the multinational corporation in his inaugural speech, 'Multi-national corporations are a phenomenon of the contemporary economy; they are here to stay and it is necessary to adjust to this fact ... It isn't all that important that multinational corporations control large industrial, commercial and financial holdings in Canada.'[44]

Norris R. Crump, chairman of cpr, director of the Bank of Montreal, International Nickel, Mutual Life, and seventeen other corporations, demonstrated how little interest most major Canadian capitalists have in Canadian economic unity when he addressed the same meeting. Crump demanded substantial changes in Canadian tariff and economic policies whose results would have the effect, in his words, of: '(1) Increasing the attractiveness of imported manufactured goods in Western Canada and the Maritimes; (2) Allowing Quebec and Ontario to integrate their economies more fully into the heartland of North America, so reducing their dependence on Western and Maritime markets; (3) Permitting Canada, particularly Western Canada, to integrate more fully with the Pacific Rim countries [i.e. Japan], which are more and more becoming their natural trading partners.'[45]

These businessmen's attitudes to the exploitation of the natural resources of Canada and the underdeveloped nations was couched in the full-blown rhetoric of the multinational ideology. As Gerard Filion expressed it: 'We are witnessing a new phenomenon in the world economy, that is the internationalization of raw materials. Heretofore, countries were rich because they possessed coal, iron ore, wood, cereals, or water power. This is no longer the case today. Japan has demonstrated that a country's chief natural resource is the brains of its managing class and the ability of its workers. The internationalization of raw materials is an advantageous phenomenon for the world economy as a whole. Every measure aimed at restricting the export of raw materials from countries that have them in abundance to those who do not counter to the general prosperity of humanity and peace between nations and men.'[46] That the 'internationalization' of raw materials is a one-way street from the poor to the rich countries appears to have escaped Mr Filion's attention.

R. Rea Jackson, Chairman of Socony Mobile Oil Company, speaking to the us National Military–Industrial Conference in 1958 was much more explicit.

In discussing the growing strategic crisis created for American capitalism by the rapidly depleting reserves of crucial metals, oil, and energy, Jackson pointed out that: 'In the old days, a country faced with such a shortage of materials would simply have moved out and grabbed colonies, under some pretext or other ... Our tradition, or at least a healthy part of our tradition, is the policy of asking for an "open door" for trade.'[47] The chief difficulty facing the US in the acquisition of raw materials by the 'open door' method was the nationalism of the countries owning them.[48] As the conclusions of the Military-Industrial Conference pointed out, to the US, 'Strategy means "the mobilization, integration, and prudent management of the political, economic, educational, technological, industrial, scientific, cultural, ideological, and spiritual resources of the entire nation." '[49] Corporate internationalism offers a crucial ideological weapon in breaking down national resistance to American acquisition of the needed raw materials. Its acceptance by the major Canadian capitalists creates a most serious threat to Canada's autonomy and, ultimately, the welfare of its citizens.

The fact that Canadian businessmen accept the ideology of corporate internationalism is not merely the result of a triumph of American propaganda. Rather, it is a reflection of their personal and corporate interests and goals as well. While a good deal is known and written about the huge degree of American ownership of Canadian industry and raw materials - the Parks, Kari Levitt, Mel Watkins, and others have made excellent contributions to that field of study[50] - much less is known of the relationships of Canadian capitalists to American capital.

Among Marxists and socialists it is often argued that Canadian capitalists are simply servants and front-men for American economic imperialism. But, in reality, the relationship is much more complex. Study suggests that a few Canadian capitalists are, at least temporarily, still members of a national bourgeoisie with few or no ties to foreign capital or business activities. Others, the majority, are deeply involved in multinational corporate business either as dependent businessmen engaged as suppliers or distributors of American goods and technology or managers of American corporate activities in Canada. A final group, again a minority, have reached the status of multinational capitalists themselves where they operate independently or as partners of other multinational interests. For the latter two groups American multinational corporate ideology serves not merely as a strategic weapon for American capitalism, but provides Canadian businessmen with an explanation and justification of their current activities and provides a goal and model for their future.[51]

Perhaps the best example of the Canadian capitalists who have achieved partnership with foreign capital at the international level is that provided in 1970 by the creation of the 'Orion' group of financial corporations owned jointly by American, British, German and Canadian banking interests – Chase Manhattan Corporation, National Westminster Bank, Westdeutsche Landsbank, and Royal Bank respectively. The function of the Orion group is to finance and manage multinational expansion in the Third World. With such enormous assets behind it (the parent banks possessed 58.7 billion dollars in assets in 1970[52]), undoubtedly it will quickly make its presence felt.

The significance of Orion's creation for Canadian capitalists lies in the fact that, at the top, multinational ideology serves their interests as much as it does those of American, Japanese, French, or German capitalists. Thus at the level of Lord Thompson of Fleet with his world-wide newspaper and television empire, E.P. Taylor, and Garfield Weston with the British and Canadian commodity cartels (which are now expanding rapidly in the United States), and Noah Timmins with his vast resource holdings, Canada has become merely a geographic location, among many, where they do business. Lesser capitalists such as the Simards, Stephen Roman, or R.A. Brown, Jr,[53] with aspirations of moving up to the multinational level, see amalgamation of their holdings with existing multinational corporations as the quickest method of reaching that level. Major Canadian capitalists do not, however, relate to national or multinational capital at a single level. They may at one time direct or manage a wholly owned American subsidiary in Canada, direct the activities of a Canadian-owned multinational corporation, and own or control one or more Canadian businesses which have no multinational interests.

Perhaps the best example of the precise relationship between the major Canadian multinational capitalists and US capital is provided by their opposition to the attempt by Rockefeller interests to expand into Canadian banking through the take-over of the Mercantile Bank. While Canadian bankers had been quite content to oversee and, indeed, to co-operate in the take-over of Canadian industries, and to manage them once they were in American hands, it was quite a different story when the Rockefeller-controlled Citibank threatened to replace them. As the Parks notes: 'The Canadian groups as well as the Canadian government involved are acting within limits defined by their idea of what the traffic will bear. They want the junior partnership and the profits following from it to continue. Any struggles with their US rivals and allies is over the division of profit.'[54]

For the indigenous Canadian capitalist who has not yet entered into multinational operations, economic nationalism and strategies in opposition to the growth of multinationalism may well make good sense, both from the point of personal commitment and a maximization of personal profits. After all, when one's financial and industrial interests are entirely in Canada, a 'buy Canadian' policy is no more than good sense. One must, however, view the nationalistic protestations of these businessmen with a certain amount of reserve since most multinational and foreign-owned corporations were once owned by Canadian capitalists who, like Stephen Roman and R.A. Brown, Jr, saw their opportunity to maximize profits by selling out to foreign capitalists.

The close relationship of government and business in Canada has been too well documented to require more than a comment upon current developments. While the two old parties have always been financed by big businessmen, and important figures in the business world such as C.D. Howe, Louis St Laurent, Mitchell Sharp, Robert Winters, and James Richardson have moved easily from boardroom to cabinet and back, currently even closer ties with business are being created at all levels of government.

Jean Luc Pepin, federal minister of Industry, Trade and Commerce, in his address to the Canadian Manufacturers Association in 1970 made it clear that he attempted to keep himself informed about business and its needs by meeting with as many businessmen and organizations as time permitted, and visiting as many plants as possible in order to get first-hand knowledge of their operations. As he put it, 'politicians and officials are generally quite keen to work with businessmen.'[55]

Pepin, however, stated that under his direction the present government had gone much farther than previous governments had in introducing capitalists into the active creation and implementation of policies within his department. To do this he had created an 'Advisory Council composed of some 40 leading businessmen, representing various sections of industry and geographic regions, with whom my officials and myself meet four times a year. This council is a very useful forum to us and I dare say to members also. Other ministers are setting up similar bodies.

'Representation progressively leads to active participation in the formulation and implementation of policies. In certain cases, we have already reached that objective, either because the evolving situation must be kept under constant review (automobile industry) or because a new strategy of development must be defined (shipbuilding, chemicals, textiles ...)

'Practically all of the operation line branches in my department have their own more or less formal committees or advisory groups.'[56]

It is little wonder, therefore, that the federal government's policies on foreign ownership and multinational dominance reflect the same approving attitudes as those expressed by the multinational Canadian capitalists.

Equally interesting is the newly created civil service training system called Career Assignment Program. Under CAP middle level civil servants are selected for a twelve-week management course then assigned to service in university or business administration for a two-year period on an exchange basis. As Pepin expressed the direction of planned development for CAP, 'Plans are to increase the number of industrial participants to 18 a year by 1971 and to have an

equal number of government employees on assignment in the private sector.'[57]
Thus, the thrust of current government planning is to facilitate the participation of capitalists in government planning and administration by training civil
servants in industrial management techniques, and presumably, providing them
with a better understanding and greater acceptance of the aims, goals, strategies, and ideology of capitalism.

In summary, the Canadian capitalist class consists of a small group of enormously powerful men whose structural relations are undergoing rapid change.
Caught up in the ideology of growth and multinationalism, the small capitalist accepts being swallowed up by a large Canadian or foreign (especially
American) corporation as an inevitable process in which his disappearance as
an autonomous capitalist is compensated for by his participation as a very
junior partner of the very powerful.

The process of consolidation of capitalism is very far advanced, but on a
multinational, not a national, basis. The huge American, British, German,
French, and Japanese capitalist structures all reach into Canada, while a few
equally powerful capitalist structures originating in Canada reach into other
countries. The ideology of multinationalism therefore has Canadian as well as
foreign beneficiaries and advocates. The power of these giants, both foreign
and domestically based, is greatly enhanced by their close association with
government, to say nothing of their ownership and control of the media, university boards of governors and other aspects of the national ideological apparatus. In their search for international economic power, they are quite willing
to accept (and indeed to advocate) the economic dismemberment of Canada
and the rape of raw materials and natural resources.

Any political strategy which is based upon the expectation of an alliance
with a Canadian national bourgeoisie is, I should think, doomed to be disappointed. The major Canadian capitalists are as committed to economic imperialism as their American counterparts, while the small capitalist dreams of
joining their ranks when the time is ripe. Moreover, the low-level branch plant
manager is, at best, a weak reed to lean on. As one observer recently pointed
out, the lower-level manager of the branch plant has no room to manoeuvre.
'He's just like any other piece of equipment in that plant. If he gives too much
trouble, then he's replaced. If he starts stomping around and saying, "Well,
dammit, we're running this show ..." then he's in trouble.'[58]

Finally, it is important to distinguish between the capitalist class, which is
composed of individuals who have names, identities, and individual as well as
class interests, from the productive apparatus (the corporations) which they
control. The enemies of the working class are not the factories, mines, and
transportation systems upon which they labour, but the system of ownership
and exploitation and those individuals who defend it and benefit from its con-

tinuance. Confusion on this point has created a dangerous situation where many young people assume that it is work, itself, which is alienating, not the structure of exploitive and dehumanizing social relations surrounding production in the capitalist system.

THE WORKING CLASSES

As capitalism has grown and developed in Canada, the composition of the labour force has changed in two distinct ways. First, a larger and larger proportion were drawn from pre-capitalist and pre-industrial occupations, such as agriculture and menial labour, into the capitalist labour market and machine-related production, and second, within the capitalist sector itself, changes in composition have occurred. Related to these changes has been the gradual decline of the status and independence of client groups such as the professional occupations.

The most striking aspect of these changes, as pointed out earlier, has been the decline and absorption of the petite bourgeoisie, especially that of the farmers. As Table 8 points out, between 1901 and 1961 farm workers declined from 40.3 per cent of the work force to 10.2 per cent. Equally important was the decline of menial labourers from 7.2 (12.0 in 1911) per cent in 1901 to 5.4 per cent in 1961. In all, therefore, those sectors which were least involved in capitalist production declined from 47.5 per cent of the work force in 1901 to 15.6 per cent in 1961. This drop in proportion has been reflected in the growth of the white collar sector from 15.2 per cent in 1901 to 38.6 per cent in 1961, and of the manual workers, outside the menial labour sub-sector, from 25.0 per cent in 1901 to 29.5 per cent in 1961. Other sectors remained relatively stable during this period.

Apologists for capitalism and technology have fastened upon the phenomenon of the rapid rise of the white collar worker as a major justification for the capitalist system, often arguing that the creation of an enormous class of middle management where status is high and alienation low effectively refutes Marxist assumptions that capitalist modes of production create a huge number of alienating tasks. Some 'futurologists' will go so far as to argue that eventually all menial (blue collar) work will be eliminated and that 'leisure' is the great problem remaining to be solved.[59] Closer analysis of changes within the major sectors as set out by census analysists, however, strongly challenge these assumptions. Moreover, analysis of income distribution suggest that within the past two decades fundamental changes have occurred within the Canadian economy which go far beyond mere occupational redistribution.

Fundamental to an analysis of these changes is the recognition that two sub-categories of labour – farmers and menial labourers – have largely disappeared.

TABLE 8

Total labour force, distributed by major occupational groups, 1901-61[60]
(percentages)

	1901	1911	1921	1931	1941	1951	1961
White collar	15.2	16.8	25.1	24.5	25.2	32.4	38.6
Manual	32.2	36.1	31.3	33.8	33.4	37.7	34.9
Service	8.2	7.7	7.1	9.2	10.5	8.6	10.8
Primary	44.4	39.4	36.3	32.5	30.6	20.1	13.1
Not stated	– –	–	.2	–	.3	1.2	2.6

TABLE 9

Work force distribution outside agricultural and menial labour sectors, 1901-61[61]
(percentages)

	1901	1911	1921	1931	1941	1951	1961
White collar	29.0	31.3	43.6	40.9	37.1	41.9	45.7
Manual or blue collar	47.6	44.9	37.5	37.6	39.9	40.0	35.0
Service	15.6	14.5	12.3	15.4	15.5	11.1	12.8
Primary	7.8	9.6	6.3	6.2	7.1	5.3	3.4
Not stated	–	–	.3	–	.4	1.7	3.1

Since both of these categories are essentially products and remnants of the pre-capitalist mode of production, analysis of the industrial capitalist sector requires an examination of proportional changes with these sectors removed (see Table 9). It is clear from the figures that the great change in composition of the labour force in the capitalist sector occurred in the 1901-21 period when the white collar sector increased from 29.3 per cent to 43.6 per cent of the work force, while the manual sector declined from 47.6 per cent to 37.5 per cent. Between 1921 and 1941 there was a general decline in the white collar sector and an increase in manual sector, which was reversed in the next twenty years. Thus, by 1961, proportions were only slightly changed from what they had been in 1921. Finally, there has been a steady decline in the primary sector even when agriculture is removed.

The white collar sector

Over the past sixty years, the white collar sector has been the most volatile group in the working class, showing both the most rapid over-all growth and the widest fluctuations. Internal analysis of its composition demonstrates the same characteristics, with the most rapid growth occurring in the professional

TABLE 10

White collar sector, proportion when agricultural
and menial labour sectors are removed from the labour force, 1901-61[62]
(percentages)

	1901	1911	1921	1931	1941	1951	1961
Proprietary and managerial	8.2	8.6	12.5	9.4	8.0	9.7	9.4
Professional	8.8	6.9	9.6	10.0	9.8	9.6	11.7
Clerical	6.1	7.1	11.8	11.3	10.6	13.9	15.3
Commercial and financial	5.9	8.7	9.7	10.2	8.7	8.7	9.3
All white collar	29.0	31.3	43.6	40.9	37.1	41.9	45.7

and clerical sectors.[63] As Table 10 shows, however, much of this proportional growth is due to the decline of the pre-capitalist sectors. Once this factor is removed a relatively stable internal distribution appears. When the white collar sector is examined within the industrial capitalist portion of the economy alone, it becomes clear that only the clerical sub-sector has experienced any large degree of growth. While other sectors have grown, they have done so at average or below average rates.

An examination of the changes in internal distribution within the white sector emphasizes the growth of the clerical sector. Made up largely of low-paid female labour (the female proportion of the clerical sub-sector has increased from 22 per cent in 1901 to 61.5 per cent in 1961), the rapid growth of this sub-sector must raise serious questions about the effects of automation on the white collar worker.

In the nineteenth century, the effects of the introduction of new technology was to reduce labour costs by breaking down complex skills into simple repetitive machine-defined tasks. This process required highly skilled technicians and supervisors but eliminated the need for crafts workers with an intermediate level of skills. While workers in the clerical and professional sectors have increased, the proprietary, managerial, commercial, and financial service sectors – the intermediate skill levels – have declined. It would seem, therefore, that the process of proletarianization-through-automation that destroyed the crafts workers in the nineteenth century may be repeated among the white collar workers in the twentieth.

While no useful Canadian study has yet been done which examines the consequences of these changes for Canadian white collar workers, a striking study has been done in the United States by Judson Gooding which suggests the direction which developments in Canada are likely to take. As Gooding points out, the most important consequence of the automation of office work has been a deep-seated and growing alienation among white collar workers: 'These workers – clerks, accountants, bookkeepers, secretaries – were once the elite at every plant, the educated people who worked alongside the bosses and were happily convinced that they made all the wheels go around. Now there are platoons of them instead of a privileged few, and instead of talking to the boss they generally communicate with a machine.

'The jobs are sometimes broken down into fragmented components, either for the convenience of those machines or so that the poorly educated graduates of big-city high schools can perform them. Despite their air-conditioned, carpeted offices – certainly the most lavish working quarters ever provided employees in mass – the sense of distance and dissociation from management has increased sharply, and the younger white collars are swept by some of the same restlessness and cynicism that afflict their classmates who opted for manual labor. All too often, the keypunch operator spends the workday feeling more like an automaton than a human being.'[64]

Moreover, whereas white collar workers used to enjoy job security, they are now as subject to the vagaries of the capitalist labour economy as are the blue collar workers. One business school professor has remarked 'White collars are where administrators look to save money, for places to fire. It's the law of supply and demand. Once you're in big supply, you're a bum.'[65]

The deterioration in white collar morale is not just a passing phenomenon born of the recent economic down-turn. For example, in the United States, Opinion Research Corporation of Princeton, New Jersey, recently surveyed 25,000 white collar workers in 88 major American companies. Their conclusions were that job satisfaction for white collar workers had markedly declined in many crucial aspects. As Judson Gooding concluded: 'There is a terrible, striking, contrast between the fun-filled, mobile existence of the young opulents of America as shown on television, and the narrow, constricting, un-fun existence that is the lot of most white-collar workers at the lower job levels. You can't buy much of what television is selling on the salaries these young workers earn; about all you do is stay at home watching those good things go by on the screen. The result is frustration, sometimes bitterness, even anger. Workers in this stratum cannot but notice that the federally defined poverty standard is climbing toward their level from below, while above them the salary needed to enjoy the glittery aspects of American life soars even higher, further and further out of reach. For many, the office is the real world, not only a livelihood but a focus of existence. They expect it, somehow, to be more than it has become.'[66]

In Canada, as in the United States, a major result of this growing alienation has been the appearance of white collar unions which have become the most rapidly expanding sector of the labour movement. Although still far from complete, the process of the proletarianization of the white collar worker must eventually have profound effects upon future class struggles.

The professionals

During the past thirty years the professionally trained person has been the greatest beneficiary among either the petit bourgeois or working class sectors. In particular, the self-employed individuals in the elite professions such as doctors, dentists, and lawyers have enjoyed enormous increases in incomes over the past twenty years. As Table 11 shows, these increases have ran far ahead of the average, with doctors heading the parade. Indeed, so rapid and so exorbitantly have doctors' incomes increased that in 1968 the 17,846 doctors and surgeons in independent practice received as much net income as did the more than half-million inhabitants of Newfoundland. While increases in income in the professional sector undoubtedly are primarily the result of higher demand created by the increased size and complexity of industrial units, the higher level of skills required in commercial and legal transactions, and the widespread demand created for health and medical services by the higher standard of living and collective medical insurance plans enjoyed by many Canadians, the creation and control of professional monopolies has contributed a good deal to their wealth.[67]

Professionally trained workers have made up a steadily increasing part of the labour force, expanding from 4.6 per cent in 1901 to 10.0 per cent in 1961; but, as pointed out before, much of this increase is simply a reflection of the over-all development of the white collar sector of the capitalist economy. Curiously enough, despite the rapid increase in numbers of professionally trained persons (in 1931 there were 238,077 professionals in the work force; in 1961 this number had increased to 634,271) and the high incomes earned by some categories of independent professionals, there has been an over-all decline in the proportion of professionals in independent practice. For example, in 1951 there were 35,138 registered nurses in the work force, of whom 3920 were self-employed; in 1961, while the numbers of registered nurses had risen to 61,553, so few were privately employed that the taxation department no longer reported the category separately.[68]

Engineers and architects – professions which have enjoyed great demand with the rapid expansion of technology – present a similar picture. In 1951 there were 24,992 professionally trained engineers and 1740 architects in the work force; of this number a total of 2210 (8.3 per cent) were self-employed. In 1961, while their numbers had grown to 35,721 engineers and 2940 architects, only 2785 (7.2 per cent) were self-employed. With the rapid proliferation of engineering schools in the 1960s, it is likely that this process will be greatly accelerated.

Even among the more independent sectors of professionals some deterioration of independence is observable. For example, the proportion of self-em-

TABLE 11

Independent professionals: comparison of incomes, 1948-68[69]

	1948	1958	1968
Total number of independent professionals	24,670	44,712	53,609
Percent of all income earners	.67	.81	.63
Average income of independent professionals	$5,551.70	$10,333.40	$19,908.20
Weighted average income (1949 dollars)	$5,723.40	$ 8,260.10	$12,827.40
Professionals income: percent average	265	313	405
Doctors' income: percent average	362	440	592
Lawyers' income: percent of average	368	385	468
Dentists' income: percent of average	246	317	397
Engineers' & architects' income: percent of average	325	409	431

ployed dentists declined from 93.5 per cent in 1951 (4310 of 4608) to 92.0 per cent in 1961 (5025 of 5463). Similarly the proportion of independent lawyers showed a modest decline from 62.0 per cent in 1951 (5600 of 9038) to 61.7 per cent in 1961 (7433 of 12,068). Only doctors and surgeons, the highest paid profession, have stood against this tendency, increasing their proportion of self-employment from 67.5 per cent in 1951 (9670 of 14,325) to 70.9 per cent in 1961 (15,088 of 21,266). Over all, the proportion of all professionally trained persons in independent practice has declined from 9.2 per cent in 1951 (35,270 of 385,676) to 8.1 per cent in 1961 (51,530 of 634,271).

The gradual erosion of their privileged positions is keenly felt by the professionals who have adopted a number of strategies to slow the loss of autonomy. For example, the medical profession staged a strike in Saskatchewan in 1962 when provincial medicare was introduced,[70] and almost repeated the performance in Quebec in October 1970. Nor are doctors alone in their uneasiness. A report presented at a recent meeting of professional engineers pointed out that an analysis by their public relations committee showed that the engineer had 'not as high an estimate of his place in society as he once did. And the public does not regard his position as highly as formerly, either.'[71]

In his examination of the petite bourgeoisie, Sandy Lockhart has argued that the proletarianization process has been masked by two factors: the transformation of the dispossessed petit bourgeois into the white collar worker within the capitalist production apparatus, and the storing up of surplus labour in the rapid expansion of faculty, staff, and students in institutions of higher education.[72] Now, of course, with the declining status of the white collar worker, and the recent surpluses in university graduates, it would appear that those transformations, in future, will be much less satisfactory, and that safety value for middle class anxiety will be closed.

The blue collar sector

Like the white collar sector of the labour force, the blue collar sector – the classical proletariat – has undergone some important changes during the past seventy years. As Table 12 demonstrates, when the proportional changes within the blue collar sector are examined, three distinct periods stand out. First, the period 1901-11 shows a huge decline in the proportion of manufacturing and mechanical workers from 49.4 to 38.0 per cent of blue collar sector. At the same time the proportion of menial labourers rose from 22.4 to 33.0 per cent. During the second period, from 1911 to 1931, the proportion of menial workers remained constant at 33 per cent of the blue collar sector, while manufacturing and mechanical workers declined from 38 to 34 per cent. The third period, 1941 to 1961, saw a remarkable reversal of the 1901-31 trends: the proportion of labourers declines sharply to 18.9 per cent in 1941 and continued to decline to 15.6 per cent in 1961, while the manufacturing and mechanical sector jumped sharply to 47.9 per cent in 1941 where it remained until 1961. These drastic shifts in proportions within the blue collar sector demonstrate the need to examine two significant aspects of Canadian economic life – immigration policy and its effects on strategies of capital investment, and the particular characteristics of capitalist development within Canada.

High immigration[73] and large-scale capital formation drastically transformed the Canadian economy from small-scale craft production to large-scale machine production based upon readily available cheap labour during the era of Macdonald's National Policy. This expansion of capital and transformation to a capitalist mode of production accelerated rapidly during the 1890-1910 period. Despite the rapid expansion of production, the enormous immigration of the 1896-1911 period (the labour force increased by 52.8 per cent between 1901 and 1911) created a huge surplus of low-skilled labourers which effectively halted the transformation towards capital intensity. Real wages dropped sharply from 1900 to 1915, and labourers' wages did not return to 1900 levels until 1925. Despite the high level of capital accumulation built up in 1910, it would appear that capital was directed into expansion of facilities rather than towards intensification of production.[74] As a result, while there had been a rapid increase in capitalization, labour productivity actually underwent a slight decrease. High levels of immigration encouraged a shift towards the use of menial labour, particularly in the mines and forests of the West. Of course, employers seized the opportunity presented by the abundance of cheap labour to reduce wages, with the result that numerous bitter strikes were fought, bringing frequent repression by the army and the creation of the federal Department of Labour as a means of social control.[75]

TABLE 12

Proportional distribution within the blue collar sector, 1901-61[76]

	1901	1911	1921	1931	1941	1951	1961
Mfg. & mechanical workers	49.4	38.0	36.4	34.0	47.9	46.2	47.0
Construction	14.6	13.0	15.0	13.9	14.1	14.9	15.2
Trans. & communications	13.7	15.8	17.6	18.9	19.2	20.9	22.3
Labourers	22.4	33.0	31.0	33.4	18.9	18.0	15.6
Total	100.1	98.8	100.0	100.0	100.1	100.0	100.1

During the 1910-20 period, and primarily as a result of the First World War, the economy was greatly diversified, particularly into the refining of non-ferrous metals. During this period, steel production almost doubled. Shortage of capital, however, as well as the continued abundance of low-cost labour reduced capital intensity almost to 1900 levels and resulted in a further decline in the manufacturing and mechanical employment sub-sector and created a further increase in the use of menial labour. By 1920, while large-scale manufacturing and capitalist production had almost entirely eliminated crafts production, still it had not created modern capital-intensive production. Rather a large and increasing proportion of the work force was engaged in essentially pre-industrial (and thereby, essentially pre-capitalist) forms of menial labour. In other words, while capitalist social labour relations had been established, capitalist industrial modes of production, in many regions and occupations, had not. On the other hand, the expansion of capitalist production and particularly the creation of large manufacturing units necessitated the creation of a large white collar apparatus to manage it. It should be noted again, however, that the size of the white collar sector is proportional to the manufacturing and mechanical sector.

The years 1920 to 1930 witnessed both the period of greatest capital expansion and the first period in which real incomes of workers began to rise above 1900 levels. While menial labour continued at a high level, within the capitalist labour sector investment, productivity and labour purchasing power all began to rise sharply. Indeed, investment per worker reached its highest point in history in 1930 as speculative fever and over-expansion gripped the economy. While menial labourers were still isolated outside the technologically advanced sectors of the industrial economy, for the first time competition for their low-wage services from the industrial sector began to pull their real wages upward. Moreover, with the huge expansion of physical plant created in the over-speculation of 1920-30, the basic facilities were established which would allow their incorporation within the capital intensive industrial sector when economic conditions warranted it. The depression delayed that process for a decade.

One of the most striking aspects of the 1930s is the huge increase in purchasing power enjoyed by those who managed to remain employed during the depression. While the general index of wages declined from 48.8 in 1930 to 43.2 in 1935 and then rose to 50.8 in 1940 (1949 = 100), the retail price index dropped from 75.2 in 1930 to 59.9 in 1935 then rose only to 65.7 in 1940. The decline in price of food and other agricultural products, of course, provided the largest part of the decline in cost of living.[77] Despite the favourable position of manufacturing workers, the extremely high level of unemployment (about 20 per cent in 1933)[78] gradually eroded the position of the menial labourers until their real incomes in 1940 fell almost to the 1900 level again. On the other hand, the average purchasing power index of all workers continued to increase, with the result that those employed within the industrial sector became a relatively high-paid labour aristocracy whose economic situation was, for the first time, markedly superior to that of the non-industrial menial labour sector.

It was the Second World War, and C.D. Howe's program of industrialization and rapid expansion of the capitalist sector through guaranteed wartime profits, which finally completed the transformation of the Canadian economy to industrial capitalism and finally incorporated most of Canadian labour into advanced modes of industrial capitalist production.[79] This process, of course, required large shifts of population from the Prairie and Maritime regions to central Canada and British Columbia, as well as a large-scale movement from rural to urban centres. By 1950, the only significant major pools of menial labour remaining were in rural Quebec and the Maritimes, with lesser pools in eastern and northern Ontario and the Prairies. This condition persists to the present.

During the 1940-50 period three additional fundamental changes occurred in the relationship of the composition of capital and labour. First, there was a sharp decline in capital intensity per worker employed. Second, productivity levelled off. And third, real average incomes of workers rose sharply although the large discrepancy between average wage rates and the wages of labourers continued. The decline in capital intensity, as Wood and Scott have pointed out, can be related to the development of tertiary or service industries which have lower capital-output and capital-worker ratios.[80]

By 1961, the capitalist economic system was virtually all-encompassing in Canada, taking in the vast majority of the work force and employing them in both capitalist social relations and in capital-oriented modes of production. The growth and development of capitalism, however, had not followed a regular pattern of growth and transformation. Rather, it had been subjected to large and dramatic convulsions in the relationship of capital and labour, each of which created a period of unrest and heightened labour consciousness.

In response to the agitation by those most deeply injured by these convulsions, a long series of government welfare programs were introduced that were aimed at reducing tensions. Since average purchasing power has risen steadily since 1921 these programs found ready acceptance by those not directly injured. Because the development of capitalism within a non-capitalist society yields enormous profits as pre-capitalist modes of production are over-thrown and replaced by more efficient methods and organizations of production, and because the new capital-intensive technology allowed the exploitation of the virgin environment of Canada to a degree never before attempted, the capitalist system could allow a high and increasing standard of living to the favoured sectors of the work force. Thus during development of the capitalist system in Canada, the capitalists have been able to stabilize the proletariat while destroying or incorporating within it the pre-capitalist formations. Moreover, one of the major consequences of the development of capitalism is a growing specialization and differentiation of production which contributes to creating and deepening divisions within labour.

As Wood and Scott have emphasized, a major long-run determinant of capital-output ratios is the size and richness of the stock of natural resources.[81] During the nineteenth century political economists reasoned that since the stock of land and resources was limited, it would be necessary, if growth took place, to increase capital investment ratios to keep pace with declining accessibility of natural resources and to augment the lessening fertility of marginal land. In the twentieth century, however, this reasoning has generally been ignored because new discoveries of easily accessible and high quality natural resources, new crops and livestock varieties, and the development of new technology which allowed the use of plentiful materials when scarce resources gave out, combined to mask the fundamental correctness of earlier perceptions.

Today, the forest and mining industries are already showing the effects of scarcity and depletion of high-quality reserves. For example, in the 1945-50 period, when there was a general decline in capital-output and capital-labour ratios, the resource industries showed a sharp increase in capital intensity.[82] This tendency continues to the present. Moreover, certain other economic sub-sectors (such as steel, automobiles, and chemicals) have shown capital intensity increases as well. Thus, while the major trend has been toward the development of a low-capital tertiary sector, other significant sectors stand against the decline of capital intensity.

The growing differentiation of capital-labour and capital-output ratios among the various industrial sectors has had significant effects on both the wage structure and the distribution of economic activity in Canada. As capital intensity rises in an industry, and as monopoly increases generally, certain segments of organized labour have found themselves in a very advantageous position vis-à-vis other sectors of labour. In industries such as mining, steel, automobiles, and chemicals, where capital intensity is high, and where it is relatively difficult or impossible to transfer operations without enormous capital loss, labour unions have won high wages. In large part, this is because high capitalization creates high fixed costs, which create losses during strikes when no production is occurring. Moreover, because of the near-monopoly situation in these sectors, the corporations are capable of passing increased labour costs on to the consumer in the form of higher prices. A similar situation exists in the construction industry. As Gilbert Burck reports: 'Although many contractors resist union demands, a contractor usually finds it easy and profitable to cooperate with unions. For so long as he cooperates, he simply bases his bids on costs and tacks on a suitable profit. If the costs of building a mile of highway doubles, so do his revenues and his profit.'[83]

In contrast to organized labour in the capital-intensive sectors, workers in labour-intensive industries find themselves at a distinct disadvantage. Where manufacturing or service industries require low levels of skills and little fixed capital for permanent facilities (such as electronics assembly and clothing manufacturing), or where competition still exists (such as in the textile and furniture industries), workers are forced to accept low wages, or to see their employer either move to a low-wage area or go out of business. Since areas with high rates of unemployment offer the best opportunities for successful exploitation of low-wage labour, government programs which facilitate the movement of labour-intensive industries into Quebec, eastern and northern Ontario, the Maritimes, or the West have the effect of fixing these areas as permanent low-wage localities.[84]

Moreover, because highly capitalized facilities are extremely costly to operate below optimal levels of production, there is a tendency among industries with capital-intensive operations to concentrate production in the most capital-intensive facilities when the volume of production falls off.[85] Because such an action causes labour costs to rise, there is a counter-tendency to move to greater and greater specialization so that aspects of an industry previously incorporated in the main production centre can, by technology, be transformed into labour-intensive operations and transferred to low-wage areas. By this mechanism hinterland areas become more and more frozen into low-skill, low-income patterns and made ever more dependent upon the metropolitan centres for economic decision-making.[86] Of course, for central Canada, this mechanism provides a two-way process when so much of Canadian industry is foreign owned. Just as high-wage, capital-intensive operations are centralized

from the Maritimes and the west to the Montreal and Toronto-Hamilton regions, so do multinational corporations (whether Canadian or American) have
a tendency to concentrate high-capital, high-wage operations in the United
States.[87]

For the workers, these movements of capital have created a profound cleavage between the well-organized high-wage capital-intensive sector and the
low-wage earners who have either weak unions or are unorganized. While the
former are, economically at least, the beneficiaries of economism and tend to
be conservative or apolitical, the latter find themselves helpless to better their
conditions; therefore they either tend toward anti-unionism (because high
wages in unionized sections force prices upward) or are open to appeals from
paternalistic politicians who promise pie-in-the-sky reforms. Thus the high-
wage sector condemns the low-income earner for his 'laziness' and his 'lack of
ambition' (which, it is claimed, causes high taxes to support 'welfare bums')
while the low-income earner fears the 'power' and 'greed' of the strong unions.
The capitalist-owned media and the well-paid influential media commentators,
of course, are delighted to enhance these prejudices and cleavages by condemning both unions and the poor. This situation is likely to continue as long
as purchasing power continues to rise for highly paid unionized workers while
low-wage workers continue to be unorganized. Only when the fragmented
poorly paid sectors are organized is greater solidarity likely to appear.

Despite their basic conservatism, not all elements among the highly paid
unionists are closed to radicalization. Despite increases in purchasing power,
the stresses of automation and the dehumanization of the workplace under
highly organized and specialized production has brought about an increasing
alienation even among the best paid workers. In a perceptive article in *Fortune*, Judson Gooding has pointed out that in American automobile factories,
'The deep dislike of the job and the desire to escape become terribly clear
twice each day when shifts end and the men stampede out the plant gates to
the parking lots, where they are sometimes actually endangering lives in their
desperate haste to be gone.'[88] But alienation goes much deeper than merely a
desire to escape the work place. It affects production as well. 'For management, the truly dismaying evidence about new worker attitudes is found in
job performance. Absenteeism has risen sharply; in fact it has doubled over
the past ten years at General Motors and at Ford ... Tardiness has increased,
making it even more difficult to start up the production lines promptly when
a shift begins – after the foreman has scrambled around to replace missing
workers. Complaints about quality are up sharply. There are more arguments
with foreman, more complaints about discipline and overtime, more grievances. There is more turnover ... Some assembly-line workers are so turned
off, managers report with astonishment, that they just walk away in mid-shift

and don't even come back to get their pay for the time they have worked ... In some plants worker discontent has reached such a degree that there has been overt sabotage. Screws have been left in brake drums, tool handles welded into fender compartments (to cause mysterious, unfindable, and eternal rattles), paint scratched, and upholstery cut.'[89]

In Canada similar tendencies are observable, particularly in Quebec where serious attempts at politicization of the workers and the creation of a 'united front' among the three major unions has been undertaken. Despite these initial signs, however, radicalization of the better paid workers is still a long way off.

Women in the labour force

Over the past sixty years, the changing nature of the economy has produced important effects on the role and status of women within the work force. As Table 13 points out, while the proportion of female workers in the work force has doubled from 13.3 per cent in 1901 to 27.8 per cent in 1961, there are some surprises involved in its distribution. For example, in spite of the songs of praise for 'Rosy the Rivetter' in the Second World War, the degree of change in the proportion of women in the manual labour sector was very small. Indeed, the male-female proportions in that sector has remained almost completely stable over the past seventy years despite huge over-all transformations.

In contrast to the situation in the manual sector, the female proportion of the white collar sector has risen sharply from 20.6 per cent in 1901 to 41.3 per cent in 1961. Moreover, when the distribution of labour within the white collar sector is examined, even more drastic changes can be observed. As Table 14 points out, the proportion of females in white collar occupations has increased in all sub-sectors except among the professionals, the best paid and most prestigious category. The most striking changes have occurred within the clerical and commercial and financial sub-sector which have tripled their proportions of female labour during that period.

It is not, however, until one examines the proportional distribution of occupations within the female white collar work force that the full impact of these changes can be observed. Thus while Table 14 demonstrated that women had maintained their proportion of the professional sub-sector and increased their proportion of the professional and managerial sub-sector from 3.6 per cent in 1901 to 10.3 per cent in 1961, Table 15 shows that these sectors have not kept pace with the over-all growth of the female labour force. In fact, with the rapid increase in the female labour force, a situation has been created where the average status of women has sharply declined. Whereas in 1901, 67.4 per cent of women were employed in the 'desirable' proprietorial and

TABLE 13

Female workers as a percentage of the labour force, and of major sectors, 1901-61[90]

	1901	1911	1921	1931	1941	1951	1961
Total labour force	13.3	13.4	15.5	17.0	19.8	22.3	27.8
White collar sector	20.6	23.8	29.5	31.5	35.1	38.1	41.3
Manual sector	12.6	10.4	10.4	8.5	11.0	11.5	10.6
Service sector	68.7	65.3	58.9	63.0	65.1	55.4	57.8
Primary sector	1.1	1.5	1.6	1.9	1.5	3.1	9.2

TABLE 14

Female workers as a proportion of all workers in white collar sub-sectors, 1901-61[91]

	1901	1911	1921	1931	1941	1951	1961
Proprietorial & managerial	3.6	4.5	4.3	4.8	7.2	8.9	10.3
Professional	42.5	44.6	54.1	49.5	46.1	43.5	43.2
Clerical	22.1	32.6	41.8	45.1	50.1	56.7	61.5
Commercial & financial	10.4	19.2	23.1	23.1	29.4	35.2	36.7

TABLE 15

Distribution of occupations within the female white collar work force, 1901-61[92]

	1901	1911	1921	1931	1941	1951	1961
Proprietorial & managerial	5.1	5.3	4.2	3.5	4.5	5.4	5.0
Professional	62.3	41.8	39.7	39.0	35.0	26.0	27.2
Clerical	22.5	30.4	38.6	39.0	41.0	49.5	49.8
Commercial & financial	10.2	22.4	17.5	18.5	19.5	19.1	18.0

managerial and professional categories, in 1961 only 32.2 per cent were in these sub-sectors. On the other hand, the clerical, and commercial and financial subsectors had risen from 32.7 to 67.8 per cent. As the director of the women's bureau of the Federal Department of Labour, pointed out, the general picture shows: 'women as clerical and office workers; sales clerks and waitresses, telephone operators; and stewardesses of airlines; but there is a dearth of planners, executives and managers in the total scene.'[93]

In contrast to the changes among female white collar workers, among male white collar workers, proportional distribution between the 'desirable' and 'undesirable' occupations has remained stable for sixty years.[94] Thus the process

TABLE 16

Female labour force participation rate, 1931-61[95]

	1931	1941	1951	1961
Married women	3.5	4.5	11.2	22.0
Single women	43.8	47.2	58.3	54.1
Other women	21.3	17.2	19.3	22.9
Total	19.3	20.3	24.1	29.5
Married women as a percentage of all women in labour force	10.0	12.7	30.0	49.8

of the proletarianization of the white collar workers described earlier consists, in the main, of the proletarianization of the female sector of the white collar workers. Male white collar workers have generally escaped the effects of this process.

Among the most significant aspects of the growth of the female labour force is the rapid increase in the number of married female workers. As Table 16 shows, the proportion of married females who are workers has risen sharply from 3.5 per cent in 1931 to 22 per cent in 1961, and married workers of all female workers from 10.0 to 49.8 per cent in the same period. This pattern has continued to the present. In 1969, 31.2 per cent of all married women were in the labour force, and married women made up 55.8 per cent of all female workers.[96] As two researchers have pointed out: 'While the labour force participation of married women in Canada and elsewhere has increased dramatically over the last few decades, the labour force participation of men, especially those in their prime working years (from 25 to 55) has remained steady at a figure just short of 100 percent.'[97]

Thus the social forces which are bringing married women into the labour force have not noticeably altered the proportion of males who are either working or looking for work. In contrast to the continued increase in participation rates in the labour force of married females, single females participation reached a peak of 58.3 per cent in 1951 and has declined steadily since that date. In 1961, the single female participation rate was 54.1 per cent, and in 1969, it was 48.6 per cent.[98]

Recent studies show that a major cause of married women entering the work force is still economic hardship. As Spencer and Featherstone concluded after a lengthy study of motivating and limiting factors: 'There is clear and convincing evidence that a married woman is less likely to be in the labour force the higher the level of family income available, exclusive of her earnings.' Moreover, 'The greater the value of debts incurred by the family the more likely the wife is to be in the labour force.'[99] Sylvia Gelber dismissed the argument that for most women a job is a pastime rather than a necessity. Adding up the estimated 331,434 women who are the sole support of their families, 925,000 single working women and an estimated 678,035 working wives whose husbands have a median income of $6454 a year, she said it is safe to assume that most women work 'because of economic need.'[100]

The rapid increase in the proportion of married women in the labour force has created deep strains in the basic unit of Canadian social organization, the male-dominated nuclear family. Canadian concepts of 'normal' family relations were imported from Europe and developed strong role attachments in which the male parent was the indespensible element of its economic existence. As married women became more deeply involved in the labour force in the past thirty years (in 1969, 31.6 per cent of married women were in the labour force) the more the 'duties' society had attached to her role as wife and mother came into conflict with her new status as breadwinner. Indeed, the more she came to accept the values of her new role as a worker, the more unjust appeared the dual demands of homemaker and worker. Moreover, it was an easy extension from the discovery that women are exploited and discriminated against in the work place to the analogy that her traditional secondary and complimentary role in the family was exploitative as well. From this logical progression came fundamental questions concerning all aspects of the female role and role conditioning, social and economic relations of female workers, and male-female relations in general. The progressively deeper involvement in the labour force by married women is likely to heighten the questioning.

CONCLUSION

Over the past seventy years fundamental changes have occurred in all aspects of class relations in Canada. With the decline of the petite bourgeoisie and the consolidation and maturation of capitalism, a new situation – one more closely resembling Marx's delineation of a capitalist economy – has emerged. Today we are entering a new era of Canadian history where the primary conflict of social forces is moving from one between the capitalist and petit bourgeois modes of production, to a conflict of capital and labour within the capitalist production system.

While the growing concentration of capital, the gradual proletarianization of all divisions of labour (and the rising discontent among workers which is the result of the proletarianization process), and the more recent phenomenon of a rapid impoverishment of the lower levels of income earners, all point toward the development of the classical Marxist model, a warning must be given. Such movements, if history is to be our guide, are matters of decades, not months or years. Therefore, those prophets who predict the immediate collapse of the capitalist system are failing to observe that it is only now reaching its full maturity in Canada. Thus while these conditions are inevitably bound to bring about higher levels of spontaneous unrest and an increased capacity among workers to understand the real nature of their exploitation, it is unlikely that the critical confrontation between capital and labour will be upon us in the immediate future. The timing of that point in history, of course, will depend largely upon the effectiveness of socialists in communicating the true state of affairs to the society around them.

NOTES

1 See various articles in *Canadian Society*, B.R. Blishen *et al.* eds. (Toronto 1968), and Charles C. Hughes *et al., People of Cove and Woodlot* (New York 1968).
2 C. Wright Mills, *The Power Elite* (New York 1959), and Gabriel Kolko, *Wealth and Power in the United States* (New York 1962). See especially an excellent article by John R. Hofley, 'Problems and Perspectives in the Study of Poverty,' *Poverty in Canada*, John Harp and John R. Hofley, eds. (Scarborough 1971), 101-16.
3 While *Capital* remains the definitive work on basic analysis of class relations within the capitalist system, there are several other works which serve as an introduction to the Marxist system of thought and analysis. Of these the *Communist Manifesto, The Economic and Philosophic Manuscripts of 1844*, and *Theories of Surplus Value* are especially valuable to the student.
4 See for example K. Marx, *Capital,* I, chap. XXV, 'Nomad Population.'
5 See especially Ernest Mandel, *The Formation of the Economic Thought of Karl Marx* (New York 1971).
6 Outstanding exceptions to this criticism is the work of L.W. and F.C. Park and Stanley B. Ryerson in English, and Gilles Bourque and his associates in French, all who have made valuable contributions to establishing the principles of Marxist analysis in Canada.
7 It must be emphasized, however, that the *Ontario Workman* represented primarily the point of view and interests of the labour aristocracy or crafts workers rather than that of the low-paid menial workers.
8 *Trades Unions Advocate* (Toronto), 13 July 1882.
9 Department of National Revenue, *Incomes of Canadians,* 1948, 1958, 1968 (Ottawa, 1950, 1960, 1970). Calculations are my own.
10 Agricultural Economics Research Council of Canada, *Rural Canada in Transition,* eds. Marc-Adelard Tremblay and Walter J. Anderson (1968), 30.
11 *Ibid.,* 31.
12 *Ibid.,* 29.
13 *Incomes of Canadians.*
14 *Census of Canada,* appropriate Years. Calculations are my own.
15 *Rural Canada in Transition,* 184.
16 Department of Agriculture, Publication 1354 (1968), cited in John W. Warnock, 'The Farm Crisis,' *Essays on the Left* (Toronto 1971), 125.
17 *Incomes of Canadians.* In 1968, 49 per cent of farmers and taxable returns. Calculations are my own.
18 *Rural Canada in Transition,* 12. Note that the definition of 'rural' population changed between 1941 and 1951. The new definition of rural gives somewhat higher totals; thus the new definition overstates (by about 10 per cent) the actual degree of change.

19 *Ibid.,* 17. See also Leroy F. Stone, *Migration in Canada* (Ottawa 1969), 53, 227. As D.A.
    Curtis points out in the latter work, some 41.4 per cent of all out-migrants from farms
    who remain in the same province will end up in the non-farm rural category. In addition
    33.0 per cent of those who leave the farm and migrate to another farm will fall into the
    non-farm rural category as well.
20 See Marx, *Capital,* I, chap. XXV, for a description of the nature and economic functions
    of an underclass in the capitalists economy.
21 For descriptions of the causes and events of this strike, see *Last Post,* I, nos. 5 and 8.
22 *Incomes of Canadians.*
23 *Ibid.*
24 *Ibid.*
25 *Anatomy of Big Business* (Toronto 1962), 43. Perhaps the most revealing study of the
    aims, methods, and function of corporate directors is the autobiography of Alfred P.
    Sloan, *My Years with General Motors* (New York 1953). As Sloan points out, the board
    of directors of GM contained both 'external' and 'internal' directors – the former repre-
    sented the shareholders, the latter were executive-level employees. He makes it clear that
    the former were in complete control of long-range policy and the latter were responsible
    for the implementation of the goals established for the corporation. The key measure of
    performance and control, he points out, was 'rate of return on investment.'
26 For example see *Grain Growers Guide,* 25 June 1913; *Macleans Magazine,* 12 Oct. 1957.
27 C.A. Ashley, 'Concentration of Economic Power,' *Canadian Journal of Economics and
    Political Science,* XXIII, no. 1 (Feb. 1957), 106. Ashley points out that directors of the
    Bank of Montreal held 13 directorships on the board of the Royal Trust, 10 on CPR, 6
    on the Steel Co. of Canada, and 5 on Sun Life.
28 See *Globe and Mail* (25 Dec. 1969). By 1971, the assets of the Bank of Montreal alone
    totalled $10,165,397,000, an increase in size of 49 per cent in just three years. See *Globe
    and Mail,* 3 Dec. 1969.
29 Ashley, 'Concentration,' 106-7.
30 John Porter, 'Concentration of Economic Power and the Economic Elite in Canada,'
    Canadian Journal of Economics and Political Science, XXII, no. 2 (May 1956), 210. For
    his study, Porter does not include the directorships of 13 corporations (10 US-owned)
    who kept no separate record of Canadian activities; nor does he include the 243 American
    and 64 British residents who are directors of the remaining 170 dominant corporations
    which are the basis of the study.
31 *Ibid.,* Appendix B, Table IV, 220.
32 *Ibid.,* Table V.
33 *Globe and Mail,* 25 Dec. 1969 and 4 Dec. 1971.
34 Porter, 'Concentration,' 220, Table IV, and *Globe and Mail* (25 Dec. 1969). Between
    1951 and 1968 assets of the ten largest Canadian-owned insurance companies grew by
    206 per cent, from $4,203,000,000 to $12,980,000,000.
35 *Globe and Mail,* 7 Dec. 1971.
36 Figures compiled from *Incomes of Canadians,* 1950, 1960, and 1970, Table 2, 'All Re-
    turns by Income Classes.'
37 Park and Park, *Anatomy,* 49-50.
38 *Incomes of Canadians,* 1970, Table 15. Calculations are my own.
39 *Incomes of Canadians,* 1970, Table 15.
40 The best exposition of the strategic need of the US to acquire control of foreign resources
    is that by R. Rea Jackson, 'America's Need for a New National Economic Strategy,' *Na-
    tional Strategy in an Age of Revolution* (the minutes of the National Military–Industrial
    Conference) ed. George B. Huszar (New York 1959), 134-43. Jackson represented the
    Rockefeller interests. See also Kari Levitt, *Silent Surrender* (Toronto 1970).
41 *Globe and Mail* (3 Dec. 1971).
42 Calculated at a 20:1 price/yield ratio from Table 15, *Incomes of Canadians,* 1969.
43 Park and Park, *Anatomy,* 51.

44 *Industrial Canada,* June 1971, 13.
45 *Ibid.,* July 1971, 49.
46 *Ibid.,* June 1971, 13.
47 Jackson, 'America's Need for a New International Economic Strategy,' 140.
48 *Ibid.,* 142.
49 *National Strategy,* etc., Appendix, 271. Although little known, this annual series of conferences, begun in 1955, offers excellent insight into the thinking of the American military-industrial élite, since virtually every branch of the American military, education,
industry, and government was represented at the highest level.
50 The following works provide an excellent introduction to the topic of American ownership: *Gordon to Watkins to You,* eds. Dave Godfrey and Mel. Watkins (Toronto 1970);
Inter-Corporate Ownership (Ottawa 1969); James Laxer, *The Energy Poker Game*
(Toronto 1970); Kari Levitt, *Silent Surrender* (Toronto 1970); L.C. and F.W. Park,
Anatomy of Big Business (Toronto 1962); *Report of the Task Force on the Structure of
Canadian Industry* (the Watkins Report) (Ottawa 1968); A.E. Safarian, *Foreign Ownership of Canadian Industry* (Toronto 1966).
51 For example, E.S. Jackson, president of Manufacturers Life Insurance Co., in his address
to the annual meeting made clear the basis for his opposition to Canadian economic nationalism. His concern was that legislating Canadian ownership would lead to retaliatory
action by other countries. With about 75 per cent of its business transacted outside
Canada – more than 50 per cent in the US alone – any legislation limiting foreign ownership might bring retaliation which would seriously affect Manufacturers Life's foreign
interests. *Globe and Mail,* 23 Dec. 1971.
52 *Fortune,* Aug. 1971, 156.
53 The Simard family are strong backers of the anti-nationalist Liberal government in Quebec. Gerard Filion, the anti-nationalist president of the Canadian Manufacturers Association, is president of the Simard-controlled Marine Industries Ltd., while Robert Bourassa,
premier of Quebec, is a son-in-law of one of the Simards. Stephen Roman attempted to
sell Denison Mines, the largest remaining Canadian-controlled uranium mine, to US interests, while R.A. Brown Jr, president of Home Oil, attempted to sell out to US interests
as well. Both the latter moves were blocked by the federal government because of the
huge public outcry.
54 Park and Park, *Anatomy,* 51.
55 *Industrial Canada,* June 1970, 25.
56 *Ibid.,* 25-6.
57 *Ibid.,* 26.
58 *Toronto Star,* 18 Dec. 1971.
59 Charles K. Brightbill, *The Challenge of Leisure* (Englewood Cliffs, NJ 1963); Ralph
Glasser, *Leisure: Penalty or Prize?* (London 1970); Norman P. Miller, *The Leisure Age:
Its Challenge to Recreation* (Belmont, Calif. 1966).
60 Noah M. Meltz, *Manpower in Canada 1931-1961* (Ottawa 1969), Table A.I.
61 Meltz, *Manpower.* Calculations are my own.
62 *Ibid.*
63 *Ibid.*
64 Judson Gooding, 'The Fraying White Collar,' *Fortune,* Dec. 1970, 78.
65 Quoted in *Ibid.*
66 *Ibid.*
67 The doctors, for example, fought for years to prevent competition by foreign-trained
doctors by rigidly excluding all but those trained in the white English-speaking world.
The current warfare by the dental profession against denturists is of a similar nature. See
for example the prosecution of denturists in Nova Scotia, *Toronto Star,* 22 Dec. 1971.
68 Meltz, Table B.I., 62, and *Incomes of Canadians,* 1953 and 1963. All figures on professional employment in this section are taken from these sources.
69 *Incomes of Canadians,* 1950, 1960, 1970. Calculations are my own.

70　For a good account of the Saskatchewan doctors' strike see R. Badgley and S. Wolfe, *Doctors' Strike* (Toronto 1967).

71　*Kitchener-Waterloo Record* (20 Dec. 1971).

72　R.S. Lockhart, 'The Proletarianization of the Petite Bourgeoisie,' MA thesis, Simon Fraser University, 1969.

73　In the mid-1820s British colonial policy undertook to create a class of landless labourers requisite to the development of a capitalist state by the manipulation of land-granting policies. See Leo A. Johnson, 'Land Settlement, Population Growth and Social Structure in Home District, 1794-1851,' *Ontario History,* LXIII, no. 1 (March 1971), 41-60.

74　Data for capital stocks and value of production is from O.J. Firestone, *Canada's Economic Development 1867-1953* (London 1958), Table 77, 209. Data income indexes are from M.C. Urquart and K.A. Buckley, eds., *Historical Statistics of Canada* (Toronto 1965), Series D1-11 and D40-59, pp. 84 and 86. Calculations which follow are my own.

75　Stuart M. Jamieson, *Times of Trouble: Labour Unrest and Industrial Conflict in Canada, 1900-66,* Study no. 22, Task Force on Labour Relations, Privy Council Office, Ottawa. See also Frank T. Denton, *The Growth of Manpower in Canada* (Ottawa 1970), 6.

76　Meltz, *Manpower,* 58. Calculations are my own.

77　Urquhart and Buckley, *Historical Statistics,* Series D1-11 and D40-59, pp. 84 and 86.

78　O.J. Firestone, Table 6, p. 58.

79　Leslie Roberts, *C.D.: The Life and Times of Clarence Decatur Howe* (Toronto 1957).

80　Royal Commission on Canada's Economic Prospects, Wm. C. Wood and Anthony Scott, *Output, Labour and Capital in the Canadian Economy* (Ottawa 1958), 269.

81　*Ibid.,* 262.

82　*Ibid.,* 263.

83　This is true in much of the construction industry as well. See Gilbert Burck, 'The Building Trades Versus the People,' *Fortune* (Oct. 1970); Restrictive Trade Practices Commission, *Road Paving in Ontario* (Ottawa 1970); L.A. Skeoch, *Restrictive Trade Practices in Canada* (Toronto 1966).

84　Recent movement of General Instrument Co. and Clairetone Electronics to Nova Scotia, Hamilton Cottons to Mount Forest, Ontario, and Sperry-Gyro from Ontario to Quebec are all examples of the mobility of low-skilled labour-intensive industries leaving areas with rising wages for low-wage areas.

85　For example, when the Dominion Steel and Coal Co. (Dosco) opened its new large-scale facilities in Hamilton, Ontario, it closed its Nova Scotia operations, even though the Nova Scotia operations were still profitable, in order to operate the capital-intensive Hamilton plant at closer to optimal production levels. The Nova Scotia plant was sold to the Nova Scotia government and workers. It continues to operate profitably.

86　An examination of the *Economic Atlas of Ontario* (Toronto 1969) provides ample evidence of this process. In particular the maps showing the movement to and concentration of the metal trades in the Toronto region provides an excellent case study.

87　The Massey-Ferguson Company provides the best example of a 'Canadian' multinational company concentrating its capital-intensive operations and centre of decision-making in the US. Tacit recognition of this process is contained in the Canadian government's creation of the Auto Pact in order to retain a minimum amount of automobile manufacturing in Canada.

　　It would appear that the only exception to this pattern of centralization and specialization occurs when entirely new capital is invested. While the General Motors plant at Ste Thérèse, Quebec, and Ford's new plant at Talbotville are examples of expansions within the central area, wholly new operations such as Volvo and Michelin Tire in Nova Scotia suggest that when new capital investment occurs in heavy industry, it may seek out low-wage areas – particularly when heavily subsidized by government grants. Since such wholly new heavy investments occur but rarely, they will probably have little effect on the over-all picture.

88　Judson Gooding, 'Blue-Collar Blues on the Assembly Line,' *Fortune,* July 1970, 69.

89　*Ibid.* For similar accounts see *Atlantic,* Oct. 1971.

90 Meltz, *Manpower*, Table A.4, p. 61. It should be noted that in the years 1921 to 1961 an average of 20 per cent of working females gave no occupational information.
91 *Ibid.*, Table A.4.
92 *Ibid.* Calculations are my own.
93 Speech to the Pioneer Women of Canada, 23 Nov. 1971, in *Globe and Mail*, 24 Nov. 1971.
94 Meltz, *Manpower*. Calculations are my own.
95 Byron G. Spencer and Dennis C. Featherstone, *Married Female Labour Force Participation: A Micro Study* (Ottawa 1970), 12. Statistics from the 1931 census are for the age group 10 and over. Statistics from the 1941-51 censuses are for the age group 14 and over. Statistics from the 1961 census are for the age group 15 and over. For a more detailed study of labour force characteristics see Frank T. Denton.
96 *Married Female Labour Force*, 13.
97 *Ibid.*
98 *Ibid.*
99 *Ibid.*, 84.
100 *Globe and Mail*, 24 Nov. 1971.

Gilles Bourque and Nicole Laurin-Frenette

Gilles Bourque is author of *Classes sociales et question nationale au Québec* and teaches in the Department of Sociology, Université du Québec in Montreal; Nicole Laurin-Frenette also teaches in the Department of Sociology, Université du Québec in Montreal

Social classes and nationalist ideologies in Ouebec, 1760-1970

translated by P. Resnick and P. Renyi

EDITOR'S NOTE: This article was originally published in *Socialisme Québécois*, no. 20, 1970. We have omitted here part of the discussion of the concept of nation and an exposition on nationalist ideologies in Quebec in the period before 1960.

THE PROBLEMS raised by the relationship between the phenomenon of social class and the national question have been the cause of much debate in Quebec, among historians and sociologists, and among members of the left who are searching for a political strategy that will reunite them with the workers. In this article, we shall first focus on the theoretical aspect of the problem. We shall try to furnish a number of elements necessary for the development of a satisfactory theory of the nation, which we feel is essential to a rigorous analysis of Quebec reality. Once we have done this, we will embark on the study of the national question in Quebec; for only then will it be possible to set out the problem correctly and to uncover the elements required for truly left-wing political action. In effect, the recent rise of nationalism poses with a new urgency the question of the organization of the radical left and the need, in order to resolve it, for a thorough and objective analysis of the national question.

THE IDEALIST FRAMEWORK –
QUEBEC SOCIOLOGICAL LITERATURE

We shall first undertake a critique of the position of the sociologists Fernand Dumont, Marcel Rioux, and Jacques Dofny. We believe that the theoretical foundation developed by these sociologists underlies all those political positions that favour joining the Parti Québécois and encourage tactical support for the bourgeoisie, without upholding the need for a specifically working-class political organization. We shall try to show that the dichotomies of social class/ethnic class and social consciousness/ethnic consciousness encompass a fundamental problem in this theory, hiding reality behind a veil of idealism. The analyses offered by these sociologists are consequently loose and tentative and too often are expressed in metaphorical, rather than scientific, language. As Michel Van Schendel wrote in a recent number of the review *Socialisme*, the concepts of ethnic class and ethnic consciousness are 'scientifically doubtful and politically suspect.'[1] We shall try to prove this by disclosing their idealist foundation and showing, at the end of this article, how they can only lead to justifying the incoherent and opportunistic strategy that encourages the left to join the Parti Québécois.

It is Fernand Dumont who most clearly expounds the idealist framework that underlies this whole approach. He writes: 'It has not been possible to bring this (the sociological analysis of the nation) back to objective, structural factors; common language, a specific ethnic group, political cohesion, etc. It was necessary to speak, like Renan, of a "collective desire to live" or to consider the nation or the tribe like contemporary ethnologists, "as the theory that its members make it themselves" (S.E. Nadel).'[2] For Dumont, therefore, in the last analysis the nation is strictly the result of its 'représentation' in the eyes of its members. According to him, the nation does not rest on a collection of scientifically analysable objective facts, but results from the pure subjectivity of the individuals who are part of it. Moreover, it is this subjectivity which seems to create the national structures out of nothing. Here, Dumont takes the opposite position to the theory of reflection in the study of ideologies. According to this theory, ideology is only the distorted reflection of given objective bases. But its reverse must lead us back to an idealist framework, because now it is the nation as an objective phenomenon which seems to become a simple reflection of its members' representation of it.

Using these premises as his basis, and arbitrarily establishing a dichotomy between ethnic consciousness and class consciousness, Marcel Rioux proceeds to write a history of Quebec by writing a history of its 'représentations.' He states: 'We can say that it is ... the predominance of one or the other consciousness at a given moment which explains the physiognomy of each epoch, the alliances and ideological struggles that appear in Quebec.'[3] The whole history of Quebec is thus explained by the ethereal relationships existing at the level of consciousness. Rioux and Dofny affirm: 'As might have been surmised, in order to analyse particular aspects of the problem of social classes in French Canada, it is necessary *to give priority to the awareness of group consciousness.*'[4] Everything takes place at the level of consciousness, whether social or national.

In Quebec, however, national consciousness has the characteristic of veiling class consciousness. Thus, we see the theme of the mask emerge: 'In all political crises, it was the ethnic "we-group" that prevailed and that masked the development of the realization of social class consciousness in French Canada.'[5] The phenomenon of 'représentations' is not placed into any relationship with 'objective bases'; history takes place at the level of relationships between two types of consciousness situated above the real facts. Moreover, what really differentiates French from English Canada is its system of values, and here Professor Rioux becomes almost a functionalist: 'If French Canada's social structure has differentiated itself almost as much as English Canada's, the former's value system and culture have remained much more homogeneous. It is this which has held back the consciousness of its social classes, and more especially, that of its working class.'[6] The important point, therefore, in studying Quebec, is to concentrate on the different forms of 'représentations' that can be distinguished there.

A PROBLEM OF 'CONSCIOUSNESS'

The explanation for this easy retreat into idealist meandering lies in yet another dichotomy, between social class and ethnic class, which according to

Rioux and Dofny is at the root of the opposition between the two types of representations to which we have just referred. We must distinguish, they say, between ethnic conflict and class conflict. They express this distinction in the following terms: while social classes do exist in Quebec, Quebec 'can itself be considered an ethnic class within Canada.'[7] For Rioux and Dofny, however, social classes are much less important as a cohesive factor than the national collectivity. As Rioux states: 'When, following Marx, Professor Gurvitch affirms that the aim of each class is to represent the global society and to claim the right to decide the fate and position of the other classes, we would think he is describing the ethnic consciousness of the Québécois; on the other hand, these characteristics seem much less applicable to the social classes in Quebec.'[8] Thus, it is the consciousness of the national collectivity that has predominated throughout Quebec history, the nation somehow embodying a principle of social cohesion more important than classes.

It appears, then, that there exist a nation and classes, a national consciousness and several class consciousnesses, although we cannot understand very well the relationship existing between these two phenomena – unless both classes and the nation are created as real phenomena by the consciousness that their members form of them. This theory is clearly pure historicism, where history is explained by the action of class-subjects who are themselves the true creators of social structures. As is often the case, this historicism goes hand in hand with a Hegelian-Lukacsian type of idealism, which bases the composition of a class-in-itself and a class-for-itself on the emergence of class consciousness. As far as the national question is concerned, given the paucacity and poor quality of research into 'the objective factors of structure,' Dumont, and Rioux and Dofny in his footsteps, can well allow themselves to neglect the economic and political factors involved, if not to deny their existence.

Thus, they are able to explain the history of Quebec as a history of the domination of national consciousness over class consciousness, and this results in some astonishing claims. Analysing the appearance of the Créditistes on the federal scene in 1962, Marcel Rioux claims: 'for the first time a certain class consciousness and a certain ethnic consciousness appear at the same time among an important part of the population'[9] – as though national consciousness had not always been class consciousness since 1760! The independence movement of the years 1830-37 was a nationalism defending the interests of the class which articulated it – the petite bourgeoisie. This class wanted to impose its 'nation' as much as to impose itself as the dominant class within the nation. The reactionary nationalism of the years 1840-1940 defended the interests and justified the domination of a minority of the traditional petite bourgeoisie, and can be explained only by the position of this minority with regard to the relations of production and socio-political relations. It is amazing, therefore, to hear Marcel Rioux claim that the link between nationalism and class ideology is a new phenomenon. Indeed, he rather prudently observes 'that it is not impossible that ethnic and social contestations are in the process of becoming intertwined and of stimulating each other reciprocally.'[10] If Marcel Rioux and Jacques Dofny perceive a new phenomenon here, it is because they have presented the nation and the representation of the national collectivity on the one hand, and social classes and class ideologies on the other, as being two relatively antagonistic realities. If they see Quebec history as the development of a simple game of attraction and repulsion between two types of consciousness, it is because their idealist foundations prevent them from explaining reality as a dialectical relationship between its actual bases and the reflection of these bases.

CLASSES AND NATIONALIST IDEOLOGIES

Must we logically conclude that nationalism is, by definition, a bourgeois ideology, whose essential function it is to produce an inverted image of the real economic, social, and political relations (the relations of domination and exploitation – that is, the class struggle)? Or can non-bourgeois nationalist ideologies exist, linked to the interests and situation of other classes within the social formation? A particular Marxist tradition tends to identify nationalist ideology and bourgeois ideology in a mechanical fashion.

The frequently cited phrase in the Communist Manifesto, 'The working men have no country,' might seem *a priori* to reduce nationalism to a bourgeois ideology. We should, however, examine the whole passage from which this phrase is taken. It reads as follows: 'The Communists are further reproached with desiring to abolish countries and nationality. The working men have no country. We cannot take from them what they have not got. Since the proletariat must first of all acquire political supremacy, must rise to be the leading class of the *nation*, must constitute itself the *nation*, it is, so far, itself *national*, *though not in the bourgeoise sense of the word.*'[11]

In this passage, Marx and Engels first recognized the existence of a structural reality which they designated by the term *nation*; and second, linked this reality to the dominant class in a social formation. That is, they linked it to the bourgeoisie (before the Revolution, while the proletariat is still a dominated class), and subsequently to the proletariat, which in assuming political power becomes the nation, becomes *national*, not in the bourgeois sense of the term, but implicitly in the proletarian sense. Thus Marx can state further: 'Though not in substance, yet in form, the struggle of the proletariat with the bourgeoisie is at first a national struggle.'[12] This concept of 'the form of the struggle' can be understood only in terms of the national features of the capitalist mode of production.

This means that the national features of the social formation (territory, state, language, national symbols), although linked to the capitalist mode of production and hence to the interests of the bourgeoisie, also *concern* the working class; they can and must belong to it and serve its class interests. The working class, because of its interests, may modify these national features of the structure; the state will be used by the proletariat and eventually disappear ... But to realize these objectives, the proletariat must first seize control of the nation and use it for its own ends. The national territory, the national state, the national language, the national heritage can be national 'in the non-bourgeois sense of the term,' serving the interests of the dominated classes, only if bourgeois domination has been abolished.[13]

We are now in a position to state that a 'non-bourgeois' nationalism, i.e. the valorization of national aspects of the social formation by and in the interests of other classes in this formation, can exist. For the nation does not exist outside classes, but as a function of classes.

QUEBEC'S NATIONAL STRUCTURE

We shall attempt to explain the structural factors that give Quebec a double class structure. Quebec is a province inside the Canadian Confederation. By definition it has a state apparatus with certain powers, concentrated principally in the cultural and social domains. On the economic plane, Quebec constitutes a regional economy characterized by a double phenomenon of colonization: (1) Following the founding of the Canadian Confederation, Quebec's economy came to be based on a type of industry using cheap labour: the dairy industry, textiles, shoes, etc. In the pan-Canadian schema, Quebec's economy is defined by its relationship to the Ontario economy.[14] (2) Beginning in the 1920s, principally because of her wealth in non-ferrous metals and water resources, Quebec became a source of primary materials for American imperialist capital. Since the last war, American investments have tended to invade many different sectors of production.

With respect to the national question, Quebec is therefore doubly interesting. We can study there, in a sort of structural condensation, the two forms which national oppression has assumed in the development of the capitalist structures of the mode of production: internal domination resulting from the ascendancy of one nation over other nations occupying the same territory; external domination (colonialist or imperialist) resulting from the exploitation of one or several collectivities by a nation not itself interested in populating the subjected country or countries. In its first phase, the creation of national states marks the ascendancy of the capitalist mode of production in different social formations. Within this construct, we can study not only the national characteristics of the class struggle resulting from the rise of the capitalist mode of production, but also the phenomenon of national domination which may result from one nation (and a dominant class within it) gaining ascendancy over other weaker nations within the same territory. Quebec is thus a dominated nation, within Canadian national structures. The English Conquest of 1760 established the structural elements, leading to the phenomenon of national domination.

Let us now examine the second of the two forms of the national phenomenon that we can find condensed in Quebec's social formation. We know that the phenomenon of imperialism, far from doing away with national characteristics as bourgeois ideology would have it, has in fact developed by maintaining the national features of the structures of dominated social groups. Imperialism has even artificially fostered these national features to strengthen its hold in countries of the Third World. We need only remember the creation of African national states at the beginning of the twentieth century, as a means for the imperialist countries to rationalize their exploitation of the colonized countries. We know, furthermore, that rather than destroying the national features of societal structures in which the capitalist mode of production is present, imperialist countries have come to terms with them, through alliance with different 'comprador' bourgeoisies. We need only think of South America. Or of Canada, for that matter, where a few years ago Gordon passed for a dangerous revolutionary because he tried to convince the Canadian bourgeoisie to pose at least some resistance to imperialist American capital. In this regard, Quebec, whose economy is increasingly dominated by American capital, reveals a local national structure subordinated to imperialist interests. The Americans, moreover, have always relied on Quebec nationalism, to a greater or lesser extent, to establish themselves in Quebec. They have always made use of the contradictions between the nationalist rural faction of the French Canadian petite bourgeoisie and the English-speaking bourgeoisie. The Union Nationale, the political organ of the rural petite bourgeoisie, always played Wall Street off against Bay Street; we need only recall Duplessis and the mortgaging of natural resources to American interests at ridiculously low prices. In the same way, as we shall see, the new faction of the petite bourgeoisie that has arisen because of technological changes in Quebec since 1945, wants to become the technocratic ruling class in the interests of imperialist capital (somehow 'civilized'!), through the Parti Québécois, seeking in this way to end only one part of the national domination from which Quebec suffers.

CLASSES AND NATIONALIST IDEOLOGIES

The colonial situation of Quebec brought about the formation of two diversified and potentially antagonistic structures: class and nation. Two theses follow from this statement that challenge the Marcel Rioux and Jacques Dofny analyses mentioned at the beginning of this article.

1. The notion of ethnic class explains no period of Quebec history. Since 1760, a diversified class structure has existed within the two nations present in Quebec's social formation. We witness opposition between classes, or factions within each of these structures: the struggle between the administration and the English Canadian bourgeoisie from 1760 to 1800; the struggle of the petite bourgeoisie against the seigneurs and clergy from 1800 to 1840; the struggle between the urban and rural factions of the French Canadian petite bourgeoisie from 1840 to 1960. The existence of this double structure does not prevent alliance between the ethnically differentiated classes; seigneurs *cum* high clergy with the colonial administration from 1760 to 1800; seigneurs *cum* high clergy, colonial adminstration, and bourgeoisie from 1800 to 1840; urban faction of the French Canadian petite bourgeoisie and English Canadian bourgeoisie from 1840 to today. Even though the most fundamental conflicts oppose ethnically different classes (French Canadian petite bourgeoisie *v.* English Canadian bourgeoisie from 1800 to 1840; French Canadian working class *v.* English Canadian bourgeoisie from 1945 to 1970), the structure does not prevent, on the one hand, the collaboration between the classes whose members are in the main from different nations, and on the other hand, the class struggle, within each nation.

The concept of ethnic class therefore cannot explain Quebec history; it merely serves as ideological coating for the independent struggle led by a new faction of the petite bourgeoisie. The nation, as we stressed above, is the effect of certain economic, political, and ideological features of the structure of the capitalist mode of production. It therefore follows that when we make use of the concept of nation, we are referring to a class structure characterized by a certain type of domination, that of the capitalist mode of production, even when we are discussing a dominated nation. An ethnic group forming a single dominated social class cannot therefore constitute a nation. We can only analyse it as a social class within the social formation and, in the case of the capitalist mode of production, the nation to which it belongs. In the case of an ethnically differentiated class, the ethnic character may be the vestigial result of another social formation; an earlier social formation in the case of conquest; another nation, where large-scale emigration is involved; but under no circumstances an 'ethnically national class' (what an abomination!). Let us stress in passing that the concept of nation has nothing to do with that of ethnic group, and that several cultural groups can exist (as is moreover almost always the case) within the same nation.

2. Within a nation, there does not exist, as Dofny and Rioux would have it, class consciousness and an ethnic consciousness that can transcend the different types of class consciousness. Nationalist ideologies can only be class ideologies. A nationalist ideology only makes sense through the class which becomes its propagandist. It is in this connection that we stated earlier that several types of nationalist ideology can exist within a social formation. In Quebec, we can thus delineate three types of nationalist ideology, which we can only explain by referring to the classes that support them:

a A conservative nationalism, defining the French Canadian nation as an entity with cultural peculiarities, enjoying certain rights that protect these peculiarities, even while participating in Canadian political structures. Within this ideology, we can distinguish two sub-types, depending on the economic vision proposed: the first was held by the seigneurs and high clergy from 1760 to 1840 and by the rural-based petite bourgeoisie from 1840 to 1960, and was an ideology more or less immune to capitalism, insisting on the agricultural vocation of the French Canadians; the second was held by the urban faction of the petite bourgeoisie who, while stressing French Canadian particularism, insisted on French-speaking Québécois participating in the Canadian capitalist economy and on the possibility of their succeeding.

b A dynamic nationalism, pointing to independence. We can here recognize the ideology of the French Canadian petite bourgeoisie from 1800 to 1837 which sought to obtain political independence with the aim of controlling capitalist development. We can also think of the new faction of the petite bourgeoisie which was formed in the 1950s, and which is now making an independentist thrust through the Parti Québécois, with the aim of making Quebec into a kind of neo-capitalist state. We shall return to this theme.

c A nationalist ideology which links national liberation to the establishment of a system of socialist self-management. This ideology, put forward by working-class militants and intellectuals, tries to reflect the aspirations of the working class and to formulate the conditions for its liberation.

We observe that these three nationalisms, though all refer to the three instances of the social formation, emphasize different features of the Quebec nation. The first type insists on the juridical and cultural features (recognition and protection of cultural rights and peculiarities). The second essentially emphasizes the political, seeking the transformation of political relationships in order to promote the economic and cultural interests of the nation. The third type stresses the need to transform relations of production in order to abolish all forms of domination (economic, political, and cultural).

There is, therefore, no nationalist ideology common to all classes in the same nation. A nationalist ideology, in and of itself, cannot mask the class consciousness of dominated classes. Rioux and Dofny forget that it is precisely the character of any dominant ideology to cover up the relationship of domination. Nationalism is only one element in a larger whole tending to fulfil the same function. We do not intend to deny that nationalist ideology can help mask the exploitation of dominated classes in a specific way. We do, however, wish to avoid the confusion which leads some to attribute this role only to the nationalist character of the dominant ideologies in Quebec. It follows from this theoretical position that we can only come to grips with the nationalist character of an ideology, (1) by relating it to other elements the ideological formation into which it fits; (2) by pinpointing its specific effects on the field of the class struggle; (3) by relating ideology to other instances in the social formation (political and economic). We shall now try to analyse, using this framework, some types of nationalist ideology in Quebec history ...

THE 'QUIET REVOLUTION'
OR THE UNITED BOURGEOIS FRONT

The period which we generally know as the Quiet Revolution (1960-64), as well as the one immediately following (1965-70), illustrates in an interesting way some of the theses which we put forward in the first part of this article. The first period saw the rise to political power of the urban French-Canadian petite bourgeoisie. This break-through coincided with the appearance and diffusion of a new nationalist-dominated ideology linked to this class. In the second period, a split occurred between two factions of this petite bourgeoisie, first at the ideological level, then at the political, with the founding of a new political group, the Mouvement Souveraineté-Association (MSA), which was to become the Parti Québécois. We shall examine these events in greater detail, analysing them according to our hypotheses.

To understand events during the two periods under examination, we must recognize the very pronounced lagging of politics and ideology behind economic events in Quebec society during the preceding period, from 1945 to 1960. During that period, the traditional petite bourgeoisie, based on an economy that was predominantly agricultural and on small-scale independent enterprise (small shops and outlets, non-salaried liberal professions), rapidly disappeared as an economic class; but despite the loss of its economic base, this class preserved its political and ideological hegemony.

The ideology of this traditional petite bourgeoisie remained much the same from 1840 to 1960. It was based on a juridical-cultural nationalism of preservation, and on a reactionary and agricultural economic-social plan. It was this ideology which still dominated, for example, under the Duplessis regime; state, church, press, and educational institutions disseminated it widely.

From the beginning of the 1950s, the urban French-Canadian petite bourgeoisie comprised the majority (compared to the previous class) in Quebec society. Its rise was due to the rapid industrialization which took place in Quebec during this period. Consequently, it came into existence in a capitalist economic context of monopolies and large public and private organizations, overwhelmingly dominated by foreign capital (American and Canadian). Until 1960, this new petite bourgeoisie had little impact on political and ideological conflicts and, despite its efforts, did not succeed in breaking the political-ideological hegemony of the traditional petite bourgeoisie. For evidence of this, we need only recall the battles waged against Duplessisism by the trade unionists, intellectuals, and writers of the epoch, clustering in a number of university faculties or around such 'avant-garde' journals as *Cité Libre* and *Liberté*.

The Quiet Revolution, in effect, resulted from the sudden collapse of the political-ideological hegemony of the traditional petite bourgeoisie, made concrete through the electoral victory of the Liberal party in 1960. The sudden coming to power of the urban petite bourgeoisie, combined with the lag that had existed in the various levels of class struggle and the rapidity with which this new class overcame it, have led many to talk of a revolution. During the next four years, this class did establish itself as the dominant one within the French-Canadian group, by disseminating and imposing its ideology, and by consolidating itself politically as the ruling class.

It is important to note the absence of any important ideological or political struggle within what we could call the 'ruling bloc' in Quebec society, during this period of so-called quiet revolution. Rather, there was a united bourgeois front, which can be explained by the almost total disappearance of the traditional French-Canadian petite bourgeoisie, and especially by the community of interests that existed during this period between the two main factions of the new French-Canadian petite bourgeoisie. There were, in fact, two factions within this class which we must differentiate, given their political importance in the subsequent events which we wish to analyse.

We can designate the numerically more important faction as 'technocratic,' for lack of a better term. In Quebec, as in several other countries, it has come into existence as a direct result of certain features of the structure of the capitalist mode of production in its advanced stage (capitalism of large private and state-run monopolies). The appearance of a technocratic faction of the bourgeoisie reveals the existence of new functions in the capitalist production process. These new functions correspond to different kinds of needs in the management, administration, organization, and planning of the production and consumption of material and symbolic goods. They connote participation in power and the greater complexity of the former direct relationship of exploitation of the salaried worker by the private capitalist owner of the means of production. We must add to this extension of functions a change in one of the terms in this relationship; the replacement of the private capitalist, in some cases, by the state – a collective capitalist entrepreneur. We suggest that this change in the structure can explain the existence of the technocratic petit bourgeois faction. In Quebec, the majority of this class are French-speaking, and they are concentrated in the public sector (for example, in Hydro-Quebec, CBC, government ministries, universities, and trade union organizations).

The other faction of the petite bourgeoisie is based, on the one hand, on private (rather than state) ownership of the means of production and, on the other, on the more classical functions of property and property control in the modern capitalist enterprise (as opposed to the new functions outlined above). This faction is numerically rather small, consisting of entrepreneurs (in industry, commerce, and services), financiers, and upper-echelon executives in large private corporations, usually Canadian or American. For lack of a better term, we can call them the 'neo-capitalist' faction.

During the period of the Quiet Revolution, these two factions of the French Canadian petite bourgeoisie had a common class practice and ideology. We shall return to the split and conflict between the factions, which was to outweigh their common interests in the subsequent period. For the moment, we shall try to analyse the common ideology of the petite bourgeoisie and the principal features of its common political practice during the Quiet Revolution.

The ideology of the French Canadian petite bourgeoisie corresponds to its class situation and to its economic and political class interests. A nationalist and neo-liberal ideology joins these two elements in an original combination. The nationalism is linked to the situation of economic dependence which the petite bourgeoisie experiences as part of the French Canadian group, a situation in which it is discriminated against as a class with regard to jobs, promotion, resources, and so on, as compared with the English Canadian petite bourgeoisie, for example. Through its neo-liberalism, it asserts its belief in free enterprise and in capitalist relations of production; and at the same time, it recognizes the necessity of state intervention in the economy, to meet the need for regulation, encouragement of capital investment, modernization, social mobilization, and so forth. This neo-liberal conception of the state is also linked to the promotion of its own interests, not simply as a petite bourgeoisie, but essentially as a dominated and underprivileged petite bourgeoisie. It would like to use the state to plan, encourage capital investment, modernize, and stabilize, with the main objective of re-establishing the equilibrium that was broken by English domination. Thus, the nationalist and bourgeois elements of the ideology are *inseparably linked* in a single class project.

We believe that most of the reforms demanded or realized by or for this class during the period under consideration can be so interpreted. The transfer back from the federal government to Quebec of certain powers or capital (the enactment of the slogan 'Maîtres chez nous'), the setting up of the General Investment Corporation, the reorganization of the educational system, the establishment of economic planning councils, both provincial and regional, the efforts to modernize the regions, the nationalization of electricity, all had the practical result of improving the economic and social situation of the entire French-Canadian petite bourgeoisie. Various means were used to obtain this objective: the creation of white collar jobs in public and private sectors, the availability of capital, better job preparation, and so on. We can add to this a number of reforms obtained from the federal government: for example, setting up the Royal Commission on Bilingualism and Biculturalism, and facilitating the hiring and promotion for French Canadians in the federal civil service.

Clearly, this ideology and practice served the interests of both factions of the French-speaking petite bourgeoisie. The technocrats and the small industrialists and financiers felt that the fact that they had discriminated against and held back from promotion because they were French-speaking petits bourgeois was the result, on the one hand, of the existence of an all-powerful English-speaking bourgeoisie, and on the other, of the reactionary politics of the traditional petite bourgeoisie.

As far as the English-speaking bourgeoisie is concerned, it is evident that the changes accompanying the Quiet Revolution were generally beneficial to them (although it did not directly initiate these changes). In this connection, we can note English-speaking support for the Liberal party, and the active and enthusiastic participation of the English-speaking bourgeoisie in several government projects. Although the aim of the implemented reforms was to promote the interests of the French-speaking petite bourgeoisie, from a nationalist ideological perspective, at the same time they served the interests of both the English-speaking bourgeoisie, whose class interests were complementary rather than opposite, and the imperialist American bourgeoisie. These classes all share an interest, in fact, in having a 'modern' neo-liberal type state established in Quebec, which, in conjunction with the federal state, can ensure the rationalization and good functioning of the capitalist economy from which they profit. Like the neo-capitalist faction of the French-speaking petite bourgeoisie, the English-speaking bourgeoisie will feel its interests seriously threatened only when the technocratic faction of the French-speaking petite bourgeoisie makes its bid for political-ideological hegemony.

This split between the two factions of the new French-speaking petite bour-geoisie became visible, ideologically, towards the end of 1964, coinciding with what has been called the end of the Quiet Revolution or the beginning of the 'reaction' (as the technocratic faction refers to it). Essentially, the conflict be-tween the two factions arose over nationalist ideology: the technocratic fac-tion wanted to push ahead with nationalist demands, while the neo-capitalist faction seemed content to maintain the ideological *status quo*, categorically refusing to go beyond those nationalist demands already realized. A number of events during the years 1964-65 – the Queen's visit to Quebec, the strike at *La Presse*, Lesage's goodwill visit to the Western Canadian provinces, the debate over the Fulton-Favreau formula, the departure of 'the three doves' for Ottawa, the Quebec government's fights with the financial cartel that un-derwrites it – illustrate the first phase in the split and conflict between the factions of the Quebec petite bourgeoisie.

THE SPLIT IN THE BOURGEOISIE
AND THE STRUGGLE FOR HEGEMONY

Throughout the period 1965-70, the internal conflict grew between petit bourgeois factions for political and ideological hegemony in Quebec society, culminating at the political level in the founding of the MSA and then of the Parti Québécois. This party was the political voice of the technocratic faction, giving coherent expression to their ideology in an articulate political program. The ideological opposition between these two factions was demonstrated, in Quebec, in the means each employed to promote its economic and political interests within the system of capitalist relations we have described. The tech-nocratic group, as a faction of the bourgeoisie, had interests as a French-speaking group which, to a certain degree, placed it in opposition to the French-speaking neo-capitalist faction and to the English-speaking bourgeoisie. It used the state as the main instrument of economic development through its role of entrepreneur-employer – hence, its insistence on strengthening the state of Quebec through political independence from Canada. (Obviously, only the state of Quebec can be this entrepreneur-employer state for the French-speak-ing technocratic petite bourgeoisie.) The main purpose of this drive was to strengthen the economic functions of the state: its role as a capitalist entre-preneur, on the one hand; the development and 'rationalization' of the eco-nomy on the other (through planning, social security, industrial relations, and so on). Pushed to its logical conclusion, the aim of the technocratic bourgeoi-sie is to establish its hegemony over the bourgeois bloc. This would become possible under a system in which state monopoly capitalism was predomi-nant.

We see once again that nationalist ideology is linked to the circumstances of a specific class. The technocratic character of this faction of the petite bourgeoisie explains its form of nationalism. Such *indépendentisme* is possible only in so far as it entails a modification in other sectors of the capitalist system of production, a modification whose specific product this faction is, as we have seen above. In the years 1950-70, this structural modification had effects analogous to those brought about in the arena of class and national conflict by economic and political transformations in the period 1800-37. In the two cases, a French-speaking petite bourgeoisie tried to assume control of the political structures by taking advantage of a change in the function of politics in the society. The 'Patriotes' tried to take advantage of the political structures set up in 1791 (the Assembly and Councils), and the rebellion corresponded to the change-over from a fur to a wood economy. The existence of a double class structure in Quebec society following the Conquest radicalized the class conflict and gave it a national character.

In the same way, the technocratic petite bourgeoisie is now trying to promote and exploit the tendency towards state capitalism that is inherent in the present phase of imperialist monopoly capitalism. It is doing this because this tendency can advance its interests as a dominated French-speaking petite bourgeoisie within a double class structure. The existence of a phenomenon of national domination in Quebec explains this propensity, unique in North America but common to a number of European capitalist countries, to translate the indicators of structural domination into politics – that is, to emphasize the importance of the economic, cultural, and ideological functions of the state.

We can thus understand the possible conflict of interest between the technocratic and neo-capitalist factions of the French-speaking petite bourgeoisie, as well as between the French-speaking technocratic faction and the English-speaking big bourgeoisie. This point of dissension is of secondary importance, in so far as the technocrats do not for a moment question the *fundamental structure* of the capitalist relations of production. But it does exist to the extent that the strengthening of the state and its economic functions (the objective of technocratic faction) can harm the interests of private capitalism in certain cases (and only in certain cases). The best example of this in Quebec is the nationalization of electricity, which was effected during the Quiet Revolution on the initiative of the technocratic faction of the petite bourgeoisie. For the most part, the conflict is only potential, and the interests of each faction are complementary and interdependent. A good example of this is the attempt by the petite bourgeoisie to establish a program of regional modernization (the Agency for the Modernization of Eastern Quebec). What happened in this case was that the local neo-capitalist petite bourgeoisie used the technocrats' participation to their own advantage. The technocrats and local small capitalists intervened jointly to quash the few efforts and to radicalize the project by helping the population to oust the local power elite, for both felt threatened by such a prospect.

The national situation, however, makes the contradiction between these two factions especially complex in the case of Quebec, for it pushes the French-speaking technocratic faction into increased support for a state capitalist economy. In fact, the class interests of the French-Canadian neo-capitalist faction may be threatened in so far as the French-speaking technocratic petite bourgeoisie can promote its interests only by strengthening the state of Quebec (independentism) – that is, by making Quebec into a real nation. The French-speaking neo-capitalist faction also needs the state of Quebec in order to improve its precarious economic position vis-à-vis the all-powerful interests of American and Canadian capitalists. The General Investment Corporation is an example of how the state serves its interests. But the French-speaking neo-capitalist petite bourgeoisie also needs the federal state, which controls some of the main economic mechanisms and looks after the integrated functioning of the whole Canadian economy. It has as much of an interest in the maintenance of the federal state as does the English-speaking bourgeoisie. Moreover, the French-speaking neo-capitalist petite bourgeoisie relies on the support of the English-speaking big bourgeoisie, to whom its economic interests are closely tied. It performs the role of a ruling class at the federal, and especially provincial, levels of government in the interests of this big bourgeoisie.

All these factors help explain the opposition of the neo-capitalist petite bourgeoisie to the technocratic faction's independentist project. More concretely, the neo-liberal Quebec state, in its present format, serves its interests. As long as the federal state and the English-speaking bourgeoisie will ensure that it is not 'too discriminated against' because it is French-speaking, it will refuse to involve itself in a class struggle of a national character. Given its class character and its economic dependence, the neo-capitalist faction of the petite bourgeoisie cannot aim at making Quebec into a nation; the 'truncated nation' suits it, at least in the short run. This does not rule out special emphasis on different national features (nationalism) – quite the contrary, in fact. But this emphasis is placed much more on cultural, linguistic, and juridical features than on political ones. Prime Minister Trudeau articulates the political consequences of this position perfectly: 'a single, united Canada, with total respect for the linguistic and cultural rights of the two groups.' Thus, each of the two factions of the new French-Canadian petite bourgeoisie has a different type of nationalist ideology, corresponding in each case to its respective interests and tactical alliances as a class faction: for the neo-capitalist faction, juridical-cultural nationalism à la Trudeau; for the technocratic faction, political independentism à la Parti Québécois.

THE WORKING CLASS AND NATIONALISM

We must ask ourselves whether there exists in Quebec a nationalist ideology emanating from classes other than the petite bourgeoisie. In the first part of this article, we put forward the hypothesis that nationalist ideological elements could be linked to the interests and activities of the working class or farmers. We think that in Quebec society, during the period under examination, these classes lacked a nationalism of their own, just as they lacked a unique ideological framework. As dominated classes within the neo-capitalist system, the working class and farmers were subject to ideological, as well as political and economic, domination. These three types of domination are necessarily interrelated, interdependent, and interlocking within the structure of all modes of production. Their ideology is that of the dominant classes; but there must be assimilated into the ideological structure certain elements that are specific to the dominated classes and which express their interests. This applies, for example, to the trade union ideology which Marxist literature terms 'economism.' Moreover, the existence of class conflict at the ideological level seems to be manifested, not as a confrontation between the ideologies of two class structures, but more as a kind of resistance by which the dominated classes can sometimes withstand the penetration of certain features of the dominant ideology. Quebec nationalism is an interesting example of this.

It can be claimed that, throughout the Quiet Revolution, the working class and farmers in Quebec were completely impervious to petit bourgeois nationalist ideology. They felt most acutely, however, the consequences of the reforms which the petite bourgeoisie initiated in its own class interests. To a great extent, the dominated classes had to pay for these reforms, through increases in income and sales taxes, the upsetting of their traditional way of life, and so forth. If the measures adopted did not go directly against the interests of the dominated classes, they still failed to meet the most important needs and aspirations of these people (employment, housing, credit, working conditions). Lacking a political organization of their own that was independent of the bourgeois parties, the working class and farmers could express their political opposition only through elections, by altering the existing balance between the bourgeois parties. Thus, acting as supporting classes for the Union Nationale, they brought about the defeat of the ruling party in 1966. We must note, however, that this ability to change the political balance does not mean that the dominated classes have political power. The proof is that the party that comes to power will continue to serve the interests of the dominant class and its factions.

Earlier we tried to show that the 'brake' applied to nationalism following the Quiet Revolution did not coincide with the election of 1966 but began in

1964, corresponding to the beginning of open conflict between the internal factions of the French-Canadian petite bourgeoisie. In terms of this internal conflict, the 1964-66 period corresponded to political domination by the neo-capitalist faction (supported by the English-speaking bourgeoisie), while the main period of the rule of the Union Nationale (1967-70) saw the establishment of a kind of political equilibrium in the conflict between neo-capitalist and technocratic factions. The main effect of this situation of quasi-equilibrium was to paralyse government action, leading many to say of the Union Nationale, 'They've done nothing!' – nothing for the working class and farmers that brought them into power; nothing in particular for the technocratic bourgeois faction; and nothing for the neo-capitalist faction, except to maintain the minimum *status quo* corresponding to their minimum common interests. It would therefore be false to say that the Union Nationale between 1966 and 1970 was (strictly speaking) the representative of a class or a class faction: politically, the Union Nationale reflected a balance between the conflicting forces.

During this period, then, the Union Nationale represented a specific product of Quebec's political structure. Between 1936 and 1960, this party had been the political voice of the traditional petite bourgeoisie, which subsequently disappeared. But the Union Nationale survived, as a result of the existence of a two-party system in Quebec, and from 1964 onward was able to capitalize on popular discontent and the split within the petite bourgeoisie. This explains its coming to power in 1966 and its repeated oscillations thereafter between independentism and federalism. These fluctuations, which many have interpreted as proof of pure opportunism, can be explained only as a function of the equilibrium that existed between the two factions of the petite bourgeoisie. The main role of the Union Nationale between 1966 and 1970 was to maintain this equilibrium. We must not imagine, however, that this political equilibrium reflects a similar economic equilibrium; economic power clearly remained in the hands of the English-Canadian and American bourgeoisies.

The technocratic faction of the petite bourgeoisie is now in the process of altering the political and ideological equilibrium between the petit bourgeois factions in its favour. This faction felt 'strong enough' to found its own political party and engage in full-scale electoral battle. The effect of this was to leave the Liberal party in the hands of the neo-capitalist petit bourgeois faction. Like all political groups, however, the Parti Québécois can come to power only through the support of a large proportion of the working class and farmers. Everything seems to indicate that this party can count on such electoral support, in the intermediate and long term (though to what extent is difficult to say). Must we therefore conclude that the dominated classes would be prepared to adopt the nationalist ideology of the petite bourgeoisie, and more particularly its technocratic faction, for the first time since 1960? We do not think the support of workers and farmers for the Parti Québécois should be interpreted in this way. It is the same kind of political phenomenon as the support given to the Union Nationale in 1966, or to the Créditistes in recent federal elections. Lacking their own ideology and political action, these dominated classes express their discontent, opposition, and aspirations by altering the equilibrium between the bourgeois parties, through electoral support for one or the other. The party's ideology or type of nationalism is not particularly important, in the end, because these classes can switch quickly from the Créditistes to the Union Nationale to the Parti Québécois, not to mention the vote for Trudeau in 1968. They will be prepared to support whatever solutions are proposed – the distribution of purchasing power, Quebec independence, or anything else – provided that the party in question can cleverly appeal to the discontent and exploitation which these classes endure.

It is from this very special perspective that the dominated classes may give significant support to the Parti Québécois; the strength or scale of this support will not alter the real reasons behind it. These classes may support independence as a possible, if not probable, way of improving their condition, or at least as a means of preventing it from getting any worse. We see that petit bourgeois nationalist ideology is associated here with interests and aspirations quite different from those to which it naturally corresponds. Reviewing Quebec history, we can find similar cases where some of the aspirations of the dominated classes were integrated into petit bourgeois nationalist ideology, an integration which was translated into support by these classes for the petite bourgeoisie's struggle. This was true of the 1837-38 rebellion, in which the peasants' participation was greatest in those regions where their economic situation was most precarious.[15] Opposition to conscription during the two world wars falls into the same perspective.

There is, therefore, no nationalist ideology or ideology with nationalist elements emanating from the dominated classes in Quebec.[16] We can discover only a number of interests, or of economic, political, and cultural aspirations, specific to the dominated classes and linked to their situation; these interests could be expressed as nationistic elements integrated into an ideology belonging uniquely to classes. We have noted the absence of such an ideology specific to the dominated classes – that is, one that is not integrated into the ideology of the dominant classes but directly opposed to them. By definition, such an ideology would be revolutionary, resulting from a situation where the conflict of the dominated classes against the dominating will have reached the revolutionary stage. We cannot analyse such a revolutionary situation or its eventuality within the framework of this article. We can only state the possibility that an ideology specific to the dominated classes in Quebec may come to exist, and that it would contain non-bourgeois nationalist elements, linked to the economic, political, and cultural interests of the dominated classes.

What form would working class or farmers' nationalism take in Quebec? We could not answer this precisely without giving way to 'sociological prophecy,' which has nothing to do with scientific analysis. Nor do we believe that we can identify the revolutionary nationalism of exploited groups 'in advance' through the ideology put forward by various movements and left-wing groups in Quebec, be it the Front de Liberation Populaire, the FLQ, the review *Socialisme*, or others. None the less, we can imagine that the revolutionary nationalism of the exploited classes would resemble to some degree the left-wing nationalism generally defined by these different groups. We can imagine that Quebec workers can achieve their liberation from economic exploitation, seize political power, affirm their culture – in short, effect a total revolution – only if they can overthrow the three forms of domination that obstruct them: the petit bourgeois classes, the colonialist Anglo-Canadian bourgeoisie, and the American imperialist bourgeoisie. Thus, the revolutionary ideology of Quebec's dominated classes will probably be anti-bourgeois, anti-imperialist, and nationalist. Through its integration into a revolutionary ideology, this nationalism will focus simultaneously on the economic, politico-juridical, and cultural features of the nation – quite unlike earlier types of nationalism, which tended, as we have seen, to stress the political features.

Clearly, this liberation of the dominated classes in Quebec society is linked to that of the North American proletariat as a whole. This double character, national and international, of the struggle of the proletariat is a specific product of the structure of the capitalist mode of production. Any attempt to deny one or the other, in analysis as well as in practice, will only impede the liberation of the working class.

THE WORKING CLASS AND NATIONALISM:
THE QUEBEC ELECTION, 1970

We must emphasize that this article was completed several weeks before the Quebec provincial election of April 1970. We do not believe that the result of this election in any way undermines our hypotheses concerning the petit bourgeois character of the Parti Québécois' type of nationalism. It was altogether predictable that the Parti Québécois would receive important electoral support from the working class – first because of the traditional electoral behaviour of the working class; and second, because of the current political crisis with which Quebec society is faced. As we have pointed out, since the dominated classes in Quebec do not have their own ideology or political formation, they can express their discontent and frustration only by throwing their weight at random into the electoral balance of bourgeois democracy. This is a game of desperation, if ever there was one; for the dominant class, camouflaged by its various factions, is always the winner. No doubt, some will reply that the dominated classes are not completely blind, and that this time they chose the lesser of two evils, 'the best of the bad parties,' and so on. We do not believe there is any reason for comfort in the fact that a more subtle, more attractive, more 'polished' petit bourgeois mystification beat out a grosser (though not by much) mystification. Let us stop believing in miracles: the Parti Québécois is not the Prince Charming, who has at last awakened Sleeping Beauty from her long slumber. The workers who supported the Parti Québécois in the 1970 election are not, on the whole, more 'politicized' and more revolutionary than those who supported the Liberal party; the Quebec working class did not take a left-wing turn, as some would like to believe, who, in their social-democratic enthusiasm, define left and right with gay abandon.

The last election represented a change, but a change initiated by the petite bourgeoisie and corresponding to its own objectives. In our study, we stressed the fact that the Union Nationale could survive politically only by making use of a temporary state of equilibrium between the two principal factions of the French-Canadian petite bourgeoisie. The collapse of this party in the last election shows that this situation no longer exists. Now that the technocratic faction has its own political party and the neo-capitalist faction has clearly rallied around the Liberal party, the internal conflicts between the bourgeoisie and petite bourgeoisie will have to be expressed through these two political groups. It follows that the working-class vote will now be divided between the Liberals and the Parti Québécois, and the farmer vote between the Liberals and Social Credit, according to the traditional mechanism of electoral behaviour that characterizes Quebec's dominated classes. Thus, the fact that a segment of the working class or of the farmers voted this time for 'new' parties (the Parti Québécois and Social Credit) is not the sign of a change in the positions or political ideology of these classes. That these two parties exist, received votes, and elected members shows a realignment of forces within the dominant class, a realignment which the dominated classes have endured, confirmed, and paid for.

The claim that the Parti Québécois has lost (or negated) its petit bourgeois character because a majority of Parti Québécois members represent working-class constituencies does not stand up to serious analysis.[17] We must analyse a political ideology, as well as the political party that expresses it, in terms of the economic, political, and cultural class interests which the actions inspired by this ideology or followed by this party defend and serve. We believe that we have demonstrated that the Parti Québécois type of nationalism (and its variations) corresponds fundamentally and directly to the interests of the technocratic faction of the French-Canadian petite bourgeoisie.

It is possible that this faction of the bourgeoisie has succeeded in imposing its ideology on a segment of the working class; for the working class, this would imply the change to a new cultural domination. But even this eventuality is uncertain; we have good reason to believe, in fact, that a segment of the working class gave its vote, but not its ideological support, to the Parti Québécois. If this were so, it would be yet another example of the political impotence of the dominated classes in bourgeois democracies.

Unfortunately, we must observe that the victory of the Parti Québécois in some working-class ridings has not only allowed the social democrats free rein in their rationalizations, but has also revived, in left-wing circles, the myths of electoralism and take-over of bourgeois political groups. Many militants who share our analysis of the petit bourgeois nature of the Parti Québécois and its ideology have begun to hope that the swing in the working-class vote to this party will allow left-wing forces to use the party to radicalize the masses or to use the masses to radicalize the party. We have to deal here not with an artificial confusion but with a real dilemma – one, moreover, that is impossible to resolve, since we have a petit bourgeois party on the one hand, and a discontented, exploited, dominated, but not politicized mass on the other. The Parti Québécois, because it is a petit bourgeois party, dominated and financially and ideologically supported by the petite bourgeoisie, cannot be the instrument of politicization and education which will lead the working class to a revolutionary break. In addition, any eventual revolutionary working-class forces could not make the Parti Québécois into a workers' party, defending the interests of the dominated classes. The Parti Québécois cannot be 'pushed to the left' from the inside; its ideology can be changed only within the narrow limits permitted by the interests of the class that supports and uses it.

In our study, we have tried to define the field of interests of the technocratic petite bourgeoisie. We have shown that this petite bourgeoisie might accept certain forms of social democratic reformism of the Swedish type, given favourable circumstances at the level of class conflict. The Parti Québécois can tolerate left-wing influence only within these limits. In the event of a revolutionary drive to force the party beyond these limits, there would be a single alternative: the petite bourgeoisie would sabotage its party. That is, it would cut off its finances and means of operation, and would withdraw all the guarantees of respectability necessary in playing the electoral game; or there would be a split between the petit bourgeois bloc, with its social-democratic–oriented working-class support, and the revolutionary bloc. The latter would be expelled and pushed out to the periphery, becoming once again incapable of achieving its objectives through bourgeois institutions.

It would be disastrous if Quebec's revolutionary militants allowed themselves a useless and costly waste of time and energy, blindly ignoring the experience of all revolutionary movements since the nineteenth century, and their own political experience in Quebec (inside the RIN, Parti Socialiste Québécois, and other groups). These experiences have proved decisively, we would argue, that the structures and political institutions of capitalist society, like all other institutions in this society, are established, maintained, and used by the dominant classes as a function of their class interests. Whatever group uses these institutions and mechanisms will only help to maintain and perpetuate them. It is absolutely impossible to modify the capitalist rules of the game if you have not first destroyed their *raison d'être.*

A NOTE CONCERNING THE OCTOBER '70 CRISIS

It was in this political climate that the Front de Libération du Québec decided to act, and its intervention revealed the contradictions that we analysed above. The weakness of the Front in both numbers and organization, as well as its lack of effective support by the people – in spite of the overt sympathy of some groups of workers, students, and intellectuals – facilitated the adoption by the federal government of extraordinary measures for the protection of the economic and political interests of the Canadian bourgeoisie, the intermediary of the imperialist monopolies. As we have seen, these are the very interests threatened by the Quebec situation. The Trudeau government used the kidnapping as a pretext for launching a repressive operation of unprecedented scope within the Canadian liberal democracy. Its purpose appears to have been twofold: on one hand, to disrupt completely any kind of leftist action in Quebec; and on the other hand, to discredit the Parti Québécois in the eyes of the people by trying to link the party indirectly to the events. In order to achieve this, the federal government relied on the provincial government, in which the Liberal party, as we have seen, is committed to the interests of federalism and of the classes which support it.

The Quebec left had no solid organization of its own, and a large number of its members belonged to the political and trade union movements controlled by the French-Canadian petite bourgeoisie. These were mainly the Parti Québécois of René Lévesque, the Front d'Action Politique (an opposition political party in Montreal gathering salaried workers under its flag for the democratization and the reform of municipal administration), the Conseil Central de Montréal (the trade union organization which was most actively engaged in socialist combat, consisting of the trade unions affiliated with the CNTU of the Montreal area), and the citizens' committees (groupings of residents of the popular boroughs for the defence of their socio-economic interests). Besides these organizations, some autonomous leftist groups must be mentioned; the number of their followers, however, was quite limited.

In spite of its weakness (numerical and political), the left nevertheless represented a certain threat to the provincial and federal powers supported by the neo-capitalist French Canadian petite bourgeoisie and the English Canadian bourgeoisie. Indeed, the effects of the existing North American economic situation are disastrous for Quebec, and the contradictions of the 'affluent society' are particularly striking in that province. The federalist forces, however, have always based their political propaganda in Quebec on what they call 'economic realities.' During the 1970 provincial election campaign, the Liberal party based its propaganda opposing the independentist ideas of the Parti Québécois on a statement affirming the possibility of economic success for French Canadians within the framework of the Federation, raising the spectre of economic depression engendered by an independent Quebec, and, more important, promising the creation of 100,000 new jobs. Economic events have clearly revealed that such election promises are a pipe dream; indeed, unemployment has increased and development has stagnated. Despite its weakness, the left found here a ground which was particularly favourable to political work, and tried to take utmost advantage of the situation in a relatively chaotic, yet quite effective, manner. A proof thereof is the relative success of the left within the Front d'Action Politique, the citizens' committees, and the Parti Québécois.

If the intention of the federalist forces was to destroy the hegemony that the Parti Québécois was trying to establish, this operation must be considered a failure. The strategy of the party is to create a centre-left bloc aiming at the independence of Quebec. This is the course followed by its leaders, who have always maintained relatively moderate positions while encouraging leftist militants to work in its ranks, at the level of the people. By attacking these militants, some elected members or personalities of the party, as well as the Front d'Action Politique in Montreal (which was more or less allied with the Parti Québécois, at least in the minds of the people), the federal government tried to undermine the hegemony established step by step by the technocratic petite bourgeoisie since the foundation of the party. The aim was to destroy its propaganda network, then active among the dominated classes, to make it lose its credibility with the voters, and to prevent undecided petit bourgeois elements from falling under its domination.

Although it may be premature at this stage to draw final conclusions, it now seems obvious not only that the operation has been a total failure but also that it has accelerated the movement toward the establishment of a hegemony of the technocratic petite bourgeoisie. Far from falling back into retreat, this group has, on the contrary, taken advantage of the events to strengthen its position, while maintaining integrally the policies adopted ever since the birth of the independentist movement. The Parti Québécois has refused to separate itself from the left, and it has drawn together the petit bourgeois opposition on the issue of the struggle against the government's repressive measures. Thus, the technocratic petite bourgeoisie seems to have emerged the victor from this confrontation and to have strengthened its positions while accelerating the movement toward the establishment of its hegemony. Its propaganda is now formulated as follows: independence with the Parti Québécois, or chaos and terrorism. The position of the Parti Québécois was strengthened particularly by the extent to which the events revealed the depth of subservience of the neo-capitalist petite bourgeoisie to the English-speaking bourgeoisie. Indeed, the provincial Liberal party has been merely a political go-between of the federal government, faithful to the economic interests of the class segments of which the Liberal party is the political voice.

Moreover, the repression hit very hard and, in the short run, disorganized those of the radical left who remained outside the Parti Québécois, refusing to adopt a conciliationist policy, the sole result of which would have been to endorse the nationalist petit bourgeois ideology. Several militant members of the FLQ and other groups are still being judged and detained in jail, often in complete disregard of the most elementary principles of bourgeois justice. It must be noted, however, that the October crisis has destroyed the Front d'Action Politique in Montreal, and that some progressive petit bourgeois members of the movement have withdrawn their support from the Front. Thus, this movement may fall under the effective control of the revolutionary militants and become the basis for a new autonomous workers' organization on the left. The new circumstances of the revolutionary struggle in Quebec – repression, censorship, and organized violence within the system – are currently forcing the Quebec left to launch itself into a struggle for socialism, a struggle which will be as hard and as radical as that of the revolutionary forces which, all over the world, are uniting in their assault against imperialism under its various 'national' masks.[18]

NOTES

1 Michel Van Schendel, 'Pour une théorie du socialisme au Québec 11,' *Socialisme 69*, no. 18.
2 Fernand Dumont, 'Notes sur l'analyse des idéologies,' *Recherches sociographiques.*
3 Marcel Rioux, 'Conscience ethnique et conscience de classe au Québec,' *Recherches sociographiques*, VI, 1 (1965), 25.
4 Jacques Dofny, Marcel Rioux, 'Social Class in French Canada,' in Rioux and Martin, eds., *French Canadian Society,* I (Toronto 1964), 309.
5 *Ibid.,* 310.
6 Rioux 'Conscience ethnique et conscience de classe au Québec,' 26.
7 *Ibid.,* 24.
8 *Ibid.,* 25-6.

9 *Ibid.,* 26-7.
10 *Ibid.,* 32.
11 K. Marx and F. Engels, *Manifesto of the Communist Party,* in Marx and Engels, *Selected Works* (London 1968), 51 (our emphasis).
12 *Ibid.,* 45.
13 We believe that we must approach the disappearance of the national features of the structure of social formations during the period of transformation to a communist society in the same way as we approach the abolition of the state. This question merits fuller treatment than we can give it in this article. We point out, none the less, that Lenin noted the need to make use of bourgeois law as long as the productive forces did not make it possible to give to each according to his needs. It seems equally clear to us that no voluntarist intervention can make the national features of social formation disappear, in so far as these too are a function of the development of productive forces, of their impact on the economic relations of production, and of their articulation at the political and ideological levels of the social formation. We must understand the increased importance of nationalism in the Soviet bloc since 1945 in terms of the existence of regional economic inequalities, linked, in part at least, to the stage of development of the productive forces.
14 In the present economic context, the result of the persistance of this type of industry is to make Quebec's economic structure relatively out-dated.
15 On this subject see Gilles Bourque, *Classes sociales et Question Nationale au Québec 1760-1840,* which has appeared in Editions Parti-Pris.
16 In this regard, we must not identify the ideology of movements claiming to 'represent' the dominated classes with the ideology and real aspirations of the classes these claim to represent. We can explain the Parti Québécois-oriented nationalism of a number of Quebec union leaders, in the Confederation of National Trade Unions or the Confederation of Quebec Teachers, or the Quebec Federation of Labour, by the fact that many of these leaders belong to the technocratic faction of the petite bourgeoisie, and by the clear affinity that exists between the economic and political ideology of the Parti Québécois and trade union ideology. For the business unionism with a participatory tendency that prevails in Quebec union headquarters, mixed or pure state capitalism, which in the last instance also constitutes the technocratic faction's political-economic project, is the true ideal.
17 People are too prone to forget, moreover, that the Parti Québécois received a high percentage of the vote in French-speaking petit bourgeois ridings where it failed to elect a member. In the working class ridings which elected Parti Québécois members, however, there was an important division of the vote among the various parties, with what was often a small share of the vote for the candidate elected.
18 For a deeper analysis of the October 1970 crisis and of the current situation in Quebec, the reader may consult several articles published in the collection *Québec Occupé* (Montréal, Editions Parti-Pris, 1971) and in the special issue of the journal *Socialisme Québécois*: 'Québec 70, la Réaction tranquille' (April 1971).

Stanley B. Ryerson

author of several books, including *Unequal Union*; he teaches history at the Université du Québec in Montreal

Quebec: concepts of class and nation

... They who control the means by which a dependent class must live, control the livelihood and conditions of that class. GUSTAVUS MYERS, Preface to *History of Canadian Wealth*

Nulle nation ne saurait obéir à une autre nation, pour la raison toute simple, qu'aucune nation ne saurait commander à une autre. *La Minerve*, le 16 février 1832

CLASS STRUCTURE, in Canada as elsewhere, is not something that is readily discernible. One arrives at a perception of it only through oblique, approximate approaches (as in Porter's *The Vertical Mosaic*), or else head-on, brutally and empirically (as on a picket-line). 'Class,' writes a contemporary social historian, 'is defined by a complex relationship of exploitation involving more than economic life alone ... Class is no more a visible datum than is surplus value.'[1] So it is quite to be expected that disclosure of the realities of class structure will entail laborious research (invisibility being no more a proof of non-reality in social science than in nuclear physics).

It is perhaps less usual that a country's *national* structure should be just about as elusive: 'Canada – two nations or one?' was Eugene Forsey's query of a decade ago; 'Canada – colony to nation' was A.R.M. Lower's title; Donald Creighton excoriates 'The Myth of Bi-culturalism'; Marcel Rioux poses 'La Question du Québec' (perhaps less well translated as 'Quebec in Question' than as 'Canada in Question'). So runs the catalogue of our uncertainties, all notwithstanding a fiat reported in 1965 under the headline: 'Trudeau believes in neither the two-nations theory nor in associate states nor in Quebec special status.'[2] It thus appears to be a singularity of Canada/Quebec, that the very nature and dimensions of the nation, of 'the national fact,' are matters of generalized dispute.

From the start we are hampered by a semantic difficulty (in French as well as in English): we must distinguish between the word *nation* in the sense (*a*) of a *political* entity, a sovereign *state* ('colony to nation'); and *nation* in the sense (*b*) of a *community* of people, linked by a common cultural-linguistic historical experience of living and working together, whether or not in possession of their own state (like the Poles partitioned among Prussia, Austria, and Russia in 1793). The former sense (*a*) applies to *countries* as state entities (the 'United Nations'), the latter (*b*) to collectivities of people. The *reductio ad absurdum* of terminological muddlement is offered by Eugene Forsey in 'proving' that the French Canadians do not constitute a nation (in sense *b*) because they lack an independent, sovereign state (sense *a*), and that Canada '*is* a nation' because it *is* such a state.'[3]

A NEW SET OF BELIEFS ABOUT CANADA

Denial of duality or its acceptance – here is the dividing line between irreconcilable definitions of the Canada/Quebec reality. The crux is acceptance (or refusal) of the French-speaking Québécois as constituting a *nation-community*, and of Canada as a *binational state* (in substance although not in structure); and of the English-speaking Canadians as a nation-community whose corporate elite is in command of the economy as well as of the state. In the alternate interpretation, the nation is the Canadian nation-state, and franco-phone Quebec is a cultural-linguistic ethnic minority 'like the others,' living in a province that is 'une province comme les autres.' *La nation québécoise* is dismissed, as was its initial manifestation, *la nation canadienne*, decried by Sir James Craig in 1810; or the *Canadiens'* 'vain hope of nationality' so blithely written off by Lord Durham in 1839.

A semantic difficulty? Rather, an unresolved national question whose his-toric persistence and intractability is reinforced by an unresolved class ques-tion: the rule of a corporate elite that can trace its ancestry to the bloc of social forces of Anglo-mercantile elements and their seigneurial-clerical colla-borators of 1774. The political power-structure of this ruling group has char-acteristically responded to francophone demands for state identity either by conceding a compromise marked by a maximum of form and a minimum of content (such as the provincial existence accorded in 1867), or by seeking the outright effacement of Québécois national identity (the 'Union' demand of 1822, the near-achievement of it in 1840). Our most recent experience of this ambivalence has been the B&B Commission, whose bicultural processional was abruptly halted by the March 1971 decision not to formulate conclusions from its massive labours, and whose very *raison d'être* is now repudiated by M. Trudeau's proclamation of something called 'multiculturalism.' At this point, the Liberal Prime Minister, abandoning even the timid cultural-dualism position of his predecessor, has blithely embraced the ultra-conservative big-otry of Professor Donald Creighton – for whom the enemy is *any* affirmation of dualism.

The threat this country faces, Creighton argued in the midst of the October crisis of 1970, is a corrosive erosion of will resulting from the propagation of 'a new set of beliefs about Canada.'[4] At the heart of this new and insidious heresy was the assertion that 'the most important fact about Canada ... was its cultural duality ...' that ethnic and cultural values were fundamental in Cana-dian Confederation, and that the chief goal of Canadian statesmanship ought to be the development of the Canadian constitution on the basis of 'an equal partnership between the two founding races.' This 'completely new idea, which formed no part in the plans of the Fathers of Confederation' has led in the direction of abandoning efforts to integrate French Canadians 'in the na-tion as a whole'; instead, the view has been toyed with that 'Québec might be accepted as the particular homeland of the French Canadian people and granted a special, separate status in Confederation.' Against such unmitigated subversion, 'our only hope of deliverance ...' Creighton concludes, 'lies in the reassertion of Canadian nationalism in its first and integral form. The vain and perilous pursuit of dualism, which was not an original object of Confederation and has nearly brought about its undoing, must be abandoned. One nation, not two nations in one, can alone maintain an effective defense of Canada.' The eager executor of this Tory imperial mandate is the Liberal, P.E. Trudeau.

The dragon of dualism (cultural as well as political) had been set loose by Lester Pearson. That Quebec might be viewed 'in a sense, as the homeland of a people' was a thought to which he had actually given utterance, as early as 1962. Even worse, by launching the vast inquiry into the relationships between the 'two societies,' he had (despite the calculated exclusion from the Royal Commission's mandate of any consideration of constitutional, state-structural elements) invited dangerous thoughts about fundamentals. Indeed, the commissioners' General Introduction (in Book I of the *Report*) was to contain a passage intimating the existence, not only of problems of cultural-linguistic and socio-economic inequality, but of an 'other dimension' altogether – that having to do with 'political equality,' indeed, with 'self-determination.' This is it:

'81. Finally, let us consider another dimension of equality between the two communities – the political dimension. This covers the possibilities for each society to choose its own institutions or, at least, to have the opportunity to participate fully in making political decisions within a framework shared with the other community.

'82. The collective aspect of equality is here still more evident; it is not cultural growth and development at the individual level which is at stake, but the degree of *self-determination* which one society can exercise in relation to another. We have in mind the power of decision of each group and its freedom to act, not only in its cultural life but in all aspects of its collective life. We are no longer concerned with the characteristics which distinguish the two communities qualitatively, or even with their respective social and economic positions, but with the extent of the control each has over its government or governments. This is the basis for the discussion of the constitutional framework in which the two societies can live or aspire to live: a unitary or a federal system; special status for the province in which the minority group is concentrated; or again, for the same part of the country, the status of an associate state; or finally, the status of an independent state.'[5]

All of which is hardly Pierre Elliott's cup of tea. It rather suggests a not unlikely rationale for the eagerness of his response to a letter from the commissioners in March 1971 (or had he perhaps actually instigated the drafting of it?). The letter set forth the grounds for their decision to abandon the drafting of the long-promised general conclusions to the *Report*. They had been unable – after eight years of labours, in the most exhaustive probe of the matter ever undertaken – to reach agreement on what they had from the outset described as 'the fundamental problems of Canadian duality.' In an unkind but ominous hint, they had the temerity to reaffirm that 'an essential element in the crisis'

was the 'conflict of the two majorities' and 'the political dimension of equality.' M. Trudeau, hastening to express his 'perfect understanding' of their de-
sistment, to reiterate his hopes for 'national unity' between what he insists on
calling 'the two main linguistic groups,' ignored the hint. Before the year was
out, he was to compound the indecent quashing of B&B conclusions by repu-
diating the very concept of duality that had been the Commission's starting-
point and frame of reference. The pluralistic fig-leaf of 'multiculturalism' is
thus henceforth to render respectable the Tory-Creighton cry: *'One nation,
not two nations in one!'*

Trudeau by his insecure intransigeance ensures the deepening crisis, not of
liberalism only, but of Canada. One might add – of the Canada constructed on
the rickety base of the colonial BNA Act, and on the corrupt and corroded
fundament of private-corporate capital, and on the irremediably 'unequal
union' of two nations, embedded in a social matrix that is obsolete. Even the
ultra-moderate liberal political scientist, Léon Dion, has come out for recognition of the right of national self-determination. Addressing the Joint Senate-
House Committee on the Constitution, Dion argued that the crisis of Canada
has taken on a new dimension with the 'rise of contestation of the established
order ... No longer is it federalism alone that is called in question, but the
socio-political order itself ... The realm of the possible has shrunk danger-
ously ...' Against this background, the issue of self-determination becomes in-
escapable: 'There is no force in the world that can prevent French-speaking
Québécois from seeing themselves as a society and a nation, original and distinct from the total Canadian reality. Conversely, few English-speaking Canadians, despite all their good will, manage to see themselves as a particular nation within Canadian reality.' Invoking the argument that has been cited in
the B&B *Report* regarding political equality, Dion urged adoption of the principle of self-determination as a cornerstone of tomorrow's political reality.[6]

A CHOICE OF EVASIONS

There are two traditional approaches to compromise whereby the issue of national self-determination may be evaded. One is the simultaneous acceptance
of cultural duality and refusal of political duality. The other is denial in practice of the binational fact in the name of provincialization. The former goes
back to G.E. Cartier's historic delusion to the effect that in 'large questions of
general interest' (the domain of the central government) 'the differences of
race and religion had no place' – that cultural-national identity was separable,
as a 'local matter,' from state structure. Liberal 'biculturalism' (at least until
its recent repudiation) has been the offspring of this conception. It is Ramsay
Cook arguing that the *entente* of 1864-67 engendered a 'nation-state founded

on the basis of an acceptance of cultural duality and a division of powers.' Or W.L. Morton, reported in Winnipeg as arguing before the B&B Commission that: 'Because Canada is a political nationality, any form of political duality must be rejected ... Because there was no one cultural nationality, there should be cultural duality to do justice to French Canada and to maintain the political unity of Canada.'[7]

The other rationalization is the 'provincialist' one. Léon Dion calls for the right of self-determination 'for Quebec and for any other province that might wish to avail itself of it' – as though each of the other provincial populations was a nation-community such as francophone Quebec. The equivocation surfaces with each dominion-provincial conference. Reporting on that at Victoria (June 1971), Anthony Westell on the one hand refers to the 'English-French crisis': 'Canada waits this morning under the shadow of Pearson's warning that failure could mean a country in fragments. The failure means, in effect, that English and French Canadians have not been able to agree on the structure of government they want for this country.' Yet two paragraphs later we are told: 'Quebec began to push for constitutional reform to strengthen provincial rights during the turbulent decade of the '60's, and the attitude was summed up in Premier Daniel Johnson's book, *Equality or Independence.*'[8] The 'catch' is right here. A push to strengthen *provincial* rights of *ten* constituent elements of one kind, when the real crisis involved two constituent elements of a radically different kind, is either self-deception or plain hypocrisy. The unequal binational union of two distinct peoples ('societies,' 'national communities,' *nations* in the sociological sense) is precisely that central fact of life and history that the 'dominion-provincial' set-up of 1867 was designed to obscure. Yet all the governments, provincial and federal, have been and remain committed to this booby-trap. Despite his ringing 'challenge to federalism' in the name of national equality or independence (1966), Daniel Johnson never got beyond the conceptual framework of the traditional federalism, cited by one commentator as 'Mr. Johnson's view of Canada being an alliance of ten provinces.' Denial of the binational reality is summed up in Eugene Forsey's gemlike formula: 'The constituent units of this country are not "French-Canada" and "English-Canada." They are the ten provinces.'[9] The built-in ambiguity of the nineteenth-century constitution has turned into a twentieth-century nightmare.

'How are we going to save our federal system?' asked a Toronto *Telegram* editorial. 'Outlook for survival as nation questioned' reports the *Globe and Mail* on the same day.[10] Could it be that a radical break with the established concept of Canada is needed, and that it is time overdue to face up to the need for an alternative concept?

Compulsive refusal by the dominant Anglo-Canadian nation-community to recognize the demand for self-determination of the other nation-community is a socio-economic as well as a political phenomenon. The position of dominance that leads Canadians to think (in English) of Canada as 'their' nation-state (with 'the French' a mere linguistic minority) is the political counterpart of their position of economic dominance portrayed in Book III of the B&B *Report*. Hence the way in which, in the October 1970 events, a crisis of legitimacy of the existing structure of the Canadian state merged with elements of a crisis of confidence in the existing social order. Symptomatic of the latter was the 'disturbingly' widespread receptivity in Quebec to the note of radical social criticism expressed in the FLQ Manifesto. Expressive of the former was the apparent acute vulnerability of the state-power centres (Ottawa, Quebec, Montreal) when faced with a serious nationalist challenge. But it was the vehemence of the 'over-reaction,' the extremism of their response, the delirium-quality of their 'apprehended insurrection' fantasmagoria, that above all bore witness to the impact of the merging of class and national issues. Here, indeed, was the belated vindication of Lord Durham's penetrating comment to the effect that with 'the greater part of them ... labourers in the employ of English capitalists,' French Canadians are 'doomed in some measure to occupy an inferior position'; with the added warning (ominous for the *status quo*) that should these people insist on preserving their identity 'the evils of poverty and dependence would merely be aggravated in a ten-fold degree, by a spirit of jealous and resentful nationality which would separate the working class of the community from the possessors of wealth and employers of labour.'[11]

'LA QUESTION SOCIALE'

Just as the unresolved national question, reflected in the turbulence of the last decade in Quebec, has stirred fresh theoretical reflection, so too has the unresolved question of social class. Concern with class structure and conflict found expression in the 1960s in two disciplines particularly: sociology and history. The colloquia held by *Recherches sociographiques* at Laval in 1965-66 on 'Le pouvoir' and on 'Les classes sociales dans la société canadienne-française' illustrate the former area. In the latter, a landmark was A. Dubuc's paper 'Les classes sociales au Canada de 1760 à 1840' (1965, 1967), which argued the hypothesis of 'la prédominance des valeurs sociales sur les valeurs ethniques' in interpreting the Conquest-to-1837 period. Notable also were the historical controversies around the theme of class forces in 1837, and the query: 'Y avait-il une bourgeoisie en Nouvelle-France?'[12] The question today would seem to be: 'Y a t-il une bourgeoisie québécoise francophone?' In any case, the argument over interpretations of class structure, class power, and class relationships has practical-political urgency for the strategies and perspectives of the national as well as the social movement. Both a 'history of capitalist development in Quebec' and a 'vertical mosaic'/'anatomy of big business' type of study are major priorities for theoretical workers on the left.[13]

Class structure in the over-all socio-economic formation of Quebec is that of an advanced monopoly-capitalism marked by certain historical peculiarities:
The ruling finance oligarchy maintains its power in association with the Catholic Church, a socio-economic hold-over from the seigneurial era and the 'traditional society' of the nineteenth century;
United States corporate ownership and control of major sectors gives the Quebec economy a satellitic character, with certain particular emphases (resource acquisition);
Industrialization having been introduced 'from outside' in conditions of Anglo-Canadian dominance dating from the British Conquest and the Britain-based Industrial Revolution, the pattern of francophone economic inferiority extends throughout, from the top oligarchy to the middle and lower levels of salaried and wage labour;
A superstructural situation of multiple conflict, deriving its contradictory impulses from all of the above, while taking on new coloration and tonalities from the radical consciousness of youth and women's revolt and from fresh initiatives in community and cultural affirmation.

After touching briefly on some of these general and particular features, we shall consider the area of class/nation interaction.

MONOPOLY CAPITALISM IN QUEBEC

In the summer of 1970, Premier Bourassa appears to have formed the opinion that doing something about 'French as the language of work' might turn out to be 'a sure way to defuse an explosive political situation.' ('English is still the predominant language of business and industry in Quebec, especially in Montreal, and almost exclusively in the upper echelons,' commented the Montreal *Gazette.*[14]) M. Bourassa called together 'representatives' of those involved. Fifty heads of business corporations were invited, and no representatives of organized labour. On being asked why the latter were omitted, he explained that he saw it as a priority to meet with those referred to by Claude Ryan as 'ceux qui ont le pouvoir de décision.'[15] These proprietors of 'the power of decision' included: the Royal Bank, Bank of Montreal, CPR, Dupont, General Motors, IBM, Coca-Cola, General Electric, Aluminum Ltd., Canadian Vickers, and Noranda Mines.

The centring of the basic power of decision in the hands of the directors of the great corporations is, of course, the essential if occult quality of the class relationship of capital and labour. As a relationship of power, and property, and exploitation, it can be grasped only obliquely, through such partial and indirect glimpses as the one just provided. The figures in the *Quebec Yearbook*[16] show 372,000 production workers in 11,000 manufacturing establishments, receiving $1.7 billion in wages and accounting for a value added of $4.9 billion – a hint at the scale of appropriation of unpaid surplus. But as Régine Robin has noted, surplus value is not subject to precise measurement – it is the expression in action of an antagonistic social relationship.

A tiny hint at the reality is contained in the Taxation Statistics (1969) that show 2.7 per cent of heads of families in Quebec earning annually $10,000 or over. These 20,000 persons include the handful who are the economic elite; what proportions are franco- and anglo-phone one can only guess. The figure for average pay of the francophone non-agricultural male worker – $3185 – cited by the B&B, is eloquent of the condition of the great mass of the labour force. In Montreal, while 'more than a third of the population suffers privation or lives in poverty, nearly half the population of the metropolitan area (48.6 per cent) can be classified as economically weak.'[17]

A function of this income disparity would appear to be 'l'inégalité sociale devant la mort': in Montreal, infant mortality rate indices stood at 16 for non-French and 24 for French, with the extreme cases of most and least favoured areas being in a relation of *one to six* – the former predominantly British, the latter French. As another indication, the maternal mortality index for Montreal as a whole is 1.4; in the working-class area of the southwest part of the city, it is 4.7.[18]

A counterpart of the concentration in the Montreal area of the financial institutions and advanced industry (as well as poverty) is the relative socio-economic underdevelopment of much of the rest of the province. Compare, for instance, the Bas St Laurent-Gaspé region with Montreal (Table 1). Or

TABLE 1[19]

	Bas St Laurent–Gaspé	Montreal area
Percentage of Quebec population	4.8	53.9
Percentage of share of personal income	2.5	64.6
Average disposable per capita personal income (direct taxes deducted)	$675.	$1,444.

consider comparative data on health conditions.[20] The index of mortality from infectious diseases shows the following range:

Montreal Island	3	Gaspé	47
Abitibi	27	Nouveau Québec	560

If the nine times higher rate of Abitibi, or the 16 times higher rate of Gaspé, bespeak an element of ethnicity as well as regional disparity in underdevelopment, the 190 times higher figure for Nouveau Québec registers the murderous fatality meted out to the Indian and Eskimo peoples, who form there a far higher percentage of the population than in any other region.

Just as secretive as class exploitation (and just as public in another way as class struggle) is the mechanism whereby monopoly capital exercises state-political power. Here the Conseil Général de l'Industrie may serve as an example. This 'council of elders' was set up by Daniel Johnson's Union Nationale government in 1969, comprising fifty-eight financial and industrial magnates. Its first president, Paul A. Ouimet (former vice-president of Iron Ore of Canada, president of the Quebec division, Canadian Manufacturers Association) is quoted as having told the Premier that 'Quebec needed a group of businessmen who would assist the government in creating a better climate.' A first step was for the Council to call before it four cabinet ministers to 'answer questions as to their views on French unilingualism and the constitutional future of Québec' (no less). That same day (13 March 1969) *La Presse* reported: 'A company president, member of the Conseil, commented to persons accompanying him: When we make recommendations to the government we fully intend that they be implemented. We now have, in the Conseil, the instrument we need to force action by government.'[21]

The Conseil de l'Industrie itself states that it is made up of '58 leading businessmen (hommes d'affaires éminents) of Quebec.' Several are prominent in the 'one-nation' Canada Committee sired by Bell Telephone and like-minded patriotic emanations. Along with a score of representatives of such foreign corporations as Iron Ore, Texaco, IT&T, Alcan, Dupont, there are ten Anglo-Canadian tycoons from Price Paper, Domtar, Dominion Textiles, Molson, Distillers-Seagram, Steinberg's, Cockfield-Brown. French Canadian business has fifteen representatives, including six of the nine from Power Corporation (Paul Desmarais, J.C. Hébert, Lucien Rolland, and others) and Laurent Beaudouin from Bombardier (Qué.).

The kind of 'favorable climate for investment' that is the quest of these public-spirited souls is not hard to visualize. James Bay and the North Shore of the Gulf of St Lawrence offer bracing prospects. The former, promising a colossal electric-power development, is to be entrusted to a mixed government and private-business set-up. On the St Lawrence North Shore, timber rights in an area twice the size of New Brunswick (five times the size of Belgium) are being handed over to that haven of orphans and widows, International Telephone & Telegraph – at philanthropic bargain rates. Duplessis' give-away of the Ungava iron-ore deposits is thus being faithfully duplicated by Bourassa.

Such is the unpleasing countenance of monopoly-capitalist rule in its US/ Anglo-Canada/Quebec configuration. It presents not a few problems of analysis, relevant to strategy. The peculiar interweave of socio-economic class and nation-community is pervasively present. Thus, the socio-economic formation enhancing Canada/Quebec is a monopoly-capitalism that is satellitic in relation to the US corporate empire, and internally oppressive in relation to 'la nation québécoise.' Class structure within Quebec is not a distinct, self-contained entity that is coterminous with the francophone nation; rather, this nation participates in a single binational structure of monopoly-capitalist relationships. Overwhelmingly Anglo-Canadian–US at the level of the top oligarchy, this corporate capitalism is predominantly and increasingly francophone-Québécois at the middle and lower levels of salaried and wage labour.

AN ELUSIVE BOURGEOISIE

Unquestionably, the big bourgeoisie in Quebec 'speaks English.' It embodies in its person not only class rule, but the dominance of that Canadian nation whose common tongue is English. Is that to say that there exists *no* dominant bourgeoisie within 'la nation québécoise'? This is one of those areas where the need for empirical study makes itself felt. André Raynauld's study of ownership of enterprises in Quebec (still unpublished!), utilized in part in Book III (*The World of Work*) of the B&B *Report,* offers a valuable starting-point. The sixty-five francophones holding impressive concentrations of directorships of banks and industries; the francophone employer group which commands 22 per cent of the manufacturing labour force in Quebec; the make-up of the Conseil Général de l'Industrie, whose francophone members include, as we have seen, not only representatives of such financial groupings as that of Desmarais-Lévesque, but a fairly strong contingent from the manufacturing sector – all constitute areas for concerted research on the 'anatomy of big business' in Quebec.[22]

Any scheme is suspect that presents the class and ethnic cleavages in roughly this manner:

A	B
(English) Canada	Québec
bourgeoisie	petite bourgeoisie
	proletariat

The disappearance of a francophone bourgeoisie is surely an optical illusion. It may be accounted for by the numerical smallness of the top elite group; but the elite is not the entire class. It is perhaps due to the cloak of invisibility so successfully assumed by the capitalist corporation that is the church temporal. Or there may even be implied an act of 'expulsion from the nation' entailing the assertion that francophone finance-capitalists are so wholly *vendus* that they really belong in the (Anglo) Canadian nation (a judgment that surely begs several questions at once, to put it mildly).

It would seem to me that the Québécois francophone nation-community does in fact include in its class structure a bourgeoisie; and that however anemic or numerically small, it provides the core of the ruling group within that community, drawing its power from the patronage (in the widest sense) of the primary ruling group in Canada/Quebec, the Anglo-Canadian finance oligarchy. Viewed from the standpoint of the over-all socio-economic structure, this small group of francophone capitalists is part and parcel of the monopolist big bourgeoisie. Viewed in terms of its nation-community, it is a politico-economic bourgeois elite whose peculiar limitations derive from the subordinate status and truncated structure of the oppressed nation. Its situation is a function of *imperialism*, Anglo-Canadian and United States. In the words of Michel Van Schendel, editor of *Socialisme québécois*: 'Imperialism is not only "external," it is "internal"; it is the very reality of class relations in national areas. The *bourgeoisie québécoise* exists, and it is a bourgeoisie of imperialism.'[23] In Van Schendel's view the Quebec case, like that of Ireland, is one of a 'marginal social formation of the dominant capitalism,' but a 'social formation fully integrated into capitalism and possessing on this basis its own bourgeoisie.' Although dominated, this bourgeoisie is more than a mere intermediary: 'It accumulates, which is something the petty-bourgeoisie does not and cannot do ... The Québec bourgeoisie accumulates ... that is its function. That is why it clusters, tries to merge its enterprises. That is why it appropriates the apparatus and power of a dominated State made in its own likeness ... We cannot, under these circumstances, accept the claim that the Québec bourgeois are so few in number (the number of individuals matters little, after all) and so assimilated to the Anglo-Canadian bourgeoisie as to be part of it. Is this not to confuse solidarity of interests with membership ...?'[24]

The implications for policy contained in a mistaken judgment of class structure can, of course, be serious. Starting out from a denial of the existence of a francophone Quebec bourgeoisie, it is possible to conclude that the main enemy of labour is 'la petite bourgeoisie péquiste': opposed to this PQ-led middle stratum stand the producers, 'la classe qui lui est antagoniste: la classe des producteurs.'[25] To make *that* the determining line of cleavage could pose curious problems for any alignment in opposition to the monopoly bourgeoisie (English- and French-speaking).

THE THEORY OF 'ETHNIC CLASS'

In addition to such a 'left' posture, an 'opposite' right-wing nationalist one can be deduced from the 'disappearance' of a bourgeoisie: the rallying of an indifferentiated, 'classless' national bloc against an equally undifferentiated adversary, 'les Anglais.' This nationalist approach is fed, on the left, by the concept of the so-called ethnic class. In this view, 'French Canada stands, in relation to English Canada, in the same position as the working class in relation to the bourgeoisie.' Marcel Rioux and Jacques Dofny introduced this concept of 'ethnic class' in a paper entitled 'Social Class in French Canada' (1962), and Rioux proposed some refinements of it in an essay, 'Conscience ethnique et conscience de classe au Québec' (1965).[26]

The suggestion that the French-Canadian 'socio-cultural entity' plays 'the same role within Canada ... as a social class' has a certain appealing quality. Not only does it seek to encompass the shifting interaction of *social* and *national*, but it points up the factor of *inequality* that is at the root of the tensions and crises in French-English relations (what Garigue describes as the interactive situation of dependence and the socially 'asymmetric' relationship of the two national communities).[27]

Why, though, should one try to *equate* the concepts of national community and social class? The valid element in the analogy (inequality) is real, but the resulting formula is not adequate to the load that is placed upon it. There results an ambiguity that blurs the specificity of class and nation and confuses their interrelationship. To try to merge the two aspects in one concept of ethnic class hinders rather than helps an understanding of their interaction.

The ethnic class concept opens the way to a sort of 'classless nationalism,' by blurring or effacing recognition of social class structure and struggle within the nation or national community – as in the Rioux-Dofny hypothetical scheme of 'evolution of class relations,' in which 'the class struggle would be concentrated at the political level where the total French-Canadian group faces the English-Canadian group' – in fact, a national and *not* a class struggle. The authors envisage, as variants, a struggle of 'the Canadian bourgeoisie against the Canadian working class without any distinction as to ethnic origin,' or an absorption of both nations by the power of the United States. None of these is clarified by the ethnic class approach. On the contrary, the problem is surely one of estimating the interaction of ethnic *and* class factors: and in this regard the Marxist approach has the advantage of making possible an appraisal of the class and national components within the framework of evolving social-economic formations.

Michel Van Schendel, in *Socialisme '69*, and Bourque and Frenette in *Socialisme québécois* have dealt most effectively with the dubious metaphor of ethnic class (see the previous article in this book). But more important, they get at what is perhaps the root of the confusion by pointing up the 'social psychologizing' of class (in Dumont, Dofny, Rioux) which tends to make consciousness and subjective 'representation of self' the determinant and originator of class, instead of the relationships founded on material production.

If the ethnic class approach dissolves classes in the nation, a seemingly opposite view is one that seeks to reassert the primacy of the socio-economic by dissolving the nation in the class. This is the conception of the nation as simply an 'effect' of class structure.[28] Such an approach misreads both history and Marxism. It implies a 'purity' of class approach that is deceptive, being purchased at the price of disincarnating the historical-social human community. There results a kind of metaphysic of disembodied 'articulations' of 'effects' and 'instances' and 'supports' in which social class itself, with its 'structure' dichotomized from its 'praxis,' languishes in a wasteland of abstraction. Carried to its logical conclusion, this metaphysic conjures out of existence contradiction, class struggle, and social revolution. It leads nowhere – or rather to a sophisticated *liberalism*.

The concepts of class and nation are not equatable. Classes embody relationships of property and work, in the context of a mode of production. The nation-community embodies relationships of a different order. Hence, while it is inseparable, historically, from class-structures and modes of production, the nation-community is more than just an 'aspect' of any one of them. This is so, because the nation-community embodies an identity, linguistic and cultural, that is not simply an 'effect' of class, however closely its evolution may be interwoven with the shifting patterns of class relations and struggles. National differences both antedate and postdate the era of the capitalist mode of production. They arose in the era of pre-capitalist social formations, as a phenomenon of social geography – initial physical-territorial isolation, clustering of human groups, emergence and crystallizing of communication. They show promise of outliving much of the epoch-long transition from private-corporate to common ownership of the economy. Maxime Rodinson, while combatting theories that attribute a sort of universal historical predominance to the 'ethnico-national' factor, has also criticized 'the vulgar-marxist theories according to which ethnico-national formations, the ideologies and organizations expressing their aspirations and over-all interests, exerted no action, had no efficacy, were pure ideological phenomena, to be reduced simply to ideologies manipulated by certain classes.' As against such a 'decidedly idealist' thesis,

Rodinson argues that class and nation are inseparably operative: 'Both factors exist concurrently, and their respective potency has to be evaluated for each period, each zone, in the light of the concrete conditions ...'[29]

TWIN-ENGINED TRANSFORMATION?

Assuredly, to hold fast at one and the same time in Quebec to the two interactive realities of nation-community and social class is far from easy. The parting of the ways of Pierre Vallières and Charles Gagnon on this issue dramatizes a historico-political dilemma.[30] The former's 'option Lévesque' has scandalized the purists by asserting the priority of state-national sovereignty as the precondition for social revolutionary change. At the same time, it leaves a gaping unanswered question regarding the prospects of a working-class and radical-nationalist bloc from which the former remains absent for want of autonomous voice. Gagnon's choice seems directed to this other (and crucial) side of the matter. But declamations about the instant conjuring up of a 'revolutionary workers' party' are not immune to certain risks. Pressures in that direction come from several groups whose common denominator combines a romantic-vanguardist mimetism with a self-defeating 'revolutionary' verbalism.

A possible advance beyond the present deadlock may entail (in this or another order) some of these:

Working-class political action, born not of mimetic 'revolutionary' gesticulation but of authentic response to needs, and moving, in terms of the actual levels of consciousness achieved, toward the project of social ownership of the economy as a majority aim reached through the successive experiences of struggle with such colossi as, for instance, Power Corporation, the Bell–IT&T, International Paper, and Union Carbide (poisoner of the air of Greater Montreal).

A bloc of labour-in-politics (a *movement*, not necessarily a machine-party) with the supporters of an independent and anti-imperialist 'nation québécoise'; a bloc of 'labour and culture,' of urban working-class and intellectuals, technicians, professionals, students, and rural anti-monopoly groups.

Resolution of the 'main enemy' dilemma (Washington? Ottawa?) through elaboration of a Québécois broadly independentist-socialist project, the realization of which would break the fused power structure of US–Anglo-Canadian imperialism at its state and socio-economic levels.

Recognition of the historical likelihood of a long-term mutation in the 'Canada' component: possible emergence in English Canada of elements of independentist (anti-US-imperialism) and social-radical solidarity with the transformations in Quebec. To rule out such an eventuality in advance is both to neglect potential allies and misjudge the toughness and complexity of the threat of an Ottawa-military operation. (In the long term, similar prospects of mutation are in the making in the United States itself. 'The Marines' as menace lack the quality of an assured eternity.)[31]

The class/nation dilemma is not to be overcome either by wishing one of its terms out of existence (it takes Trudeau to do that with both of them!), or by decreeing a rigid temporal priority for the solution of one rather than the other. The working-out of the social-class and national-liberation struggles will assuredly involve a whole range of pervasive areas of contestation that cannot be underestimated, much less ignored. They include: the penetration of the crises of class and nation-community by the issues of poisoning of the environment; cultural alienation and educational impasse; the revolt of youth; women's liberation; defence of democratic liberties threatened by a neo-fascist, anti-labour 'law and order' offensive of the ultra-right.

Marx's 'old mole' of history has its own way of burrowing unexpected tunnels – lateral ones included. While some of these latter may be taken momentarily for some sort of tangential escape-hatch, the basic over-all direction will assert itself. Since each and all of the new areas of contestation derive from the fundamental structure of corporate-business society, its exploitive colonialism, its historic misanthropy, they are likely to act as catalysts of national as well as social transformation. In combination they are the ingredients of historical dynamite.

NOTES

1 'La classe se définit par un rapport complexe d'exploitation qui n'engage pas que la seule vie économique ... Pas plus que la plus-value n'est directement lisible, la classe n'est un donné qui se voit.' Régine Robin in *La nouvelle critique*, mars 1970.
2 Gilles Lesage, *Le Devoir*, 23 Oct. 1969.
3 'Canada: Two Nations or One?' *Canadian Journal of Economics and Political Science*, Nov. 1962.
4 Address to Canadian and Empire Clubs, Toronto: *Globe and Mail*, 17 Nov. 1970.
5 General introduction, Book I, *Report of Royal Commission on Bilingualism and Biculturalism*, sections 81-84, pp. x/iv-x/vi.
6 *Le Devoir*, 2-3 April 1971.
7 *Winnipeg Free Press*, 17 May 1965.
8 *Toronto Daily Star*, 23 June 1971.
9 *Canadian Forum*, Nov. 1964.
10 24 June 1971.
11 *Lord Durham's Report*, C.P. Lucas, ed. (Toronto, 1912), II, 292-3.
12 Cf. *Economie québécoise* (1969); C. Nish, *Les Bourgeois Gentilshommes de la Nouvelle-France* (1968); L. Racine and G. Bourque on F. Ouellet's economic and social history (in *Parti pris*, IV, 5-6). Other studies include Gérald Fortin: 'Le nationalisme canadien-français et les classes sociales' (*La Revue d'Histoire de l'Amérique Française*, mars 1969); in the ongoing debate on the Rioux-Dofny thesis of the 'ethnic class' (in *French Canadian Society*, 1964), M. Van Schendel, 'Pour une théorie du socialisme au Québec,' *Socialisme québécois*, no. 18, and in no. 20 by G. Bourque and N. Laurin-Frenette,

'Classes sociales et idéologies nationalistes au Québec (1760-1970),' a new version of the same appearing in nos. 21-22 under the title: 'La structure nationale québécoise.' In this latter issue also, Luc Racine et Roch Denis: 'La Conjoncture politique québécoise depuis 1960,' and Van Schendel, 'Impérialisme et classe ouvrière au Québec.' And in *Québec occupé* (Editions parti pris, 1971) contributions on class structure by M. Pichette and by Hélène David, Louis Maheu, and E. de Ipola.

13 Cf. V.I. Lenin, *Development of Capitalism in Russia* (1894); M. Dobb, *Studies in Capitalism Development* (1963).
14 *Gazette,* 3 July 1970.
15 *Le Devoir,* 30 June 1970.
16 (1971), 518.
17 *Troisième Solitude,* Etude du Conseil du Travail de Montréal (1967), 26.
18 *Parti pris,* 2, no. 3 (1964); J. Henripin, in *Recherches sociographiques* II, i (1961), 'Montreal, la ville des autres.' Maternal mortality: *La Presse,* 16 Oct. 1969.
19 In *Un Parti à fonder:* documentation PQ (1968).
20 Rapport du Service de Démographie, Gouvernement du Québec (1965).
21 *23 dossiers de Québec-Presse* (1971), 14.
22 A number of groups are working in this field: notably, the researchers of *Socialisme québécois,* and le Centre de Recherche pour l'Indépendance du Québec, authors of 'Le Gouvernement de l'industrie': texte préliminaire.
23 M. Van Schendel, 'Impérialisme et classe ouvrière au Québec,' in *Socialisme québécois,* 21-22, pp. 156 ff.
24 *Ibid.*
25 Péquiste: supporter of the PQ Parti Québécois.
26 'Social Class in French Canada': in Marcel Rioux and Yves Martin, *French-Canadian Society,* 1, *Sociological Studies,* 307-18 (Carleton Library no. 18, Toronto 1964); paper translated from *Revue française de sociologie,* III, 3 (1962). M. Rioux: 'Consciencé ethnique et conscience de classe au Québec,' in *Recherches sociographiques:* 'Les Classes sociales au Canada français,' VI, 1 (1965), 23-32. (Colloque de l'Association internationale des sociologues de langue française; also in *Cahiers internationaux de sociologie,* XXXVIII, 1965).
    Part of the argument in this paper appeared in a review article of the author's 'Questions in Dispute,' *Marxist Quarterly,* 15 (Autumn 1965). (Translations are the author's.) The passages that follow are from the author's 'Comment on the Rioux-Dofny concept of ethnic class,' Socialist Studies conference, Calgary, 1968 (mimeographed text).
27 *L'Option politique du Canada français* (1963), 146: 'La situation de dépendance entretient l'asymétrie sociale dont elle previent et par laquelle elle se perpétue.'
28 Cf. N. Poulantzas, *Pouvoir politique et classes sociales* (1968).
29 *Partisans,* no. 61 (Sept.-Oct. 1971), 159.
30 P. Vallières, *L'Urgence de Choisir* (1972); C. Gagnon in *Le Devoir.*
31 *Status-quo* Canada, or 'Canada as we have known it,' has a poor life-expectancy. Few are the states that have been saved by earnest fatuousness; and such, alas, is the quality of our rulers' pious invocations of a 'national unity' that is held able to avert US absorption by perpetuating Québec's subordination. Is this to say that there is no good in our northern 'Nazareth'? Or even that there is no such place, and that the Canadian nation-community whose common tongue is English amounts to no more than a polite (and impolitic) fiction? To this particular archaic Canadian, at least, such a judgment is as false and shallow, in its own warped way, as the 'national-unity' litany of the anglo-imperial elites. There *is* some humus of an historic identity from which some things have sprouted, and a certain residual tough-rootedness remains. Why else would the American take-over encounter resistances, however sporadic and thinly scattered?
    Cf. *One Country or Two,* ed., R.M. Burns (1972), particularly the essay by John Meisel, whose perception of the anglophone Canadian phenomenon adds a dimension to a little-explored reality. In this symposium volume, serious consideration by some Anglo-Canadians of the possibility of alternatives to *status-quo* Canada constitutes something of a landmark.

Gary Teeple

'Liberals in a hurry': socialism and the CCF-NDP

THE EPITHET 'liberals in a hurry' was Prime Minister St Laurent's endearing recognition of the CCF's adherence to a liberal vision of society and the state. His observation, likely one of the more insightful by any Canadian prime minister, unveiled the essence of a program which the CCF called socialist. The program of the CCF, despite minor changes, always maintained the liberal notion of a society of self-seeking individuals whose inter-relations were regulated by the state. In this same vision, the role of the state lay in defence of the 'commonwealth,' maintenance of justice, and building and keeping certain public works and institutions which no individual could undertake profitably. The state functioned to provide an atmosphere in which independent producers could flourish and where individuals could pursue 'the good life.'

This notion of the state was clearly reflected in the platforms of the CCF throughout its development and the acceptance of individualism was implicit in the CCF commitment to the institutions of bourgeois (liberal) democracy. Despite the change in name from the Co-operative Commonwealth Federation to the New Democratic party, adherence to these notions of state and society persisted.[1]

What the CCF-NDP calls socialism is an extension of the principles of liberalism. From this fact, it can be shown that the policies and actions of the party lead it in one direction – towards state capitalism,[2] and not to the creation of a workers' state as envisaged by Marx and Engels. If the struggle for socialism and independence in Canada is to be won, the nature and limitations of the CCF-NDP notion of socialism must be examined.

ORIGINS OF THE CCF: THEORY AND PRACTICE

To know the origins of the CCF is to understand its past and current political policies and practices. Present at the formation of the party were the elements which have made it a successful social democratic party and a persistent opponent of any movement towards developing a class analysis of Canada, an analysis which would form the basis of the struggle for revolutionary socialism inside and outside Parliament. The formative elements of the CCF can be delineated as follows: a section of the Progressives known as the 'Ginger Group' in the House of Commons, a part of the Western Labour Conference especially the Independent Labour Parties (ILP) in the West, and the League for Social Reconstruction (LSR). The social gospel of Protestantism was a major philosophical influence adding much to the tone and content of the founding document. How each of these came together to form the Co-operative Commonwealth Federation is not the question at hand; rather, their notion of socialism and how to achieve it are of interest here as they constitute the origins of CCF theory and practice.

The liberal reformist character of the CCF is evident in the two groups which formed its nucleus in 1932, the Ginger Group and the two labour representatives – J.S. Woodsworth and W. Irvine – in the House of Commons. The Ginger Group was an off-shoot from the Progressives, a group electing 65 members to the federal House in 1921, which Underhill described as 'never quite able to make up their minds whether they were a new political party, or whether they were an independent left wing of the Liberal party, or just what they were politically.'[3] The Progressives were far from being a socialist party: they were not class-conscious; rather, they were populist and reformist; they were as one historian has labelled them, 'crypto-Liberals.'[4] It is from this 'party' that there emerged the so-called Ginger Group, 'acclaimed for the "ginger" it provided in Parliament, for its catalytic effect on the old parties.'[5] Its role as it saw itself was to prod, to embarrass, to cajole the ruling party into enacting social reform. The Ginger Group was clearer than the Progressives in one major aspect: it wanted to put an end to private monopolies and institute in their place a 'publicly controlled economic order.'[6] The way to do this they felt was through the building of a third party which, when elected with a majority, would legislate massive reforms. This argument was consistent with what became CCF philosophy. It was not class-conscious, it sprang from liberal-democratic ideals, and it accepted the paternalism of social reformism.

Shortly after its formation in 1924, the Ginger Group began to work with the two labour representatives in the House. Their common ground was the belief in liberal social reformism. Although they represented labour, both of these MPs, like William Ivens and James Simpson who were also founders of the CCF, had come to labour-politics through the Protestant church. It was through the church that came much of the moralism in the CCF 'analysis' of capitalism. All of these men – Woodsworth, Irvine, Douglas, Coote, King Gordon, and others – were Protestant clergymen. This dedication to Christianity brought elements not only of moralism but also of liberalism to the CCF. They were strongly attached to the notion of liberal democracy and they were motivated by a Christian social gospel to reform the state, end the inequities of capitalism, and create a co-operative society.[7]

The goal of a society based on co-operative principles has the aura of socialism. But this goal in the minds of Woodsworth and company was to be established by legislation from Parliament, it was initiated by the humanitarianism of the gospel which was inescapably paternalistic; and it follows that the people were the receivers of reform, not the active, creative initiators.

The vision of a co-operative commonwealth did not originate in the social evangelism of Protestantism, but in the philosophy of the British Labour party and the Fabian socialists. It was carried to Canada by returning students (such as Woodsworth himself) and by British immigrant unionists. The Fabian and

and Labour party views were strongly represented in the CCF by the Independent Labour parties of Manitoba and Saskatchewan, the Dominion Labour party of Alberta and the Socialist party of BC.[8] The ILP was 'distinctly Fabian in outlook'[9] having been organized largely by M.J. Coldwell, a student of Fabianism.

A concurrent philosophy of 'labourism' marked the labour parties or sections of which helped to form the CCF. The political strategy of this notion was straightforward: 'elect more labour representatives to the halls of the legislature.'[10] One labour historian suggests that this philosophy sought the allegiance of any party so long as their elected representative argued for legislation 'in the interests of organized labour.'[11] Socialism was not their goal. The 'parliamentarians,' those sections of organized labour which were 'labourite,' formed the workers' representatives in the original CCF.[12] Those labour groups which advocated Marxist revolutionary socialism were (to a large extent) involved during the twenties with the Communist party of Canada.

Fabian socialist theories, while central to many of the labour groups which joined the CCF, were advocated most openly by the League for Social Reconstruction (LSR). The League came into being in 1932, largely at the instigation of Frank Underhill who wanted to create a 'Canadian Fabian Society.'[13] The LSR, like the Fabians, was to provide the research, the intellectual groundwork, for a new reform party whose role was to curb the corruption of the old parties and to expand the tenets of liberal democracy to include a greater acceptance of social responsibility. As the theoreticians of the CCF, the task they set themselves was research and education, for it was through greater understanding of the problems of capitalism that the party could appeal to the people of Canada and 'change' that system by winning a majority in parliament.

By the early 1940s, it has been argued, the last of the 'radicals' in the CCF 'had become convinced that only constitutional, orderly change could build a better society.'[14] But it is difficult to assume, aside from the early rhetoric which contained some Marxist-sounding phrases, that the CCF was ever anything but a liberal, social-democratic, reform party. The chief architect of the Regina Manifesto was Underhill, who remarked that 'John Stuart Mill I never got beyond,'[15] who saw politics in terms of 'counterweights' and who could write, 'I never doubted that socialism must be liberal (with a small l).'[16]

Millian theories and Fabian socialism present no contradiction; indeed, the work of J.S. Mill can rightly be considered as very influential in Fabian writings.[17] And it is plain that the literature of the Fabian socialists was closely read by the groups which formed the CCF in 1933. Both the labour parties (especially the ILP) and the LSR, the two most important long-term influences, were open and enthusiastic about their adoption of Fabian theories. For this reason, it is of value to digress briefly in order to examine the content of Fabian socialism – the heart of what became CCF socialism.

In the development of socialist theory, it can be said that the Fabians did two things: they were among the first who called themselves socialist to be anti-Marxist, and they elaborated the liberal notion of socialism in which state intervention in society was interpreted as 'collectivism,' the *intelligent* woman's socialism.[18] Thus, the Marxian labour theory of value was rejected entirely. Sidney Webb argued that the worker produced only the equivalent of his wage. He substituted the labour theory of value as the basis for a 'collectivist economy' with a theory of land-rent taxation gleaned from Ricardo and a theory of 'confiscated interest.'[19] Moreover, Marx's theory of the class struggle and proletarian revolution were held in great disdain by the Fabians. As one economist wrote, 'They think of socialism as a mere extension of the ideals of bourgeois democracy, and they would be quite content with a logical development and application of the principles which at present govern society.'[20] Socialism for the Fabians was not a class doctrine; it was a kind of gift, a humanitarian gesture, from a 'well-educated,' 'intelligent' group to the people as a whole.

For Marx, the struggle for socialist revolution would take place in the midst of recurring capitalist crises, and on the basis of increasing alienation and impoverishment of the working class. For the Fabians, revolution was out of the question; indeed, socialism was to be seen all around, it was materializing without conflict, its very victims (the bourgeoisie) seemed to approve of it.[21] It was everywhere, this Fabian socialism – in the form of museums, parks, roads, streets, fire engines and so on, not to mention public baths and wash houses. All it required was interpretation as socialism and a demand for 'its wider extension.'[22]

'Socialism,' then, was blossoming; it needed to be 'discovered,' not fought for. The Fabians were not simply 'collectivists,' however; they took their liberalism seriously and argued not just for a more egalitarian state, but for one to be run by experts, to be the epitome of man's rationalism. Control of the state was to be held by an 'aristocracy of talent.'[23] Planning was to be efficient, rational, moral (for the greatest number) and, above all, expert.[24]

The anti-Marxism and extended liberalism which characterized the Fabian Society became, through the LSR and ILP, the philosophical biases entrenched in the CCF-NDP from its inception. The Fabians like their Canadian off-shoot, the CCF, criticized the capitalist system only from a moral point of view. By ending the corruption and extending the ideals of bourgeois liberal democracy, they reasoned, a truly moral and rational society could be set up. There is little in this view to suggest that the system is exploitative beyond the cry that the politicians are misusing the state for the purposes of certain groups or classes, and there is no demand for change beyond reforming what exists in terms of liberal, social responsibility – to wit, increasing the role of the state.

With the labour theory of value dismissed and a class analysis of society spurned, the CCF had no real basis on which to analyze capitalist exploitation. Confronted with poverty, unemployment, and other manifestations of the profit system, the party could only argue it was bad and suggest the problem lay in monopoly control and not in the system itself. The rejection of the analytical tools needed to understand the problem did not allow Fabian and CCF socialism to develop beyond moralistic liberalism.

PARLIAMENT AND REASON:
THE ROAD TO CCF-NDP SOCIALISM

Holding the notion that socialism consists of nothing more than the desire to rectify the misery created in the bourgeois world by means compatible with that system, the CCF could insist in its founding document that it did 'not believe in change by violence.' With a blind eye to the violence of the state against the working class, it sought to achieve its goal of political power 'solely by constitutional methods.' Parliament and elections – the liberal, democratic method – were the exclusive means by which the CCF chose to bring about its brand of socialism. For the CCF-NDP, therefore, Parliament has never been examined as a central organ of Canadian capitalism for obscuring the class struggle and in co-opting the elements of moderate dissent. It has been, in essence, a major political prop in perpetuating the rule of our 'compliant' bourgeoisie.

In 1961 at the founding of the NDP, the acceptance of Parliament as the only road was profound: indeed, Stanley Knowles offered praise in the superlative: 'as a means of achieving democracy [Parliament] is one of the best instruments man has devised. But they [the people of Canada] know that if it does not function as it should it can fail to fulfil its high purpose. Canadians really want their Parliament to function properly; they want it to be the most respected public institution in the land.'[25] But all was not well with Parliament – it had to be restored to 'its proper functioning.' The academics in the LSR clearly analysed what was wrong with it. Parliamentary democracy was becoming less liberal, and therefore, it was failing. They argued that the Conservative and Liberal parties represented business corporations and when elected to office ruled in their interests.[26] The power of corporation monopoly was growing and the 'people's' interests were becoming more subordinated to those of business. What democracy needed, wrote this Canadian facsimile of the Fabian society, was socialism; that is, CCF-NDP socialism – the notion that the state was an instrument of the party in power and, with a mere change of political party, could be organized in the interests of the 'people,' not the capitalists.

The CCF-NDP has never critically examined the role of Parliament beyond suggesting that its liberal character was falling victim to capitalist monopoly interests. The democracy that the LSR wanted to save and expand was liberal democracy, the form of state control produced 'by developing capitalist market societies.'[27] Without doubt, it was and is a form of class domination despite the enfranchisement of the working class. While the CCF, like the NDP today, could see the control that the ruling class had over the 'party in power,' it understood that control as a perversion of the ideals of liberal democracy[28] not the essence and logic of its development.

Acceptance of the tenets of liberalism has important implications for the political method of a party. The belief that Parliament is the sole arena for the struggle for power is rooted in this acceptance. Classes in this view are simply groupings of people with similar interests. There is no dialectical vision of class conflict, no admission that classes might be active, creative forces struggling in their own right. Instead, there exist group interests – farmer, worker and middle class interests – which in the final analysis reduce to a 'basic community of interest,' namely, inadequate living standards, individual helplessness and lack of opportunity.[30] The truth contained in this description is not seen as means of moving classes to action; rather it is a CCF prescription for voter appeal. Classes are passive bodies; the only conceivable form of activity is an individual one – the casting of a ballot. Thus, a 1935 CCF pamphlet could begin with: 'Smash the Big Shot Monopoly' and end with 'A Vote for the CCF is a Vote for Yourself.'[31] More recently, the Ontario NDP leader, Stephen Lewis, could only suggest to several thousand workers protesting proposed changes in Ontario labour legislation that they vote NDP in the next election. The core of a political philosophy that would admit to this one 'solution' is paternalism based on the liberal vision of social inertia where the 'people' must be ministered to via the state – they are not creative, active beings capable of direct democracy.

This affirmation of parliamentarism means the CCF-NDP obscures the nature and potential of the struggle between the working class and the ruling class, consisting principally of American corporations and their Canadian complement – transportation and financial conglomerates. The party's perception of capitalism is an ailing liberal democracy and the solution is proposed only within the confines of liberal theory and practice – individualism and parliamentarism. In contrast, the revolutionary socialist, according to Engels, viewed elections and bourgeois democratic institutions as 'opportunities for the working class to fight these very state institutions.'[32] For a Marxist party to enter into bourgeois politics was not to abandon the class struggle, but to carry it into the arena of parliamentary politics. The structures of liberal democracy were to be used to advance this struggle; they were not to be accepted on their own terms and for their own ends.

As profound liberals, the leaders of the CCF believed the rationality of individuals to be central to their program. With the denial of class struggle, this notion became the chief premise underlying CCF political action. If men were rational, they could be educated and made to understand via speeches and pamphlets the superiority of CCF socialism over capitalism. Learning in the course of struggle with capitalists was ignored because it led to class consciousness, the antithesis of CCF politics. Frank Underhill, the clearest proponent of liberalism in the movement, wrote in 1934 that in order to consolidate itself the party must 'develop new techniques of public education and propaganda.'[33] Several years later in 1941, David Lewis wrote that he had a 'very deep conviction that if we could only find a way of getting our message graphically to the people, we could obtain support to an extent which we don't even dare dream of.'[34] In 1948, a *Handbook* from the national office advocated building the party by 'persuading people to support the program of the CCF.'[35] Although NDP party literature for educational purposes today is almost non-existent, the party still adheres to this view.

Education, persuasion, reason – these were the means by which the party sought to enlist supporters and bring socialism into being through the institution of parliament. But if the 'people' could not be convinced, as it seems they still have not been, the use of reason could be applied in other quarters. Parliament was for the CCF 'a forum in which representatives of the people legislate by process of rational argument.'[36] Even if it remained a small minority party, the CCF felt that its pressure on the government to institute reforms was a sign of its 'rightness' and success.[37]

Parliament is the route, reason the means, and reform the solution. CCF-NDP socialism can be defined as state intervention to resolve the inequities of a system which at bottom is accepted. Thus, it is no wonder that whenever the state moved to mitigate the worst effects of the vagaries of our capitalist system, even in the most minimal of ways, the CCF could suggest socialism was on the march. Like the Fabians, the CCF saw its socialism being enacted all around and took pride in pointing out how it had helped the Conservatives or Liberals to recognize their 'responsibilities.' The old age pension, unemployment insurance, family allowances, housing legislation, better labour legislation, and so on were all part of what the CCF considered progress towards socialism. Woodsworth commented on R.B. Bennett's formation of the radio commission in 1933 by suggesting that the 'principle' involved was what the CCF had been advocating. And further, he said: 'We have a good example of how the CCF Government would function in the Hydro.'[38] A prominent labour and CCF leader, James Simpson, announced in the same year that 'the Conservatives of Canada have been preeminently the sponsors of great Socialistic undertakings.'[39] In 1960, Frank Underhill remarked that 'this expansion of state activity has been going on all the time since Confederation in our history, and that is a kind of socialism.'[40]

During the thirties and forties, the CCF at the federal level could 'reason' with the government to enact social reforms where there were none to alleviate the worst effects of capitalism. The last decade has found the NDP calling for better social welfare (most aspects of which have some legislation) and raising indignant cries over the abuse of Parliament.[41] There is much room for better social legislation in Canada, but the point is that the party which sees its major goal as being achievable through reforms will always have its program preempted by the larger parties. The Conservatives and Liberals do offer social palliatives, albeit not as encompassing as the NDP, but through the haze of propaganda at least equally as attractive.

Dedicated to liberal democracy, the institution of Parliament, and gradual change through social reform, the CCF-NDP has found co-operation with Marxist groups intolerable. As defenders of liberal-democratic means and goals, it was imperative to be 'respectable,'[42] and contradictory to be revolutionary. In order to maintain this image of respectability so crucial to a social democratic party in parliament, the CCF waged a long struggle against the Communist party. In politics and in the trade unions, the CCF and its union allies fought the development of 'extra-parliamentary' and 'non-labourite' activity frequently sponsored by the Communists.[43] Whatever criticisms may be levelled at the Communist party for its role in the development of working class consciousness, its intentions were to build such consciousness. CCF-NDP ideology and practice have been clearly antithetical to the establishment of a militant consciousness. Trade union demands and other political activity have been channelled into election issues. Revolutionary activity was anathema to liberal democracy; it admitted to working class interests and the subordination of individual to class action in the struggle for revolutionary socialism.

This belief in the principles of liberal democracy and social reformism has made the CCF-NDP a major buttress for the colonial, capitalist system in Canada. The party has subordinated the class efforts of workers and farmers to electoral activity under the pretense of representing their interests in the 'democratic' way. Adherence to these principles, however, has meant not only the rejection of class struggle, but also continual compromise in the party program. The CCF-NDP has accepted the notion of class only in terms of group economic interests which could be incorporated into an election program. Thus, the more groups or 'classes' the party might appeal to on the grounds of representing their interests, the more votes could be won and the more 'success' the party would enjoy.

From the first the party sought to qualify its program and temper its rhetoric. At the Regina convention in 1933, J.S. Woodsworth carefully pointed out that CCF socialism was not working class socialism or 'Marxian Socialism'; it was to be a 'Canadian type' based on liberal principles.[44] By 1936, the party leadership decided more farmer votes could be won without the reference to socialism in campaign literature.[45] In subsequent years the word was used less in the hope that more voters would be attracted to this 'moderate' and 're-spectable' party. The CCF position on public ownership was dramatically toned down a mere five years after the Regina Manifesto, again with hopes of obtaining more votes among small businessmen and farmers.[46]

In 1933 the Manifesto declared that the CCF was not going to 'rest content until it ... [had] eradicated capitalism' and 'socialized' financial institutions, transportation, communication, power, and other 'services essential to social planning.' In 1956, the Winnipeg Declaration declared only the 'subordina-tion' of capitalist ventures to 'social planning.' Eradication of capitalism was no longer necessary, and now the CCF would 'not rest content' only until everyone was 'able to enjoy equality and freedom,' 'human dignity,' and 'op-portunity.' By 1961, the NDP had lost sight of the word 'capitalism,' and even the CCF panacea, socialization, had been greatly qualified. In the 1970 On-tario NDP party program, the closest reference to government ownership is concerned with the expansion of Crown corporations into areas of the eco-nomy which private enterprise has not exploited. As for 'socialization,' the program states: 'Using scarce capital simply to change the ownership of exist-ing resource operations from private to public would neither create more jobs nor result in a substantially greater return to the people beyond what could be obtained by adequate taxation.'[47]

So much for CCF-NDP socialism. Today, the NDP offers nothing more than an expanded reform program – even the rhetoric and call for pervasive govern-ment ownership have gone. The depression years allowed for strong words against the system that had collapsed; yet the CCF remained 'respectable' be-cause its protest was based on the defence of prevailing liberal values. The years following the Second World War were marked by fervent anti-commu-nism, the growth of a 'white-collar' sector in the working class, and the expan-sion of welfare legislation – all of which conspired to 'outdate' the depression Manifesto. The CCF responded in 1956 and 1961 by moderating its rhetoric and program. As Lipset put it: 'The winning of votes, particularly the decisive marginal votes of the middle class, calls for a policy of ideological opportu-nism and grandualism.'[48] Such is the nature of the CCF-NDP road to socialism.

STATE OWNERSHIP: CCF-NDP SOCIALISM

For the CCF-NDP, society has always been seen as a loose cluster of individuals and groups whose inter-relations are regulated by consent through a state. The modern liberal-democratic state is considered an organ representing the views of the majority of individuals; it stands at the head of society and arbitrates the social relations. The actual situation, however, was thought by the party to be a perversion of this ideal. Like the Fabians before them, the party leaders argued that the state had been usurped by 'big business'; it no longer represented the majority of the people. In the words of the 1933 Manifesto: 'Power had become more and more concentrated into the hands of a small irresponsible minority of financiers and industrialists and to their predatory interests the majority are habitually sacrificed.' Monopoly capitalists perverted the ideals of liberal democracy and brought in their wake a system marked by 'injustice and inhumanity.' The CCF blamed all the attendant miseries of capitalism on this monopolistic control of Parliament and other state institutions perpetuated by the alignment of the 'old parties' with 'capitalist interests.' The way to restore the ideals of liberalism and to put an end to the 'evils' of capitalism was to secure CCF control over the state. With control, the party would 'socialize' the 'principal means of production and distribution'; that is, take over key industries and services and plan an economy to serve the interests of the people.

The problem was a moral one. Liberal democracy was being led astray, and individual freedom was being subordinated to the interests of big business. Injustice and inhumanity were pervasive, and security for the farmer, worker, and small businessman was tenuous.[49] In short, the appeal for change was based on moral considerations – which could include national concerns, especially when the sell-out of Canada had become so obvious in the 1960s. The Regina Manifesto moralizes about the lack of justice and humanity in the present system and promises uncorrupted reason and altruism in its place. In the 1956 Declaration, it was argued that 'Canada [is] Still Ridden by Inequalities,' that 'Capitalism [is] Basically Immoral' and the promise was 'for a Just Society.'

Nowhere is there an analysis of what *causes* these 'evils' under capitalism except the plaintive observation that the wrong people are in charge of the state, and that their 'share of the pie' is too great. In dismissing Marxism – the labour theory of value, historical materialism, and class struggle for socialism – the CCF-NDP can analyse capitalism only at the level of moralism. Having a deep attachment to liberalism, the party can only lament its demise – and suggest that a system in which the state would become the chief owner of production and distribution would renew liberal-democratic values. It is frequently the case that those who espouse liberal (bourgeois) democracy, but feel a paternal compassion for the 'less fortunate' and want to end the greatest abuses of market liberty, have seized on the panacea of state capitalism.

Chief among the reasons why the CCF has called itself socialist are the two sections of the Regina Manifesto calling for 'Socialization of Finance' and 'Social Ownership.' It is in these sections that the CCF originally outlined its program of state ownership of a wide number of industries and services. The Manifesto did not call for a complete socialization of the economy; it called for state ownership of the 'natural resources and the principal means of production and distribution.' The rationale for this partial socialization was to save the 'main industries ... from the wasteful competition of the ruinous over-development and over-capitalization which are the inevitable outcome of capitalism.' In other words, public 'management' and planning of the major industries and services were to end the wasteful and irrational aspects of capitalist production and to distribute the accrued wealth more equitably.

The major responsibility for managing a socialized corporation was to be placed in the hands of a 'planning board'; and almost as an after-thought the Manifesto adds that workers 'in these public industries must be free to organize in trade unions and must be *given* the right to participate in the management of the industry' (emphasis added). In short, the state through the planning boards was to have ultimate control over the 'publicly owned' means of production. It was not to be a state controlled by workers, but a state which took the place of the capitalist – running the economy more efficiently than under its capitalist owners but still hiring workers and appropriating the products of their labour.

It is clear from this description of the state that the CCF in what is considered its most radical statement viewed the problem of capitalism largely as the inefficiency and irrationality of competition. Capitalist production was not seen as being exploitative of the worker as Marx analysed it. That is, a system of production in which a 'portion of the laborer's output produced in working beyond the time necessary for supplying the substance of his personal needs,' which Marx called surplus-value, belonged 'not to the laborer but to those who hire him and determine his conditions of work.'[50]

If the central problem of capitalism was its irrational and inefficient nature, it could be solved, the CCF argued, by a system of rational and efficient planning. According to this vision, the state would be the embodiment of rationality having 'a small body' of experts planning the economy at the highest level with 'boards' and 'commissions' of 'competent' managers or professionals at the head of each industry. The worker was to have a 'share in the control of industry,' but his role in this vision never strayed beyond the limits of trade unionism; that is, the struggle for higher wages, more security, and better working conditions. In short, the relations of production remained the same as under capitalism – the workers remained workers but the means of production now were owned by the state.

Several events moved the CCF to abandon progressively its 'take-over' policies. The very year the CCF was formed saw F.D. Roosevelt elected to the presidency of the USA and the ushering in of his New Deal. Soon to follow was R.B. Bennett's 'new deal' in Canada. Thus, in the midst of the most dramatic failure of capitalism, governments took initiative in restoring order to the chaotic and faltering capitalist system. A mere three years later (1936) John Maynard Keynes published his thesis that through a system of government regulations and 'partnerships' with business the chances of economic depressions could be lessened and unemployment held at a constant low level. Soon after the appearance of Keynes' theory, the Second World War broke out. The necessity of war production forced the allied governments to increase the role of the state in the economy. Following these three events the CCF never looked back. 'Take-overs' were not necessary, the laissez-faire capitalist system appeared to be transforming itself. Governments assumed an increased role in social welfare and labour legislation, and took over certain essential transportation, communication, and service industries.

It was unnecessary for the CCF-NDP to look back on 'socialization'; its very dream was being realized in the form of the so-called 'mixed' economy – government and private corporations 'in partnership.' The liberal philosophy of a latter-day Keynesian, John K. Galbraith, became the ideological successor to the Fabian socialism of the Regina Manifesto.[51] The difference being small, the transformation was smooth.

In the Manifesto there was described a society in which 'the financial machinery' and major monopolistic industries and essential services were centrally controlled by the state. Those industries and services which were not essential or monopolistic, as well as 'the family farm,' were to be protected and encouraged. It was a vision where the state removed the impediments to a liberal market society of small farmers and small businessmen – and labour unions – and insured individuals against poverty and lack of opportunity through a comprehensive welfare scheme. Despite the laments of the more 'radical' members of the present NDP, the vision of the Regina Manifesto has changed little over the years. That the NDP today is limited to demands for more social legislation is testimony to its acceptance of the Galbraithian analysis of modern society. The 1933 call for 'socialization' has changed but only in deference to the apparent 'natural' coming of the goal. The mixed economy is what the CCF always envisaged.

From a bourgeois point of view, the mixed economy – the Keynesian welfare state – appears to be a move towards socialism. To have the state remove certain industries and services from the control of 'free-enterprise' raises concern among capitalists about the limits of production of goods and services for private profit. But the concern is dampened by the realization that the state intervenes largely in unprofitable or high risk ventures, and never at a loss to the owners. Moreover, where the state initiates an industry or service it is often non-competitive (like the postal service and production of hydro-electric power) or near monopolistic (like the CNR and Air Canada). In short, state ownership of certain means of production and distribution does not produce a 'mixed' economy but rather an economy better serviced by the state in the interests of the capitalists.

To a social democratic party, such as the CCF-NDP, the substitution of private ownership with state ownership, state planning of production and distribution, and a national welfare scheme are the criteria of a socialist society. This 'solution' implies that state ownership is qualitatively different from private ownership of the means for making money. Moreover, it suggests that the central problems of capitalism are the inequality of justice, opportunity, and standard of living. If such a position is valid, it means that the exhaustion of socialism comes with a full employment program, state economic planning, and welfare 'from the cradle to the grave.' But can it be accepted that there is nothing beyond this vision for the working class; indeed, is state ownership and state planning the socialism of Marx and Engels?

From the point of view of the worker in a capitalist society, there is but one way to subsist and that is to sell his ability to work to the capitalist for wages. The effect of selling his labour power or ability to work reveals the two chief characteristics of a capitalist system as analysed by Marx and Engels. First, while the worker sells his labour power for a daily wage, the *value* of that wage is produced for the capitalist within a few hours of work. But the worker must complete his day's work and thus having laboured to produce the value of his own wage he must work more hours to fulfil his 'contract.' This 'surplus labour,' then, produces a 'surplus value' – a product or number of products worth more than his wage – 'which cost the capitalist nothing, but yet goes into his pocket.'[52] Surplus value is the essence of the wealth which the capitalist accumulates (his capital accumulation). Second, by selling his labour power the worker alienates part of his very humanity, his ability to work, for once sold it belongs to the capitalist. Likewise, the product of his alienated labour stands as an alien object.[53] It is a commodity which to be used must be purchased by its producer, the worker. Neither the worker's labour-power nor the product of his labour is his own in a system of commodity production; that is a system of 'production for exchange on the market.'[54]

Thus, capitalism for Marx and Engels was characterized by the accumulation of wealth based on wage-labour and human alienation stemming from the system of commodity production where one class owned the *means* to produce commodities and another could but sell their *ability* to produce them. The point of struggling for socialism, in this view, was not simply to end the inequities and uncertainties of capitalism and replace it with a planned economy, but to end a system which marked progress and success in terms of capital accumulation[55] and which embodied human alienation in the pursuit of this accumulation of wealth.

The advocates of state ownership suggest that centralized control and planning are the answer to providing the material needs of the workers. Even if the argument is accepted, the question of wage-labour and alienation still remain. Does state ownership of the means of production and distribution, of part of the economy or the whole of it, lead to the elimination of capitalist relations of production (that is, wage-labour) and alienation? For Marx and Engels, this question was answered in the negative. 'The transformation' of individual capitalists, Engels wrote, 'either into joint-stock companies and trusts, or into State-ownership, does not do away with the capitalistic nature of the productive forces.'[56] The modern state in any form, he suggests, is the major prop for maintaining the capitalist system – it is 'the ideal personification of the total national capital.' And the more it takes over sectors of the capitalist economy, 'the more does it actually become the national capitalist.' Thus, in a state-owned industry or state-controlled society 'workers remain wage-workers' and the class position of the former capitalists is usurped by the government and its planning boards. Such a system is state-capitalist not socialist.

In other words, all state-controlled systems are marked by capitalist relations of production. The state represents the interests of either a capitalist class of 'coupon-clippers' or a privileged bureaucracy. In such a system, it is the government and not the capitalist which pays the worker a wage and which expects to appropriate a value (in products) worth more than the amount of the wage. This surplus value is assigned and distributed according to the plans of the state. For the worker, the relations of production remain the same under state-capitalism as under capitalism. He sells his labour power to the management of an enterprise and must use his wages to buy 'commodities from management of other enterprises.'[57] The alienation of the worker's labour power and the product of his labour are not eliminated. As one writer concluded, 'Formally, there is not much difference between private-enterprise and state-controlled economies, except for the latter's centralized control over the surplus-product.'[58]

To conclude that the state-controlled system does not change capitalist relations of production or solve the problem of alienation is to suggest that the socialism envisaged by Marx and Engels must have been much different from what was advocated by the CCF. Socialism for them meant the end of wage-labour and alienation. It was the very opposite of state ownership; it was the overthrow of the state and the institution of working class control, not a state bureaucracy of planning experts. This seizure of power by the working class meant the abolition of the 'State as State.' That is, the class exploitation resting on the capitalist mode of production required the state to protect the relations of production and keep the working class in its place.[59] Once the working class has seized the state the means of production fall into its hands, and consequently, the 'production of commodities is done away with,' that is, the system of wage-labour, the rule of capital as embodied in a capitalist or state-capitalist managerial class. It followed that, at the same time, the conditions giving rise to alienation disappeared.

Aspects of the Marxian notion of socialism were embodied in the early rhetoric but not the program of the CCF. The party progressively abandoned its radical-sounding language and even parts of its program until it offered only to do 'better' than the other parties. Yet, it remained the only 'respectable' party considered to be on the left – and a safe place for academics. By 1969, with the NDP stagnant, unemployment high, and the American take-over ever more obvious, there arose a small group of university teachers within the NDP who sought to make the party more 'radical.' They issued a manifesto which decried American imperialism in Canada and urged a struggle for socialism in terms very similar to the Regina statement of 1933.

THE WAFFLE

The distinguishing characteristic of the Waffle is its goal 'to help transform' the New Democratic party into 'a truly socialist party.' It is this objective which colours all of its policies and which largely determines the direction of its activities. Such a goal contains many assumptions about the NDP as well as about the nature of the socialism that the Waffle claims to be working for.

Chief among these assumptions is the notion that the NDP is mildly socialist and that in being so it can be made into 'a full socialist party.' If by socialism is meant Fabianism, it can be agreed that the NDP has moderated its original position[60] in favour of a Keynesian analysis of capitalism. Given this 'dilution' of Fabianism, there might be an argument for moving the party back to its 1933 statement. But from a Marxist point of view, state capitalism and not socialism is the essence of this CCF platform. The class struggle in theory and in practice is rejected and fought against by the CCF-NDP. The analysis of capitalism as a class system based on exploitation by wage-labour and producing pervasive human alienation is nowhere touched upon in CCF-NDP literature. The party's criticism of capitalism is limited to moralizing on the condition of 'the people'; it is not an understanding of why the working classes are alienated and exploited. Thus, it cannot be assumed that the NDP is socialist in a Marxist sense; indeed, it is anti-Marxist.

As for the question of socialism, the Waffle has made an assumption about itself. It has assumed that it is socialist without ever stating the essence of its notion of socialism beyond one which is strikingly similar to that in the Regina Manifesto. The Waffle Manifesto calls for: 'extensive public control over investment and nationalization of the commanding heights of the economy such as the key resource industries, finance and credit, and industries strategic to planning our economy.' As an extra, 'workers' participation in all institutions' is tagged on. As in the CCF-NDP program there is implicit here the notion that the state once in the 'proper' hands will grant the workers the right to participate in their places of work. Workers' control of the state is never considered. Moreover, the Waffle has never outlined how it hopes to achieve socialism. Is proletarian struggle or is Parliament to be the chief means for establishing socialism? If both means are in order, does one receive priority or are they of equal weight? Other troublesome questions are apparent. The Waffle has presented no class analysis of the structure of Canadian society and little analysis of the NDP which it hopes to transform. Without a class analysis of Canada the Waffle clearly is not Marxist. If this is the case, how can the Waffle be characterized? The answer can only be as a non-Marxist, left wing of a social-democratic party. It is a group whose ideas differ in 'degree' but not in 'kind' from the 'mixed economy' or state-capitalist theories of the parent NDP.

It is also assumed by the Waffle that the NDP has a working-class base. The notion of a working-class base is not easy to fathom given that the NDP is an organization for fighting elections; in other words, the base must refer to those who vote NDP or those who hold party office or both. Regarding party office, it is apparent that only a very small percentage of CCF-NDP officers have been or are from the working class. Most of the officers are former teachers, clergymen, welfare workers, lawyers, and trade union officials.[61] With the stress on planning by experts in CCF-NDP documents, their interests seem to be well represented by the party. Working-class interests, on the other hand, are to be serviced. As for electoral support, from the few voting studies that have been done in Canada, it is clear the party is well supported in ridings where unions are strong. Whether or not this constitutes a working-class base for the party, however, remains an open question when it is realized that trade unions in Canada represent less than 30 per cent of the total work force and that the Liberal party consistently draws a large percentage of the working-class vote. On these grounds, could it be argued that the Liberals have a working-class base?

It is recognized that the NDP is tightly linked to the trade union movement. But what does this link mean? Social democratic parties have traditionally sought the support of organized labour and, in many cases,[62] with this support, they have formed governments. In government or out, however, the link between social democracy and organized labour has meant greater integration of the union movement into the capitalist system. Capitalists have always reigned where social democratic governments have held 'power.' The reason why the Canadian Labour Congress – in essence, the coalition of American-based unions in Canada – has affiliated with the NDP is to win political concessions in the form of 'better' labour legislation. Such labour-legal changes are tolerated by the capitalists and give union leaders an ever-increasing sense of participation in the system: Concessions can be made, even the demand for workers' 'control' or share in management can be tolerated, as long as productivity does not decline and ownership of property and profit is not challenged. In other words, as long as concessions are the limit of the demands, as long as the capitalist framework is not in dispute, toleration can be practised, even encouraged, as a means of integrating the union leaders and the top strata of well-paid unionized workers into the system.

This being the nature of the link between the NDP and the CLC, it makes sense from a Marxist point of view to fight it, to expose it for misleading the struggle for socialism. The Waffle chose to ignore the reformist nature of 'business unionism' until the fall of 1971.[63] Yet when attacking this aspect of trade unions in Canada, the Waffle Labour Committee obscured the role of the AFL-CIO as a willing partner to American imperialism.[64] The Committee rightly argues for rank-and-file control of the labour unions to combat the bureaucracy and philosophy of 'business unionism.' But unions independent from American domination is a position that must parallel the development of a militant and class-conscious trade union movement in Canada. The Labour Committee pamphlet[65] does not touch upon the ignominious role of many international unions, which can best be described as labour imperialism.

Because this issue is not squarely faced in the pamphlet, the argument for an independent trade union movement is made to rest on the flimsy position of *stifled* 'initiative and self-determination in political and economic action' and, moreover, is obscured in the call for 'an independent working class.' It is no doubt true that trade union activities in Canada are stifled, but this 'analysis' of the effects of international unions in Canada is hardly sufficient even as a beginning. As for the phrase, 'an independent working class,' it can only be asked, what does it mean?[66]

These are the assumptions which have permeated the Waffle. In short, it has not examined the nature of the NDP or its relationship to it, choosing instead to silence criticism with presumptuous statements about the 'socialist' NDP, its labour base, and the political impotence of the numerous 'mini-left' groups outside the party. All are fatuous arguments because they are based on the assumptions the Waffle holds about the NDP.

Although this is too brief an examination of the Waffle, it is still possible to suggest the major effects it has had since its formation in 1969. As the left-wing within a social democratic party, the Waffle does not disagree fundamentally with the notion of socialism of the NDP or the chief means by which the party seeks to achieve it – that is, through Parliament. Yet giving the impression of being 'more socialist,' anti-imperialist, and even Marxist, this left-wing draws a considerable number of discontented social democrats back into the party, and more importantly, it attracts some of the most progressive workers, unionists, and socialists to the NDP. In the final analysis, it is the right-wing of the party which profits – despite what it thinks or its worries about respectability. It profits because the electoral machine is strengthened by the membership of the Waffle – albeit, with the Waffle's 'promise' of more radical ventures.

The Waffle, however, is due some credit for helping to develop a consciousness of the colonial nature of Canadian society. Although, this left wing has attempted to link the struggle for independence from the United States with socialism, these two struggles are linked only in name because the Waffle has not moved beyond democratic liberalism.

Because the stated aim of the Waffle is to transform the NDP, its political activities have been largely restricted to party affairs, and consequently, it has spent most of its time organizing for conventions and elections. Little has been attempted in the way of organizing sections of the working class to help them fight the foreign and domestic capital which exploit them. Its extra-parliamentary activities have been restricted to unconnected conferences and demonstrations where issues were raised on a 'one-shot' basis. It has been this goal of the Waffle which has allowed it to be little more than a few small committees and a mailing list.

The task of transforming social democratic parties is a dubious undertaking.[67] It is difficult to imagine Fabian social democracy being wrenched from the characteristics fundamental to it – moralistic liberalism and political opportunism. In working with or attempting to change such parties, a critical awareness of these characteristics is essential. Without this understanding, there can only be confusion. It follows that the principles and motives of those wanting 'more' socialism from a liberal political platform become as questionable as the principles and motives of the party whose program they want to change.

NOTES

1 This change in name was not accompanied by any change in policy. The NDP founding document differs little in content from the 1956 Winnipeg Declaration. The union affiliation that came about in 1961 was a mere formalization of what had been going on for several years.

2   State capitalism refers to the concentration of some or all of the means of production
    and distribution – that is, the factories, mines, banks, and so on – in the hands of the
    state. In a 'moderate' sense, it refers to the role of the state in managing certain essential
    (and usually unprofitable) enterprises such as electric power and water systems, for the
    benefit of private business and to enable large populations to concentrate around these
    businesses.
3   F.H. Underhill, *In Search of Canadian Liberalism* (Toronto 1960), 160.
4   W.L. Morton, *The Progressive Party in Canada* (Toronto 1950), 200.
5   S. Knowles, *The New Party* (Toronto 1961), 24.
6   *Ibid.*, 26.
7   For an argument on the relation between left-wing Protestantism and liberalism see:
    A.R.M. Lower, *This Most Famous Stream: The Liberal Democratic Way of Life* (Toronto
    1967), 132; W. Young, *The Anatomy of a Party: The National CCF* (Toronto 1971), 28:
    'The CCF was to be a movement of men and women motivated by Christian ideals, volun-
    teering their services and determined upon the reformation of society to achieve the co-
    operative commonwealth'; David Lewis and Frank Scott, *Make This Your Canada* (To-
    ronto 1943), 86: 'Growing numbers of people find the processes and results of monopoly
    capitalism the absolute antithesis of the Christian ideal of the dignity of man and regard
    the democratic advance toward social ownership as a partial fulfilment of that ideal.'
8   For his admiration of Fabian reform policies see J.S. Woodsworth, *Toward Socialism:*
    Selections edited by E. Fowke (Toronto 1948), 26-7. The theories of Henry George,
    Edward Bellamy, Thorstein Veblen, and Robert Blatchford also found strong exponents
    in these labour parties. None of these theories suggests anything but reform through legi-
    timate channels.
9   Young, *Anatomy of a Party,* 21.
10 M. Robin, *Radical Politics and Canadian Labour: 1880-1930* (Kingston 1968), 274.
11 *Ibid.*
12 There were avowedly Marxist groups at the formation of the CCF, but it is clear that
    their views did not prevail.
13 F.R. Scott, 'F.H. Underhill and the Manifestos,' *Canadian Forum* (Nov. 1971), 8.
14 G. MacInnis, *J.S. Woodsworth* (Toronto 1953), 276.
15 C. Berger, 'F.H. Underhill and the Tenacity of Liberalism,' *Canadian Forum* (Nov. 1971),
    13.
16 Underhill, *In Search,* xiii.
17 M. Cole, *The Story of Fabian Socialism* (Stanford 1961), 28.
18 A parallel and not unrelated anti-Marxist movement developed in Germany under Eduard
    Bernstein. See P. Gay, *The Dilemma of Democratic Socialism* (New York 1962).
19 C. Gide and C. Rist, *A History of Economic Doctrines* (London 1950), 605.
20 *Ibid.,* 607.
21 Indeed they must have, for the state did reward them – Sidney and Beatrice Webb be-
    came Lord and Lady Passfield. Similarly, several CCFers have been rewarded by the Cana-
    dian state, for example, Senator Eugene Forsey.
22 E.R. Pease, *The History of the Fabian Society* (London 1925), 240.
23 *Ibid.,* 247.
24 *Ibid.,* 249. Pease writes: Fabianism 'has not defended the state as it is, but rather urged
    the need for a state which is based on democracy tempered by respect for the "expert".'
25 Knowles, *New Party,* 97.
26 *Democracy Needs Freedom,* by the Research Committee of the LSR (Toronto 1938),
    25-7.
27 C.B. Macpherson, *The Real World of Democracy* (Toronto 1965), 35.
28 Young, *Anatomy,* 73. See also Underhill, *In Search,* 229, who lamented the demise of
    liberalism: 'We Canadians have been mainly spectators at this tragic process of the disin-
    tegration of nineteenth century liberal democratic values.'

29 Engels remarked on the Fabians this way: 'This socialism of theirs is ... represented as an extreme but inevitable consequence of bourgeois Liberalism.' *Marx and Engels, Correspondence, 1846-1895* (New York), 505.

30 Lewis and Scott, *Make This Your Canada,* 96.

31 Young, *Anatomy,* 89.

32 K. Marx, *The Class Struggles in France* (New York 1964). See Introduction by Engels, 21.

33 Young, *Anatomy,* 198.

34 *Ibid.,* 100. It appears that they did not dare to dream.

35 *Ibid.,* 181.

36 *Ibid.,* 249.

37 The party reasoned, as Young put it that 'the aims of the movement could be achieved piecemeal without the necessity of political power.' *Ibid.,* 249.

38 G. Pierce, *Socialism and the CCF* (Montreal 1934), 59.

39 *Ibid.,* 60. The Toronto *Star* captured the essence of CCF socialism when it wrote: 'Toronto is the centre of Applied Socialism in Canada, with its publicly-owned street railways, ferries and electrical services. Canada has a great Socialistic enterprise in its nationally-owned railways, and joins with Ontario in another fine example of Socialism, the Old Age Pensions. In Ontario there are such Socialistic undertakings as Mother's Allowance and Workmen's Compensation.' 5 Dec. 1933.

40 CBC, 'The Radical Tradition,' 1960, p. 11.

41 Knowles, *New Party,* 31. As Stanley Knowles wrote of the pipe-line debate of 1956: 'True the legislation got through. But the government that disregarded the rules to gain its will went down. The electorate showed its concern for Parliament, and it might well be said of the CCF that even though it too suffered a setback in the process, this was one of its finest hours.'

42 Young, *Anatomy,* 251.

43 *Ibid.,* chap. 9, and also G. Horowitz, *Canadian Labour in Politics* (Toronto 1968), chap. 3.

44 MacInnis, *J.S. Woodsworth,* 274 and 277.

45 S.M. Lipset, *Agrarian Socialism* (New York 1968), 162.

46 *Ibid.,* 173.

47 *New Democratic Party/Program for Ontario,* 1971, 48.

48 Lipset, *Agrarian Socialism,* 194.

49 D. Lewis, 'How Much Welfare Does Social Responsibility Demand?,' in I.A. Litvak, ed., *The Nation Keepers; Canadian Business Perspectives* (introduction by L.B. Pearson) (Toronto 1967), 66-7.

50 William Ash, *Marxism and Moral Concepts* (New York 1964), 32.

51 In a book edited by Litvak (*The Nation-Keepers*) T.C. Douglas and David Lewis each wrote an article extolling the virtues of government in a mixed economy. Douglas wrote with enthusiasm how government could devise 'new vehicles to mobilize private savings for industrial investment' and would enter into 'a productive partnership with private industry' (50) while Lewis quoted from Galbraith to justify government spending as mitigating the social problems of capitalism (24).

52 F. Engels, *The Condition of the Working-Class in England,* in K. Marx and F. Engels, *On Britain* (Moscow 1953), 20.

53 K. Marx, 'Alienated Labour,' in *Karl Marx, Early Writings,* ed. T.B. Bottomore (New York 1964), 123.

54 P.C. Roberts, *Alienation and the Soviet Economy* (Albuquerque 1971), 17.

55 P. Mattick, *Marx and Keynes: The Limits of the Mixed Economy* (Boston 1969), 281.

56 F. Engels, *Socialism: Utopian and Scientific,* in K. Marx and F. Engels, *Selected Works,* II (Moscow 1949), 136.

57 Mattick, *Marx and Keynes,* 289. The strikes by Polish dock workers in the recent past suggests strongly that they are and see themselves, in relation to the state as workers in relation to a capitalist. The demands were similar to those of any striking trade union in the

West. Marx (in 'Critique of the Gotha Program') pointed out that the trade union was 'the real class organization of the proletariat, in which it carries on its daily struggles with capital.' This is precisely the reason trade unions remain in the Eastern European countries and why they are included in the CCF vision of socialism. The accumulation of capital through wage-labour remains a fundamental aspect of these systems. They are at bottom state-capitalist and workers must have their own 'class' organizations to represent their interests in the face of the state-capitalist.

58 *Ibid.,* 289.
59 Engels, *Socialism,* 138.
60 As found in the Regina Manifesto.
61 L. Zakuta, *A Protest Movement Becalmed* (Toronto 1964), 36 and 59.
62 Notably in the United Kingdom and closer to home, Saskatchewan and Manitoba.
63 Except to call for 'the revitalization and extension of the labour movement' (see the Waffle Manifesto).
64 This point is well established in two articles in this book; namely, those by J. Scott & R. Howard and C. Lipton.
65 See the pamphlet, 'A Socialist Program for Canadian Trade Unionists,' issued by the NDP–Waffle Labour Committee, 10.
66 As a final note to the Waffle trade union policy, it should be pointed out that to assume that it is wise to attempt to transform the NDP because it is tied to the unions is a failure to realize that only the highest level union bureaucrats are involved in the party ruling circles. Thus, to suppose changing the party would influence the unions is to argue for radicalizing the unions from the top down. In contrast, what is needed is the building of a militant rank and file movement which would fight the imperialist role and bureaucracy of the large international unions in Canada. For this policy, control of the NDP is not required.
67 An alliance between a Fabian party and socialists for certain limited goals would allow for political action on grounds defined by clear principles. The approach of the Waffle implies compromise and opportunism; hence its name and its inability to take a position on anti-imperialist questions such as sovereign Canadian trade unions.

Appendix

The ideological foundations of Social Democracy and Social Credit
by R.T. Naylor

THE EMERGENCE of the CCF and Social Credit movements can only be understood in the context of the patterns of Canadian colonization of the West. The annexation of the western territory to the Canadian Confederation in 1871 was planned by a coalition government at the time of Confederation, but by 1871 the Clear Grit element, representing Ontario agrarian liberalism, was virtually eliminated from that coalition, and with it the free-land and open frontier philosophy. The process of dispelling Clear Grit influence from the federal government was completed by the Red River rebellion which unseated William MacDougall and resulted in the Manitoba Act delivering the West, complete with its lands and natural resources, into the hands of the CPR-Hudson's Bay Company-Bank of Montreal-Tory party alliance.[1] The Canadian frontier was thus effectively closed and new forms of Clear Grit-petit bourgeois liberalism emerged in the West to try to open it again.

C.B. Macpherson has suggested a 'model' for the analysis of the Social Credit movement in Alberta based on two structural characteristics of the Canadian West during the first few decades of this century: 1, its relatively homogeneous class structure, i.e. a majority of income earners were petit bourgeois; 2, the colonial character of the economy. Given these two characteristics and given that Alberta (and Saskatchewan) were creations of the federal government, he deduces the alienation of the western provinces from the orthodox eastern-based two-party system and the need to generate strong, unified folk movements with the political power to stand up to the federal government and eastern big business.[2] What cannot be explained with this model is why Alberta followed the Social Credit movement while neighbouring Saskatchewan, with identical structural characteristics, followed the CCF. We shall attempt to resolve this contradiction, but first some clarifications of the Macpherson schema are needed.

The alienation of the West from the old two-party system cannot be assumed to be an absolute. It germinated in the 1896-1911 period when Laurier betrayed his constituents and capitulated to eastern big business on the tariff issue.[3] Third-party movements, however, did not become the sole recourse of the West until the defeat of reciprocity in 1911. Note also that Macpherson's two structural characteristics are really one and the same. The petit bourgeois base reflects the character of the economic colonialism suffered by the West. It reflects the fact that eastern big business was predominantly mercantile in its orientation – commercial banks, railways, land speculation companies, retail chains, elevator companies. In so far as eastern business impinged upon the West its strength in the sphere of exchange and distribution, rather than production, served to create the petit bourgeois base which it exploited. Thus, these colonial economies of the West can be regarded as 'simple' market societies[4] not characterized by alienation of surplus through wage labour, but rather alienation through adverse terms of trade due to an asymmetry of bargaining power vis-à-vis the eastern mercantile haute bourgeoisie. While the 'Liverpool' prices of grains were set by world market conditions and were thus beyond control, farm movements sprang up to try to establish some control over those price and cost factors which were accessible – brokerage and insurance costs, bank charges, freight rates, etc.

Given these characteristics, how can one reconcile the rise of 'agrarian socialism'[5] in Saskatchewan with the victory of the Social Credit movement in Alberta? One way is to attempt to impute the difference to variations in the backgrounds of the immigrants who peopled the West.[6] Manitoba, settled from Ontario, inherited an orthodox Clear Grit tradition and hence was not alienated from normal political procedures of the Dominion. Saskatchewan was settled largely with British working-class immigrants who brought Fabianism with them; while Alberta was largely peopled by American farmers who imported American populism. In light of the brevity of the period under consideration this explanation may be of some use in explaining the subjective attitudes of the leaders of the movements and even of some of their followers, but it fails to explain the objective appeal these movements held for the petit bourgeois class as a whole, why this class should attach itself to one movement or the other. For 'attach' it surely did: the CCF was not an agrarian socialist movement. The farm base was simply co-opted by the Fabian leadership of the CCF. The farm adherence to the CCF in Saskatchewan was opportunistic; it followed Fabian leadership not because it was Fabian but because policies were proposed which appealed to the objective class positions of the farmers. As to the contradiction between Social Credit and CCF emerging from identical conditions, it ceases to exist once these movements are viewed in terms of objective class standards rather than subjective standards of the leaders. The two movements are indistinguishable. For the farm constituency, the policy proposals of both groups were identical.

Heresy! The CCF 'socialist' humanitarianism equated to the crypto-fascism of the Social Credit? Underneath the rhetoric and public posturing of the leadership, however, they are similar. Social democracy and Social Credit in Canada sprang from identical constituencies, exhibiting exactly the same objective class attributes. Both emerged as movements designed to break down eastern mercantile dominations. Social Credit took strong aim directly at the banking cartel; the CCF generalized its antipathy to the whole eastern mercantile sector. Both sought to interfere in the realm of circulation, distribution, and exchange to equalize bargaining power between East and West. Both favoured low tariff and trust-busting policies to turn the terms of trade in favour of the West. Both supported the family farm as an economic institution and the extension of the co-operatives, and hence accepted, and even promoted petit bourgeois and bourgeois modes of production.

While the family farm is unambiguously a petit bourgeois institution, the co-operative is frequently lauded by social democrats as a purveyor of 'social-ism.' In reality the co-operative principle applied in the West was perfectly representative of petit bourgeois philosophy and policy. The capitalist mode of production based on alienated labour power is accepted by the co-op: pro-fit on alienation is still the driving force, with the objective being to divert this profit into the hands of the petit bourgeois group who form the co-op, rather than letting it be usurped by the eastern capitalist. At the same time the one-man one-vote principle, regardless of the number of shares of the co-op held by the individual, also illustrates their desire to keep private property and capitalist production intact while correcting bargaining power. Underneath both Social Credit and the CCF, and indeed the NDP, lies the grand old princi-ple of social democracy – that production and distribution can be separated, that distribution can be altered, reformed, corrected while the mode of pro-duction is left untouched.

The idea that production and distribution can be dichotomized, an idea which is central to social democratic and liberal reformist theory, derives from the ideological founder of liberal democracy, John Stuart Mill.[7] According to Mill, the laws governing production, i.e. the bourgeois mode based on the wage contract and private capital accumulation, were sound, but the laws of distribution could act in a perverse manner. The role of the state was to inter-fere with distribution – to redistribute income from the rich to the poor and to rectify imbalances of power and their consequences through factory legisla-tion, etc. Universal manhood suffrage was a means to this end. Mill was a lib-eral reformer who accepted the petit bourgeois principle that the state should step in to rectify asymmetries of bargaining power and to change the distribu-tion of income and power that resulted from those imbalances. These petit bourgeois concepts were assumed to be applicable to a fully fledged industrial system.

Of more recent influence than Mill on social democratic theory was the work of John Hobson, another English political economist who followed in Mill's tradition.[9] Hobson, while rejecting the labour theory of value, accepted that an economy produced a certain amount of surplus value over and above the 'cost' of maintaining the *status quo* level of economic activity, and that this surplus tended historically to grow, relatively as well as absolutely. How-ever, surplus could be either 'productive' or 'unproductive,' the first largely entrepreneurs' profits or necessary incentives to capital formation, the second the result of monopoly power and hoarding of productive resources, especially capital. Excessive amounts of capital controlled by a few individuals were to Hobson the chief evil of the system leading to crises, industrial stagnation, and imperialism. The bourgeois mode of production, the industrial system *per se*, was perfectly healthy provided it could be freed from the monopoly of control of a handful of financiers. The solution was state interference with the distribution of income.

John Stuart Mill and John Hobson were the most influential political economists in shaping modern concepts of social democracy and the welfare state. It is interesting to compare their theoretical framework with that of Major Douglas, the founder of Social Credit.[9] The gist of the Douglas theory, contained in the infamous $A + B$ theorem, was that total incomes generated by the productive system (A) always fell short of the total value of production (C), by a factor (B) consisting of raw material costs etc., but especially of credit costs which do not return as income to individuals. The financier is the principle bogey man in the Douglas system, with a vested interest in maintaining artificial scarcity. The industrial system itself is given a clean bill of health, and state intervention is to take the principle form of issuance of additional 'money' of an amount (B) to rectify the imbalance left by the industrial system. To do so required the economic extermination of the financial class. Douglas's theory, then acknowledges the same fundamental problem – distribution – and looks forward to the same basic sort of state interference to rectify it, as did Mill and Hobson. Private property and the capitalist mode are unaltered.

Last in this regard let us note briefly that John Maynard Keynes fits directly into the Mill–Hobson–Douglas tradition of regarding the bourgeois mode of production as fine by itself and seeing the origins of crises and so on in imperfections in the distribution of income and the monopoly power of a small group of financiers.[10] The role of the state becomes that of redistributor of income and power. Keynes favoured inflationary credit policies to ensure 'the euthanasia of the cumulative power of the capitalist to exploit the scarcity value of capital,'[11] and regarded interest payments in excess of some low level as a form of modern-day usury.

To reiterate the principles we have seen as being common to social credit, social democracy, and modern welfare capitalism alike: 1, a belief in the fundamental efficacity of the bourgeois mode of production based on surplus value alienated through wage labour; 2, a distaste for monopoly power; 3, a belief that the rules governing distribution can be altered without changing the mode of production; 4, a belief that the role of the state is to rectify imbalances of power between income groups, professional groups, or socioeconomic classes. This rectification of imbalances of bargaining power serves to offset the impact monopoly power has on the terms of trade, and this principle is seen in farm co-operatives and business unions alike. It is the concept underlying the collective bargaining process being guaranteed by law.

In the final analysis social democrats will even turn to positive state activity, that is, nationalization of industry, to alter the terms of trade. But note that far from being a socialist measure, nationalization in the sense of substituting state ownership for private, leaving the mode of production unaltered, is a petit bourgeois measure aimed solely at rectifying imbalances of market power or improving the functioning of a market economy. Since the mode of production remains bourgeois, the state being substituted for the private capitalist, nothing is done to alter the fundamental attribute of capitalist production – the alienation of surplus value through the wage contract. As for Crown corporations, as that great Canadian social democrat, C.D. Howe, put it, 'They are not public enterprises; they're *my* enterprises.'

The earliest statement of the ideological foundations of the CCF-NDP in western Canada emerged from the Sayer's trial at Fort Garry in 1849, when the Métis, having broken the Hudson's Bay Company monopoly, streamed from the courtroom shouting, 'La commerce est libre! La commerce est libre! Vive la liberté!'[12] The perspective and ideology of the NDP have yet to evolve beyond that point.

NOTES

1 It is one of Canadian history's great ironies that the Clear Grits, who through their stooges, the Canadian Party, fomented the Red River rebellion, should be knocked from the echelons of power by the results of the uprising. See esp. G. Stanley, *The Birth of Western Canada* (Toronto 1960), and C. Martin, *'Dominion Lands' Policy* (Toronto 1938), for accounts of the rival classes involved.
2 C.B. Macpherson, *Democracy in Alberta* (Toronto 1953), esp. 6-20, 21.
3 See esp. E. Porritt, *The Revolt against the New Feudalism in Canada* (London 1911), for an account of the Laurier sell-out and predictions, surprisingly accurate about the nature of western protest. See also W.T.R. Preston, *The Life and Times of Lord Strathcona* (Toronto 1914 approx.) esp. 279-80 on Sir Richard Cartwright. For a fuller account see R.T. Naylor 'The Rise and Fall of the Third Commercial Empire of the St Lawrence,' this volume.
4 C.B. Macpherson, *The Political Theory of Possessive Individualism* (Oxford 1962), 51-3.
5 The term is that of S. Lipset, *Agrarian Socialism* (New York 1968), a thoroughly confused and confusing account of the CCF in Saskatchewan.
6 Cf. W.D. Young, *Anatomy of a Party: The National CCF* (Toronto 1969), 15-16.
7 See esp. *Principles of Political Economy,* and *Essays on Some Unsettled Questions of Political Economy,* chap. II.
8 Hobson has written a large number of volumes. Two of the best and most representative are, however, *The Industrial System* (London 1927) and *Imperialism* (London 1902).
9 On Social Credit monetary theory see Macpherson, *Democracy in Alberta*, and R. MacIvor *Canadian Monetary Banking and Fiscal Development* (Toronto 1958).
10 J.M. Keynes, *The General Theory of Employment, Interest and Money* (London 1961), 372-3.
11 *Ibid.,* 376.
12 See variously, Stanley, *Birth of Western Canada*; Martin, *'Dominion Lands' Policy*; or E. E. Rich, *The Hudson's Bay Company*, III (Toronto 1962), for accounts of the trial and its consequences.